Rationality and Power

MORALITY AND SOCIETY
a series edited by Alan Wolfe

BENT FLYVBJERG

Rationality and Power

DEMOCRACY IN PRACTICE

Translated by Steven Sampson

THE UNIVERSITY OF CHICAGO PRESS
Chicago & London

Originally published as *Rationalitet og magt*, vol. 2: *Et case-baseret studie af planlægning, politik og modernitet*. Copyright © 1991 by Akademisk Forlag and Bent Flyvbjerg. The current English translation is a revised and updated version of the original Danish book.

The University of Chicago Press, Chicago 60637
The University of Chicago Press, Ltd., London
© 1998 by The University of Chicago

Printed in the United States of America
07 06 05 04 03   3 4 5
ISBN: 0-226-25449-6 (cloth)
ISBN: 0-226-25451-8 (paper)

Library of Congress Cataloging-in-Publication Data

Flyvbjerg, Bent.
     [Case-baseret studie af planlægning, politik og modernitet.
     English]
     Rationality and power : democracy in practice / Bent Flyvbjerg ; translated by Steven Sampson.
          p.   cm. — (Morality and society)
      Translation of : Case-baseret studie af planlægning, politik og
modernitet
     Includes bibliographical references (p.   ) and index.
     ISBN: 0-226-25449-6 (cloth) — ISBN: 0-226-25451-8
(paper)
     1. Ålborg (Denmark) — Politics and government.   2. Democracy —
Denmark — Ålborg.   I. Title.   II. Series.
JS6185.A53F5913 1998
320.4489´5—dc21   97-17204
                                                                       CIP

⊗ The paper used in this publication meets the minimum requirements of the American National Standard for Information Sciences—Permanence of Paper for Printed Library Materials, ANSI Z39.48-1992.

For Maria Kristine

SINCE MY INTENTION IS TO SAY SOMETHING THAT
WILL PROVE OF PRACTICAL USE TO THE INQUIRER,
I HAVE THOUGHT IT PROPER TO REPRESENT
THINGS AS THEY ARE IN REAL TRUTH, RATHER
THAN AS THEY ARE IMAGINED.

Niccolò Machiavelli

THUCYDIDES, AND . . . THE *PRINCIPE* OF MACHIAVELLI,
ARE RELATED TO ME CLOSELY BY THEIR
UNCONDITIONAL WILL NOT TO DECEIVE
THEMSELVES AND TO SEE REASON IN *REALITY*

Friedrich Nietzsche

Contents

Preface

Research and writing are not possible without the support and collaboration of others. In this Preface I wish to extend my thanks to the many persons, organizations, and institutions who helped make this book possible.

A special thanks must be given to the many interviewees, informants, and organizations who placed their experiences, time, and archives at my disposal. It is indicative of the assistance I received among all parties—government and private—that none of my requests for interviews or access to primary documents were ever refused, including internal or confidential documents.

Special thanks are due also to Alan Wolfe and Steven Lukes. Alan Wolfe is one of those rare Americans who reads Danish; he encouraged me to publish the original Danish version of the book in English and suggested that I submit the translation to the University of Chicago Press. Steven Lukes twice invited me to present my work at the European University Institute in Florence and to seek feedback from faculty and students; he also made valuable suggestions for improving the manuscript. In revising the book and in finding a publisher, I received much appreciated encouragement and suggestions from Erik Allardt, Robert A. Dahl, Andreas Faludi, John Forester, John Friedmann, Clifford Geertz, Anthony Giddens, Patsy Healey, Alasdair MacIntyre, Seymour Mandelbaum, James G. March, Alan Pred, Arpad Szakolczai, James Throgmorton, Martin Wachs, and Aaron Wildavsky. Two University of Chicago Press reviewers provided highly useful comments for preparing the final version of the manuscript.

Hubert Dreyfus, of the University of California at Berkeley, persuaded me to study power and learning processes when I thought I would be immersing myself in the problems of hermeneutics and structuralism. C. Roland Christensen and José Gomez-Ibañez of Harvard have shown me unique hospitality, and by their example have taught me to appreciate the case study as a research and teaching method. Several years ago, in preparing a methodological paper for this book, I benefited from comments by Daniel Bell, Richard Bernstein, John Friedmann, Hans-Georg Gadamer, Anthony Giddens, Alasdair MacIntyre, Lisa Peattie, Martin Wachs, and Aaron Wildavsky.[1] My colleagues at Aalborg University, Finn Kjærsdam and Hans Gullestrup, read large portions of a first draft of this book, and their comments were invaluable in helping to improve the original Danish version. For their helpful comments on various parts of the book, I also wish to thank Henning Bender, Inger Bo, Jens Erik Christensen, Jeppe Gustafsson, Gorm Harste, Niels Helberg, Karsten Friis Johansen, Ib Jørgensen, Anker Lohmann-Hansen, Morten Rugtved Petersen, Jørgen Primdahl, Neal Richman, Janne Seemann, and Bo Vagnby. Ib Jørgensen also provided a stimulus to my work by continually calling my attention to relevant research literature.

Librarian Anni Busk Nielsen carried out a monumental task, at times like a detective, of procuring the books, articles, and reports on which this study is based. Leon Jarssen at the Danish Road Data Lab, Finn Palmgren Jensen of the Danish Country-Wide Air Monitoring Program, and Paul Lauritzen of Copenhagen's City Engineering Directorate have all offered invaluable assistance in providing data for the evaluation of the outcomes summarized in Chapter 19. Lilli Glad, Vibeke Bo Jensen, Dorte Madsen, and Birthe Nørskov transformed my drafts into readable manuscripts.

Research for the book was carried out with support from several funding agencies. A three-year research scholarship from the Danish National Research Council provided me with the necessary freedom to conduct the research. Support from the Danish Social Science Research Council made possible an intensive concluding phase of writing-up. My research was also supported by the Fulbright Commission, the Carlsberg Foundation, the Denmark-America Foundation, the Egmont H. Petersen Foundation, Knud Højgaards Foundation, and by a Christian and Ottilia Brorson Travel Grant. Finally, Aalborg University provided generous support via the Consistorium's Research Committee, the Faculty of Technical and Natural Sciences, and the Department of Development and Planning. Translation of the revised and updated Danish manuscript into English was made possible by grants from the Danish Social Science Research Council, the Cowi Foundation and the North Jutland University Foundation.

Steven Sampson not only translated the book into clear, readable prose. He warned me from the outset that my involvement in the translation and its adaptation to English-speaking readers would be on the order of writing a new book. I did not believe him, but he was right. As an experienced scholar and writer, Steven Sampson also suggested valuable improvements in the original text. Douglas Mitchell, senior editor at the University of Chicago Press, provided precious guidance and support in seeing the book through the printing process.

Roger Grandy lent me his house in Big Sur, providing a perfect environment to work on the manuscript.

Finally, I wish to thank my family and friends, whose love and care has sustained me and my work.

Responsibility for any errors and omissions in this book remains mine alone.

Bent Flyvbjerg

Aalborg
June 1997

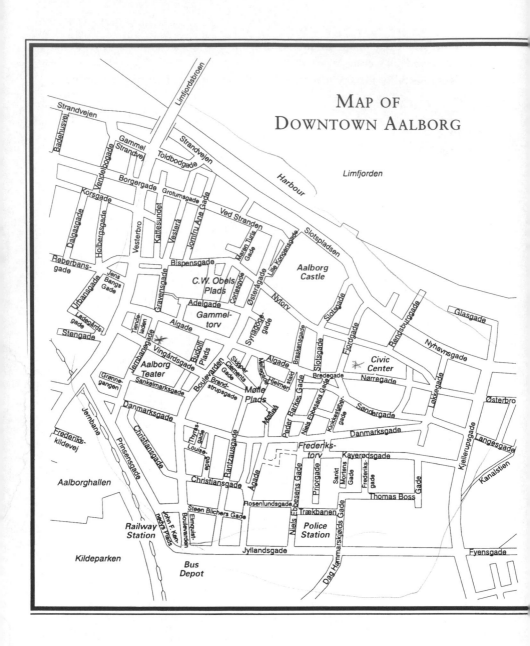

MAP OF
DOWNTOWN AALBORG

Limfjorden

One

IN SOME REMOTE CORNER OF THE UNIVERSE

"Have courage to use your own reason!"—that is the motto of
enlightenment.

Immanuel Kant

In some remote corner of the universe," begins Nietzsche in one of his
early essays, "there once was a star on which clever animals invented
knowledge. That was the most arrogant and the most untruthful moment
in 'world history.'"[1] In this book I will take the reader to a remote corner of the
universe, to a star like Nietzsche's. The action takes place in the Kingdom of
Denmark, that is, nowhere and everywhere. Here, too, knowledge was invented. How, why, and the consequences of this knowledge constitute the tale
of this book.

THE ISSUE: RATIONALITY AND DEMOCRACY

My major aims in writing this book have been threefold. First, I wanted to do
an empirically deep and richly detailed case study of modernity and democracy—as manifested in modern politics, administration, and planning. Given
the current state of the subject in which I am interested—the dynamic relationship between rationality and power—empirical depth as well as attention
to detail is required to develop our understanding further. My second objective has been to carry out the study drawing upon an intellectual tradition
largely ignored by the Enlightenment, a tradition that starts with Thucydides
and continues with Machiavelli and Nietzsche to Michel Foucault. Finally, it
has been my aim to present my findings in the form of a narrative that would
help readers move about in the dense case material, so as to provide them with
the basis to form their own judgments about the case and its implications.

In the Enlightenment tradition, rationality is typically seen as a concept that is well-defined and context-independent. We know what rationality is, and rationality is supposed to be constant over time and place. This study, however, demonstrates that rationality is context-dependent and that the context of rationality is power. Power blurs the dividing line between rationality and rationalization. Rationalization presented as rationality is shown to be a principal strategy in the exercise of power. Kant said that the possession of power unavoidably spoils the free use of reason. We will see that the possession of more power spoils reason even more, that the greater the power, the less the rationality. The empirical study is summed up in a number of propositions about the relationship between rationality and power, concluding that power has a rationality that rationality does not know, whereas rationality does not have a power that power does not know. I will argue that this asymmetry between rationality and power forms a basic weakness of modernity and of modern democracy, a weakness that needs to be reassessed in light of the context-dependent nature of rationality, taking a point of departure in thinkers like Machiavelli, Nietzsche, and Foucault.[2]

Is this, then, a book in the anti-Enlightenment tradition? The answer to this question is a clear yes and no. No, if by anti-Enlightenment one means being opposed to central ideals of the Enlightenment such as freedom, justice, truth, etc. I fully share these ideals, and I find them worth striving for, something which should be clear from the book. Having lived most of my life in a part of the world where there originated free, universal education, the public library, the folk high school, the cooperative movement, the parliamentary ombudsman, and other institutions essential to a well-functioning democracy, I have deep respect for Francis Bacon's dictum: "Knowledge is power." Bacon's idea is fundamental to modernity, democracy, and Enlightenment: "Enlightenment is power." Hence, the more enlightenment—the more rationality—the better. Yet there is a problem here. The problem lies with the normativism of many modernists and, indeed, with the project of modernity itself. Much of modern politics, administration, and planning—and many theories about these phenomena—emphasize the ideals of modernity but do not examine modernity as it is actually experienced. Modernity's elevation of rationality as an ideal seems to result in, or at least to coexist with, an ignorance of the real rationalities at work in everyday politics, administration, and planning. In *The Prince,* Machiavelli spells out in no uncertain terms the dangers of the normative attitude when he says that "a man who neglects what is actually done for what should be done learns the way to self-destruction."[3] With the problems and risks of our time—environmental, social, demographic; globally and locally—Machiavelli's dictum remains acutely relevant today. Whereas the focus of modernity is on "what should be done," I suggest a reorientation toward "what is actually done." In this way we obtain a better grasp—less idealistic, more grounded—of what modernity and modern democracy are and what kind of strategies and tactics may help change them for the better. Taking this approach, we must be willing to accept the possibility that when we examine how knowledge, rationality, and power work in real life, we may end up standing Bacon on his head.

This book must be seen, therefore, as anti-Enlightenment, if we mean by this term being against the general outlook of the Enlightenment on how social and political affairs work, and ought to work, and if we mean being against the instruments that the Enlightenment tradition envisions to achieve its ideals. The Enlightenment is sorely lacking on these points, much to its own detriment, due partly to its failure to understand how power operates. Champion thinkers of the Enlightenment—like Plato, Kant, and Jürgen Habermas—are useful for theoretically justifying Enlightenment ideals. However, when we move from justifying ideals to understanding how modernity works in practice, and to implementing and practically defending the ideals, these thinkers are weak. Then we are better helped by so-called anti-Enlightenment thinkers like Nietzsche and Foucault because they are practical thinkers of power. I maintain that if one takes Enlightenment ideals seriously, one needs to understand the Enlightenment in anti-Enlightenment terms, that is, in terms of Nietzschean will to power and Foucauldian rationality-as-rationalization. We should not conclude that because Nietzsche and Foucault criticized democracy and other Enlightenment ideals, we, as democrats, cannot use their thinking to understand democracy better and to work for more democracy. To be a Nietzschean democrat is not a contradiction in terms but a real and productive possibility.

THE CASE: AALBORG

At the core of this book is an in-depth case study of politics, administration, and planning in the Danish town of Aalborg, located in northern Jutland. Aalborg will be to this study what Florence and Tuscany were to Machiavelli's—no other comparison intended.[4] Aalborg is the main, urban administrative and commercial center for northern Jutland, a region of a half-million people. A typical medium-sized European city, Aalborg has a high-density historical center several centuries old. When the case opens, the center has for decades had to adapt to an ever-increasing number of cars, which have transformed, and even destroyed, substantial parts of the city's historical center. Now city officials have decided that the car will have to adapt to the city. They initiate what will become known as the "Aalborg Project," an award-winning scheme that later will be recommended by the Organization for Economic Cooperation and Development (OECD) as a model for international adoption, on how to integrate environmental and social concerns into city politics and planning, including how to deal with the car in the city. The new approach will bring to a halt Aalborg's passive accommodation to unceasing demands for more office space, shopping space, road space, and parking space, leaving little space for anything else—or so is the intention. The new approach of the Aalborg Project also will become one of the town's most sensitive and enduring political and planning issues for a decade and a half. As one participant will later say about the Aalborg Project, "It just keeps going. It goes on and on." What follows in these chapters is what Nietzsche calls the *wirkliche Historie,* real history, of the Aalborg Project and what Machiavelli calls the *verita effettuale,* effective truth, of how rationality and power have shaped it.

"All the problems of politics, of social organization, and of education have been falsified through and through," Nietzsche says, "because one learned to despise 'little' things, which means the basic concerns of life itself."[5] I take the Aalborg case to be one of Nietzsche's "'little' things," a "discreet and apparently insignificant truth," which, when closely examined, reveals itself to be pregnant with paradigms, metaphors, and general significance, what Nietzsche in typical immodest fashion calls "cyclopean monuments."[6] Applying the Nietzschean approach to Aalborg, we will find that the most particular also reveals itself to be the most general. Nietzsche may have declared the death of God, but God fooled him; God is still in the detail. So is the devil, as we shall see. To understand the story of Aalborg is to understand central aspects of modernity and of modern politics, administration, and planning. Thus, Aalborg is not presented as a case of "something rotten in Denmark." It is put forward as a case of the more pervasive problem of how to make democracy work in a modernity that is strong on democratic ideals but weak on their realization. With Denmark being one of the oldest, and probably also one of the best functioning welfare state democracies in the world, the Danish case demonstrates just how seriously we should take Bernard Crick's observation that to call governments "democratic" is always a misleading piece of propaganda.[7] We may want the democratic element in government to grow greater, but it is still only an element tempered by other elements that we need to take into account when working for more democracy. In this book, our focus will be on democracy in relation to these "other elements."

In addition to being a metaphor of modernity, the Aalborg case, in laying open the dynamics of rationality, power, and democracy, helps elucidate contemporary and classical debates about these phenomena and their relevance to social and political science and philosophy. Finally, Aalborg is offered as a reference point against which rationality, power, and democracy elsewhere can be compared. Others will be able to ask practical questions like, "Do we have an instance of Aalborg here?" "How close to or how far from it are we?" And, as people in Aalborg have asked on the basis of the original Danish version of the book, they can pose the question, "Is this what we want?" Here, the Aalborg case also may be of interest to those working with emerging democracies in Eastern Europe, the former Soviet Union, and developing nations. The case is a lesson in the importance of endurance: democracy is not something a society "gets"; democracy must be fought for each and every day in concrete instances, even long after democracy is first constituted in a society. If citizens do not engage in this fight, there will be no democracy. In this way, the story of Aalborg may be used not as a model but as a guide for situational ethics and practical action. After all, we tell stories in order to do things differently.

THE INTELLECTUAL TRADITION: THUCYDIDES, MACHIAVELLI, NIETZSCHE

The insight that reasoning quickly turns into rationalization and that dialogue becomes persuasive rhetoric under the pressures of reality is already present in detail in Thucydides. Machiavelli, who, like Thucydides, had experience with the practical employment of power, worked out this insight reflectively and began developing a concept of power with an emphasis not only on power as an entity that is conquered and held based on force and law but also on power as "strategies and tactics" exercised in more subtle ways. The view of power as "strategies-and-tactics" was advanced substantially in the interpretation of Nietzsche, who described himself as being closely related to Thucydides and Machiavelli.[8] And with Foucault, who, unlike Nietzsche, had the skills and temper of a historian, the "strategies-and-tactics" view of power was put to practical historical and empirical use in Foucault's famous studies of imprisonment, insanity, and sexuality.[9]

In this book, the strategies-and-tactics view of power is employed in a study of contemporary affairs using social science research methodology.[10] Despite differences in time perspective, substance, and methodology, this study shares with Nietzsche's and Foucault's approaches a view of power as productive and positive and not only as restrictive and negative.[11] Power in Aalborg is a dense and dynamic net of omnipresent relations. It is not simply localized in "centers," nor is it something one can effectively "possess" and regulate by law. The central question, in addition to who has power and why they have it, is how power is exercised. Power is studied with a point of departure in small questions, "flat and empirical," in Foucault's words, instead of based on "big questions."[12] The Great is found in the Small as mentioned above. Most important—and this I take to be the main contribution of Nietzsche and Foucault to the study of power and modernity—knowledge and power, truth and power, rationality and power are seen as analytically and politically inseparable, leaving the actual relationship between these phenomena open to empirical test.

In sum, when using the strategies-and-tactics approach to the study of power, the main question is not only the Weberian "Who governs?" posed by Robert Dahl and most other students of power-as-entity, though this question is still important. It is also the Nietzschean question, "What 'governmental rationalities' are at work when those who govern govern?" In this book, therefore, we will focus on the less visible mechanisms of the modus operandi of power, mechanisms which turn out to be relatively independent of who holds power and who governs and which in this sense show themselves to be more fundamental.

A key concept in the book is what I call *Realrationalität,* or "real rationality." Machiavelli made clear that an understanding of politics requires distinguishing between formal politics and what later, with Ludwig von Rochau, would become known as *Realpolitik.* No such distinction has been employed in the study of rationality. I will argue, however, that distinguishing between formal rationality and *Realrationalität* is as important to the understanding of modernity and of modern politics, administration, and planning as the distinction between formal politics and *Realpolitik.*

With the *Real* approach to understanding rationality and politics, and with the power-as-strategies-and-tactics view of power, the dynamics of conflict and struggle become the center of analysis. In most societies, conflicts have been viewed as dangerous, corrosive, and potentially destructive of social order and therefore in need of being contained and resolved. There is evidence, however, that social conflicts themselves produce the valuable ties that hold modern democratic societies together and provide such ties with the strength and cohesion they need; that social conflicts are themselves pillars of democratic society.[13] Governments and societies that suppress conflict appear to do so at their own peril. For example, a basic explanation for the deterioration and loss of vitality of the Communist-dominated societies may be their suppression of overt social conflict. From a Nietzschean and Foucauldian point of view, suppressing conflict is suppressing freedom, because the option to engage in conflict is a part of freedom. It follows that if societies that suppress conflict are oppressive, social and political thinking that ignores or marginalizes conflict is potentially oppressive, too. And if conflict sustains society, there may be good reason to caution against an idealism that ignores conflict and power. This is the main reason for placing conflict at the center of power as understood in this book. We will see that such a conflict-centered approach is corroborated by the findings from the Aalborg study.

THE METHOD: NARRATOLOGY

A Wittgensteinian approach is used in telling the story of Aalborg; that is, the emphasis is on narratology before epistemology.[14] Wittgenstein utilized the following metaphor in describing his own use of the approach employed here:

> In teaching you philosophy I'm like a guide showing you how to find your way round London. I have to take you through the city from north to south, from east to west, from Euston to the embankment and from Piccadilly to the Marble Arch. After I have taken you many journeys through the city, in all sorts of directions, we shall have passed through any given street a number of times—each time traversing the street as part of a different journey. At the end of this you will know London; you will be able to find your way about like a born Londoner. Of course, a good guide will take you through the more important streets more often than he takes you down side streets; a bad guide will do the opposite. In philosophy I'm a rather bad guide.[15]

In this book, I will take the reader through the streets and alleyways of Aalborg. We will explore the city firsthand instead of reading maps of it; we will investigate the actual practices of politics, administration, and planning before their rules; and we will not be satisfied by learning only about those parts of the practices that take place in public. We also will enter behind the closed doors of government and interest-group decision making. For readers who stick with the minutiae of the Aalborg story from beginning to end, the payback will be an awareness of issues of democracy, rationality, and power that cannot be obtained from "maps," that is, summaries, concepts, or theoretical formulae. Achieving such awareness is central to developing judgment and expertise in political and administrative affairs and in carrying out research into such affairs.

The Wittgensteinian approach to narratology does not mean that summaries and generalizations from the case study cannot or should not be attempted. My own attempts at this can be found in Chapter 20 and consist of a grounded theory of the relationship between rationality and power.[16] In telling the Aalborg story, however, I have demurred from the role of omniscient narrator and summarizer in favor of gradually allowing the story to unfold from the diverse, complex, and sometimes conflicting stories that the actors in the case have told me. I have made every effort to be thorough and fair, which involves a vast accumulation of source material covering the different perspectives represented in the case, and which also involves extensive use of feedback from actors and colleagues before finalizing the text of the case. This approach leaves ample scope for readers to make varying interpretations and to draw diverse conclusions. Thus, in addition to the voice of the actors and of myself, there is space for the voice of the reader in deciding the meaning of the case and in answering that categorical question of any case study: "What is this case a case of?" I encourage the reader to occupy that space.

As explained previously, modern ideals and modern realities are at the center of the narrative. Generally speaking, we are poorly equipped to deal with the relationship between ideal and reality, partly because the very language we use to understand reality—the written and spoken word—is itself characterized by rationality and coherence, whereas reality is often characterized by power and fragmentation. "Through words and concepts we are now continually tempted to think of things as being simpler than they are," Nietzsche says. "There is a philosophical mythology concealed in *language*" (emphasis in original).[17] Michel Serres puts the matter even more succinctly. "Language has a disgust for things," he says. Modernity and modern democracy, too, have a disgust for things and conceal a philosophical mythology. In what follows we will attempt to get beyond this mythology by examining the practices of modernity and democracy. We will look at what people actually do, not only what they say they do nor their stated reasons for doing it. In short, we will focus on practices rather than discourse and theory.

Using this approach, the Aalborg case is depicted not in terms of codes but in terms of events, simply recording what happened on such a day, in such a place, in such a context. Events are then structured into a narrative by the conventional means of time, place, actors, and context. The narrative is developed with two plots, the immediate plot of actors and actions, and the conceptual plot of the relationship between rationality and power and what this relationship means to modernity and democracy. The narrative gains direct practical and political implications by demonstrating the contingent character of institutions and practices and thereby creating the possibility of changing them. No phenomena can have only one narrative or a single genealogy, just as no historical situation can be explained as having emerged out of total necessity. Narratives not only give meaning to our past experiences, they also help us envision alternative futures.

Two

THE AALBORG PROJECT

Am Anfang war die Tat.
Johann Wolfgang Goethe

In Aalborg, Denmark, on an autumn day in the late 1970s, a group of high-level city officials gather for a meeting. Only one item is on the agenda: initiation of what will eventually become an award-winning project recommended by the OECD for international adoption, on how to integrate environmental and social concerns in city politics and planning, including how to deal with the car in the city. From the very outset the stakes are high. Making the car adapt to the city in the scale now envisioned is something never before tried in Denmark. The project which begins on this day will become known as the "Aalborg Project" and will become one of Denmark's most lauded, and most controversial, urban projects for the next decade and a half. The actors involved will include the business community, grass-roots organizations, political parties, the largest private corporation in all of Denmark, the trade unions, the police, various local and national consultants, interested citizens, the media, the Danish Town Planning Association, North Jutland County, the Office of Public Health, and several agencies of national government, including the Environmental Protection Agency and the Danish Environmental Appeals Board, the OECD, and the Aalborg City Council and its administration. On this, the first day in the life of the project, however, only a handful of people know about its existence, and only a select few are present at the creation. (An overview of the main actors in the Aalborg Project can be found in Appendix A.)[1]

THE WILL TO INNOVATE

The people present at the first meeting are the city engineer, the chief of city planning, the city architect, and the director of the Aalborg Bus Company. The first thing this group of leaders does is to form an Executive Committee for the project with themselves as the only members. Subordinate to the Executive Committee, a Task Force is established containing one staff member from each leader's area of responsibility. From the outset, the Aalborg Project is designed as an interorganizational and interdisciplinary project. The Office of the City Engineer, the Planning Office, the Office of the City Architect, and the Aalborg Bus Company are involved in both the Task Force and the Executive Committee for the project. The city engineer's representative in the Task Force is made the project leader and secretary to the Executive Committee. The Executive Committee is led by the city engineer himself. One member of the Task Force describes the mood at the start of the project and comments upon the interdisciplinary cooperation:

> For me there was a rare agreement between the desire to make a contribution and the desire to work *far beyond* normal working hours. We did this *very* much, three or four of the five or six who were in the Task Force. It was also like this with the attitude we had to the problems [of the city]. What kind of solution were we actually heading toward? For it is one thing to be willing to exert an extraordinary effort to get some problem solved. But it makes it much easier to get results if there is a unity of spirit in the group, and there was. We worked extremely well together. In fact, since then I don't think we've had a group as good as the Task Force . . . A good start and good cooperation, which is something we definitely had, is something very, very powerful and difficult to stop.[2]

A three-year plan is developed for the Aalborg Project. The first year will be spent on developing two plans for downtown Aalborg, one for traffic and environment and one for land use. During the second year, the project will be approved by the City Council, and action will begin on detailed planning of individual subprojects. Finally, the third year will see the implementation of the required physical changes in the city and the official inauguration of the completed project.

Eventually, the Aalborg Project will consist of a large number of subprojects and plans. From early on, however, it is clear to those involved that a central priority will be public transportation. Their mission will be to improve the services of the welfare state by subsidizing and planning for better transit.[3] A year before the Aalborg Project began, the municipality had purchased the city's bus company from an ailing private operator in order to gain control over the provision of this service to the public. The plan is to expand and reorganize the city's bus system. A new bus terminal, with more than 2,000 arriving and departing buses a day, is planned as the hub for the system. The terminal will be the largest single subproject within the Aalborg Project. In addition to the bus terminal, two other planned projects are particularly important at this time: a new civic center, and a new "buses only" street through the city center.[4] The civic center complex is to house the City Council, the Municipal Library, a childrens' library, rooms and facilities for exhibitions and meetings, and a restaurant. With a certain symbolism that does not escape the general public, the City Council decides to build the civic center directly on a piece of land originally cleared for a major road link through the city. Creating the right-of-way for the road had leveled parts of Aalborg's historical center and triggered such controversy that a moratorium was declared on further road construction in the center.[5] The City Council has now made sure that the right-of-way will never be used for its original purpose, physically demonstrating its change in policy by blocking the right-of-way with the civic center and by forcing the town to develop around it. The bus street running through the civic center will provide increased access for public transportation to both the civic center and to the city center in general. Together, the three projects will considerably alter the future appearance and everyday life of Aalborg.

As the bus terminal is the single largest subproject in the Aalborg Project, and the single most important concern of the Task Force at the outset, I have chosen to make a closer examination of the technical analyses and political decisions affecting the location, size, and design of the terminal.

CONDITIONING THE FUTURE

At the start of the Aalborg Project, the Task Force takes it as a given that a bus terminal must be located in downtown Aalborg and that it will be placed at Nytorv, Aalborg's historical town square, and the adjacent street of Østeraagade (gade means "street") (see map facing Chapter 1). It is not clear why the Task Force assumes the terminal's location as a given.

The changing role of public transportation in Aalborg is indicated by the increasing amount of money spent on bus service. From the year when the Aalborg Project begins until four years later when the bus terminal opens, the municipality's total expenses for city buses will triple, while the subsidy will increase ten times.[6] Public transportation is thus a considerable growth sector during these years. As mentioned, a goal of the Aalborg Project and of building the bus terminal is to support and control this growth, to manage the effects of several new bus lines, more passengers, and more buses in the streets.

Aalborg's bus system is the "hub and spoke" type: all bus lines meet at the city center. New bus lines and additional buses running on existing routes will therefore entail a considerable increase in the number of buses in the center. In the narrow streets of the historical center, this leads to increased pressure on scarce road space. Moreover, the buses in Aalborg operate on what the bus company calls "the correspondence model." Bus schedules are planned so as to enable passengers to transfer from one line to another. Buses thus meet simultaneously at the same place in the city center with a pause of three to five minutes, allowing the passengers to transfer to another line, before all the buses again drive away from the transfer point simultaneously. A logical consequence of the correspondence model is that the expansion of public transport becomes especially space demanding in the city center, thus necessitating a bus terminal. Yet the location of the terminal—at Nytorv and Østeraagade, as advocated by the responsible city officials—remains unexplained.

One possible explanation is that prior to the birth of the Aalborg Project the city government already had plans to bring the buses together at Nytorv-Østeraagade. At a Municipal Administration (*Magistrat*) meeting four and a half years before the start of the Aalborg Project, it was announced that "representatives of the Aalborg Bus Company have declared themselves in accord with and interested in the establishment of the aforementioned bus route [the 'buses only' street through the city center] *with the intention of establishing a bus terminal in the Østeraagade-Nytorv intersection*" (italics added). According to a planning consultant who worked for the city at that time, the idea for the bus terminal came from planners working for the municipality, and the intent was to ensure better penetration of the downtown area by public transportation. The planners managed to have the "buses only" street placed on the planning agenda by making it a prerequisite for the architectural competition for the civic center. When the Aalborg Project was initiated, the "buses only" street and the civic center were under construction. The bus street now points literally toward Nytorv as a logical location for the bus terminal. One of the involved Task Force members explains:

> *Planner:* They started with the bus terminal by building the "buses only" street. If they ended up [locating the terminal somewhere else than at Nytorv]—and this is not mentioned anywhere [in minutes, memoranda, and other documents]—then it would have resulted in somebody having made a mistake, right? If someone had figured out that the bus terminal must be placed somewhere else, then [the "buses only" street] would have been a wrong decision.
>
> *Interviewer:* What do you mean?
>
> *Planner:* Then you would in fact have had a bus street, you know, invested in a bus street under [the civic center], where very few buses would be running [be-

cause some other location of the bus terminal would result in another routing of buses].

Even though Nytorv-Østeraagade thus seems destined to become the home of the bus terminal, three months after the start of the Aalborg Project the Task Force begins to discuss other possible locations. Aalborg's city architect has aesthetic and environmental concerns about placing such a large construction in the midst of Aalborg's historic center. First, the terminal would be placed right next to protected, historical buildings. For example, the entire length of one of Aalborg's few architectural treasures of international repute, the Renaissance-style Jens Bang Stone House from 1623, would be covered up to the second floor by waiting buses several times per hour.[7] Second, the terminal would be placed in an already congested traffic environment, where the buses could be expected to create problems in relation to pedestrians, bicyclists, and cars. Finally, the municipality is fully aware that the management of Aalborg's inter-city regional bus station and several private bus owners who operate the intercity buses want an eventual city bus terminal to be placed at the intercity bus station, which, as in most Danish towns, is located at the train station. By locating the city bus terminal at the train station, the intercity bus managers and operators hope to obtain better coordination and transfer possibilities between local, regional, and national bus and train traffic, in addition to increased revenues for the intercity bus station due to increased activity. Therefore, the Office of the City Architect considers moving the proposed terminal away from Nytorv-Østeraagade and now begins to survey other locations.

Officials of the Aalborg Bus Company react strongly to this turn of events. They quickly compose a two-page "Memorandum Concerning the Aalborg Bus Company's Demands for the Bus Terminal."[8] These demands are of interest for two reasons. First, it is the only time in the course of almost fifteen years and tens of thousands of pages of documents regarding the Aalborg Project that one part of the city administration has put forth genuine demands to another part and to the planning process itself. Second, it is worth noting that placing the bus terminal at Nytorv would fulfill all the bus company's demands, even if the memorandum never explicitly cites Nytorv. The demands from the Aalborg Bus Company can be summarized in four main points, here quoted from the memorandum (all italics in the original):

(1) The "most important question" to the bus company is "to ensure" that the terminal "be located at *the most important destination for bus passengers,*" which for the company is "*the network of pedestrian streets*" in downtown Aalborg.[9] (2) Furthermore, the bus company wants buses to "*stop at the terminal simultaneously*" in order to "provide the possibility for a comfortable transfer between bus lines." But the bus company "cannot tolerate" that the stop at the

terminal is longer than three minutes "due to those passengers remaining on the bus." As it takes up to one minute for passengers to exit a bus, this leaves two minutes for walking time between buses, which, when restated as walking distance, translates into a need that all bus stops should be "*located at a distance of less than 150 meters* [from each other]." (3) The bus company points out that it is "not physically possible" to include suburban and intercity bus lines in a city bus terminal located by the pedestrian streets. To make possible transfers between the different types of bus services, the bus company suggests, therefore, that "*a centrally placed transfer area with contact between city buses and other buses should be found.*" This suggestion will later result in the planning of yet another large bus terminal in the city center. (4) Finally, the bus company points out that "a draft plan for bus routes has made it probable that the needs of the city bus network will be met if possibilities are reserved for the *simultaneous placement of 20 city buses at the terminal.*"

In the photocopy of the memorandum I examined, and which stems from the archives of the Office of the City Engineer, no less than nine handwritten figures resembling exclamation marks are written in the margin next to the demand that the terminal be able to hold twenty buses. The question of the *size* of the terminal will be discussed later. Here we will continue to focus our attention on its *location*.

Why does the Aalborg Bus Company make demands at all? And why use the term "demands" only here and not in other issues in the project? On this point the responsible government official, Aalborg's chief planner for public transportation, who is a member of the project's Task Force and subsequently also of the Executive Committee, comments:

> *Chief planner for public transportation:* I don't really remember why I used such a strong word. But, in fact, we viewed these things as quite serious. For as I began by saying, this work [the Aalborg Project] was to a great degree caused by the fact that we were getting a bus terminal, and getting a better arrangement for the buses. We also got the impression that from the municipality's side they were interested in getting good work done and good conditions for the buses. They were willing to spend money on it. That's probably why we have tried to express in such unambiguous and strong language what we thought was necessary in order to obtain good conditions for the buses.
>
> *Interviewer:* But these "good conditions," could you only achieve them at Nytorv?
>
> *Chief planner for public transportation:* No, perhaps not, for the demands you mention are related to the number of buses and maximum walking distance and things like that. We could also get [good conditions for buses] in the harbor areas or at the Railroad Station Square, as long as we are only talking about space [for

the buses]. And I don't think that we use the word "demand" in connection with the other things, that is, regarding questions about travel times and other conditions which in our view make locating the terminal at Nytorv the most desirable option.

The chief planner for public transportation is correct that demands 2, 3, and 4 do not point specifically toward the Nytorv solution. The first demand, however, which explicitly calls for the terminal to be located close to the pedestrian street network, would exclude locating the terminal at either the train station or harbor area.

The bus company's demands startled the other members of the Task Force. One staff member recounts:

I really fell over that word "demands." We discussed it in [the Task Force], and [the Aalborg Bus Company] said that it could just as well have been "preferences." But they *said* "demands." We objected to this in the Task Force because if you evaluate various placement options, there will be some sites where some of the demands cannot be met, and other sites where other demands cannot be met [with the exception of Nytorv, where all the demands can be met; this is the critical point]. There will always be a trade-off between advantages and disadvantages. [The chief planner for public transportation] accepts this, of course. But there is no doubt that most likely it is not a coincidence that he has written "demands" . . . Of course this emphasizes—how should we say it— their preferences, or their proposals for the placement of the bus terminal [at Nytorv].

The bus company's demands obtain a permanent effect on subsequent planning activity in the Aalborg Project because they are ratified by the Executive Committee as prerequisites and criteria in the city architect's evaluations of alternative placement possibilities for the bus terminal. The result, therefore, seems predestined, and the evaluations, as we will see later, become more ritual than real.

ACTORS AND STRUCTURES IN TRANSIT

What enabled the Aalborg Bus Company to present genuine "demands" and have them respected by other city administrative organs? Why does the bus company have so much power?

Three factors—structural, organizational, and individual—can explain why. First, it has already been noted that public transportation was a significant growth sector at this time—in Aalborg and in all of Denmark. In contrast, the activities of the municipality's Technical Department, containing the offices of the city engineer, planning, and the city architect, are all related to construction and are all in deep recession at this point in time, like construction-related activities in the rest of Denmark and in most of Europe. The recession and the aftermath of the 1973 oil crisis begin to have an impact on the power balance between the Aalborg Bus Company and the Technical Department. The bus company obtains increasing patronage and increasing subsidies, whereas the Technical Department is weakened by budget cuts. Here, too, money adds greater weight to an argument, helping it to become a "demand."

Second, the Aalborg Bus Company is an independent public utility company under Aalborg Municipality with responsibility for, and control over, a significant capital and operating budget. The bus company, like other utilities, is sovereign in decisions that concern budgetary considerations. To the extent that the bus company argues that a given decision is necessary in order to meet its budget, and that other decisions will strain the budget, it will be difficult or impossible for other administrative organs to oppose these arguments. And this is exactly the tactic used by the bus company when it argues in favor of the correspondence model and the bus terminal's location at Nytorv: it insists that placing the terminal in locations other than Nytorv would entail longer driving times and thereby increased operating expenses.

There is also a third, personal, source of the bus company's influence: that it is organizationally placed directly under Aalborg's charismatic, social democratic mayor.[10] At this time no other politician in Denmark draws more personal votes in the municipal elections, and no other mayor is more powerful.[11] For the time being, then, the bus company's representatives in the Task Force and Executive Committee have at least as much formal political authority behind them as the entire Task Force and Executive Committee, which is placed under the alderman responsible for the Technical Department and which as mentioned subsumes the three offices of city engineer, planning, and city architect. Here it should also be said that even though the mayor and the alderman are formally equal with respect to their responsibility for their different departments, the post of mayor is more prestigious and more visible to the public than that of alderman. The mayor's visibility, his many personal votes, his charisma, and his ambition make his area of responsibility especially strong both within the city administration and in the community at large. Finally, the mayor, who has the nickname "Bus-Marius"—his full name is Marius Andersen—was himself employed by the Aalborg Bus Company in his youth and is an enthusiastic advocate of public transportation. The mayor was the key figure in the municipality's acquisition of his former employer and in the subsequent major expansion of public transportation. The mayor explains in his own words:

Interviewer: Does it make a department stronger to have a direct connection to the mayor, as the Aalborg Bus Company did?

Mayor: I would certainly say that it is not a minus. But it is clear that in the decision about just that major issue you are asking about [locating the bus terminal], it does not mean anything, for it is still the City Council which in the final instance must approve these things. This issue was both discussed and approved by the City Council, more than once even—discussed, that is . . . We in the Social Democrat group, where I was a member, of course,[12] believed that in order for things to move rapidly, [public transportation] must be under the control of the mayor. And then it was probably also taken into account that in my sweet youth I was employed on the buses.

Interviewer: Yes, you were known as "Bus-Marius"?

Mayor: Exactly, and I still am. So I think that this has meant a great deal. There is no doubt about that. We had many different plans for what we believed needed improvement. And finally, we must also remember that the pressure was enormously great, in that we had run up against all this with oil prices and gasoline prices and such, where the citizens were demanding better public transportation. So just as quickly as I got the plans, and we [the mayor and the Bus Company] could agree on this thing and that thing, they were sent to the Municipal Administration and the City Council. So it's true, things went fast. This is also because especially in the Planning Office [for Public Transportation] I had [the chief planner for public transportation] and then I had one of my people from the Economic Office. And these two, they were really a good team. I owe them a lot for the contribution they made. I was both pleased and proud of them. We cooperated well, so there was nothing like their having to wait when they came up with something. They practically had first priority in getting access [to the mayor].

POWER'S EXPECTATIONS

The two staff members "came up with" the above-mentioned preference to site the bus terminal at Nytorv-Østeraagade. This preference is then backed by the highest political quarters, that is, by Aalborg's mayor and by the alderman in charge of the Technical Department. Again, the mayor explains:

Mayor: I don't think we should hide the fact that we have always considered Nytorv to be the most suitable hub for all public transportation. Therefore we believed that Nytorv was the place for buses . . . I think that all of us who had something to do with the buses—and when I say "us," I think not only of the politicians, but also of the staff—that we believed it would cause a lot of damage if we chose somewhere else [than Nytorv]. When all is said and done, it turns out that the hub is at Nytorv. You feel that this is where you want to go. Because it is so close to all things, public offices, but also the daily shopping trip and many other things, of course . . .

Interviewer: Was placing the bus terminal at Nytorv something you had decided upon in advance in the First Department [in the Mayor's Office]?

Mayor: Perhaps I would not say in the First Department because it was more the experts in the Bus Company under the First Department. It was the First Department, of course, but it was the Bus Company itself. There we agreed, and we have never been in doubt that it should be placed at Nytorv.

Interviewer: Did the alderman for the Technical Department agree to this?

Mayor: I think he agreed with us. I am quite certain.

The mayor's belief is correct. The alderman for the Technical Department, who had gone along without there apparently being any kind of genuine agreement, elaborates:

Personally I had no doubt that in Aalborg there were so many old traditions linked to Nytorv and so much—what should we say—in connection with planning, with respect to business and to the citizens who came to shop, that Nytorv was the right place.

In direct continuation of this quote, the alderman then proceeds to discuss the evaluation of the alternative siting possibilities for the bus terminal being carried out by the Office of the City Architect:

Quite frankly, I must admit that the evaluation [of alternative siting possibilities] was perhaps of a character that it should demonstrate as soon as possible that the other locations were not really well-suited.

Three

BACON AND NIETZSCHE COME
TO NORTHERN JUTLAND

> The will to truth requires a critique—let us thus define our own task—
> the value of truth must for once be experimentally *called into
> question*.
>
> *Friedrich Nietzsche*

STAYING "ON TRACK"

Given the mayor's and the alderman's agreement regarding the exact location of the bus terminal, the city architect's anxieties about aesthetics and environment have little political or technical impact. These anxieties were the original reason for undertaking evaluations of alternative placement options for the terminal. The evaluations, however, become mere rationalizations of a political decision made in advance. The decision to locate the bus terminal at Nytorv is not explicit at this stage, just as no politicians are directly involved in the planning process at this time. Nevertheless, certain political attitudes become prominent in the course of the work. Witness the following example, from an interview with Aalborg's chief planner for public transportation:

> *Chief planner for public transportation:* We didn't draw on the mayor as someone who stood behind us [the bus company] pounding the table . . .
>
> *Interviewer:* But in the Executive Committee and the Task Force did you call attention to the fact that the mayor wanted the Nytorv option?
>
> *Chief planner for public transportation:* No, I didn't, because I have never discussed this with the mayor. It just wasn't necessary. It might have been necessary to discuss it with him if the evaluations looked as if they favored a completely different site. Then I would certainly have gone in and discussed his views with him. But as long as we—allow me to say—kept things on the track where I knew that he agreed with us, there was no reason to go in and discuss whether we ought to opt for something else.

The most important means of keeping the decision process "on track" was, first, the bus company's set of ostensibly neutral demands for placing the bus terminal at Nytorv, as described in the previous chapter. The demands were neutral only in the sense that the precise desired location was never named specifically. A second important means by which the decision was kept on track was the technical evaluations of alternative placement possibilities for the terminal, for which the bus company's demands were ratified as prerequisites and evaluation criteria. This chapter focuses on how these seemingly neutral evaluations form part of the relations of power which underlie the Aalborg Project.

DECISION FIRST, RATIONALIZATION LATER

Four months after work with the evaluations began, a twenty-six-page memorandum is completed, the main conclusion of which is that the bus terminal should be located within the geographic area corresponding to downtown Aalborg.[1] No one has ever suggested or expected anything else. Since the memorandum says nothing about specific placement options for the bus terminal within the downtown area, it is, in effect, an empty exercise that does not advance the decision regarding placement of the terminal any further.

The situation is altered, however, with a second memorandum which appears about a week later.[2] In three pages and nine maps, seven possible locations for the bus terminal are mentioned: (1) Nytorv-Østeraagade, (2) the Railroad Station Square (Banegaardspladsen), (3) the southern part of Østeraagade, (4) Gabelsgade-Nytorv, (5) Budolfi Square (Budolfi Plads), (6) the northern part of Østeraagade toward Castle Square (Slotspladsen), (7) in the area of the block Boulevarden-Algade-Budolfi Plads-Vingaardsgade. The evaluation of the seven placement possibilities with reference to the bus company's demands occupies a page and a half and fails to make any final conclusion about a preferred placement of the terminal. The memorandum states, however, that locations (3) through (7) do not meet the requirements for twenty separate bus stops within the terminal area. Thus, only Nytorv and the Railroad Station Square are viewed as real options. The memorandum concludes that placing the bus terminal in Nytorv will create problems for pedestrians in this area and will cause problems for vehicles delivering goods to certain shops and businesses.

The two memoranda are incomplete. They are a long time in the making, and their collective content—a long text about a nondecision, followed by a short one on the real problem, but again without any recommendations—is clearly unbalanced. In addition, neither memorandum tackles their primary task: to rationally argue for the best placement of the bus terminal in the city center. This may be due to the fact that the author of the memoranda has divided loyalties. On one side stands his chief, the city architect, who is skeptical about the Nytorv option. On the other the much more powerful coalition of the mayor, the alderman for the Technical Department and the management of the Aalborg Bus Company, who all want precisely the Nytorv option implemented.

Regardless of the reasons for the incomplete nature of the two memoranda, it transpires that even before the technical evaluations of placement options for the terminal have been completed, the Aalborg Project's Task Force decides to locate the terminal at Nytorv anyway. At the same time, however, it is decided that the evaluation work must be continued, but it is transferred from the Office of the City Architect to the consulting firm working for the Technical Department on the overall design of the Aalborg Project. Minutes of a Task Force meeting summarize the situation: "The Task Force agreed upon selecting the Nytorv-Østeraagade intersection as the city bus terminal. [The consulting firm] will elaborate a report which describes the advantages and disadvantages of the proposed locations for the city bus terminal."[3]

What happens, then, is that the decision regarding the location of the bus terminal is made simultaneously with a decision about elaborating the technical basis for that very decision. The idea that this seems a topsy-turvy way of operating met with laughter in an interview with the head of (and secretary to) the Task Force:

> It sounds mystical . . . Of course [the two decisions] contradict each other, that's clear. It must have been a bad secretary [the interviewee himself] who did not censor it out [of the minutes of the meeting] [laughter].

As concerns the transfer of the evaluation work to a consulting firm, the Task Force member who up to this point has been responsible for the evaluations at the Office of the City Architect explains that the transfer was aimed at increasing the credibility of the decision:

> We wrote a memorandum. The memorandum still does not have the necessary traffic engineering expertise and needs to be supplemented. The mere fact that it is done by [the consulting firm] means that it obtains this expertise.

Those desiring a location at Nytorv might also see it as an advantage that the work is transferred out of the Office of the City Architect, as it was the city architect who originally expressed doubts about the Nytorv option. In any case, after the consulting firm takes over the evaluation of alternative locations, work proceeds rapidly. Six days after the Task Force has decided to propose Nytorv and delegate the evaluation work to the firm, the consultants have completed a memorandum on the advantages and disadvantages of eight different location options.[4] Not surprisingly, Nytorv is pointed out as the best site for the bus terminal. The consultants write:

> In our opinion, a review of the suitability of the eight selected city bus terminal sites results in favor of the Nytorv-Østeraagade intersection. In relation to the above review, there is as such *nothing which speaks against* a placement [of the terminal] at this site. The other sites must be discouraged due to the following *main objections* . . . [italics added].[5]

The objections cited include lack of central location, inadequate capacity, too great a walking distance inside the terminal, negative environmental effects, poor entrance and exit possibilities for traffic, and poor visibility. Of interest here, however, are not so much the contents of the specific advantages and disadvantages but the structure of the entire argumentation. The Nytorv-Østeraagade option is discussed in terms of the *advantages* of a bus terminal on this site, while for the remaining locations emphasis is placed on their *disadvantages*. One can, of course, call this an evaluation of advantages and disadvantages, but it is a quite unique form of evaluation in which the advantages are evaluated for a single option—Nytorv—while for all the other options it is the disadvantages which are highlighted. The consequences are obvious. This unique evaluation method appears not only in the consulting firm's internal memorandum but also in the official final report on the bus terminal presented to the City Council and to the public. In this final report, the evaluation method and its results are edited even further, such that every mention of disadvantages for Nytorv and of advantages for the seven remaining location options are now left out.[6]

The city architect's reservations about deficiencies in the Nytorv option—aesthetic, environmental, and functional—are totally absent from the report. They reemerge later, however, in the political treatment of the overall project design now underway, just as the alternative options to Nytorv show themselves to be unwilling to quietly fade away. But this is a subject for the future. For now the Executive Committee for the Aalborg Project approves the Task Force's recommendation that the bus terminal be built at Nytorv, and the draft designs of a terminal at this site are begun.[7]

The disagreement between the Office of the City Architect and the bus company regarding the location and size of the bus terminal had the seeds of open confrontation. As we shall see repeatedly in this study, however, confrontation is actively avoided in the Aalborg Project. In this case, the city architect and the Technical Department adapt themselves to the bus company's demands for a larger, more centrally placed terminal, despite the fact that these demands are neither technically nor economically documented.

While interviewing two Task Force members who were the main actors in the evaluation of the bus terminal, I called their attention to the fact that both the procedure and the content of the technical evaluations seem unbalanced:

> *Interviewer:* To me it seems you use a strange sort of evaluation method.
>
> *Task Force member:* It certainly is. There is no doubt that from the start, Aalborg Bus Company simply pointed toward Nytorv as the site where the bus terminal was to be located. Of course it has been the object of discussion both in the Task Force and in the Executive Committee, where it is then decided that the analysis of the location options must be carried out. And where it may sometimes be, I don't know, probably difficult to execute such an analysis completely and fully when in reality there are people involved who have already made their views known in an especially hard and uncompromising way. And it is certainly correct, I would also say, that if I read through this [evaluation of the bus terminal's location] that I would also think, "Well, yes, all this sure seems completely strange." I was so deeply involved in the case at that time that I thought it sounded acceptable. [The consulting firm] apparently did so, too. It is they who are listed as the authors. So I cannot really say anything else than I certainly also think now, several years afterwards, that this sounds strange.

Asked the same question, the second Task Force member responds in similar fashion:

> *Task Force member:* It is reasonably clear regarding the demands which the Aalborg Bus Company has formulated that they really were based on the question, "What functions can be carried out at Nytorv?" The evaluation has then consisted of how the other placement options could fulfill these needs compared with Nytorv. And it could certainly be that if other demands had been formulated, or other points of departure were taken, that some other result would have emerged. Then our elaboration of [these location options] would of course have led to something else . . . But we knew full well that the bus company's wishes were entirely clear: when we started they wanted Nytorv. But I think really that when we started we were perhaps more critical about a location down there [at Nytorv] and leaned more toward a location at the railroad station. Those were the two alternatives. What did we actually write about the train station? [Reads aloud from the evaluation report:] "Furthermore, location must be completely central in relation to the pedestrian streets." That's right. It is really fantastic that this is written here. But from the demands made [by Aalborg Bus Company], it's correct. If this is a prerequisite, then [a location at the Railroad Station square] is no alternative . . .

Interviewer: In the Task Force you all agreed to propose Nytorv to the Executive Committee. At the same time you decided that a memorandum had to be written which should describe the advantages and disadvantages. In terms of a normal logical sequence I would think that it should have been the reverse.

Task Force member: Yes, that's entirely clear. The problem in this planning is time pressure. There is, in fact, a set schedule for when a bus terminal at Nytorv-Østeraagade must be established. And whether starting to look at the other [location possibilities] is a plot, or what it really is, I think can be questioned. The memorandum we wrote lacks a more planning and traffic-related evaluation of the different location options, for we had no chance to carry out such things.

Interviewer: But isn't this just good old fashioned manipulation? To make a decision on something and then say, "Let's make a memorandum which shows that it is the right decision."

Task Force member: I wouldn't say that. But you know, it might look kind of strange, right? [Laughter]. And that's correct—it might, well—of course it resembles—hmmm, you know—rationalization, right?

At this point in the interview this Task Force member clearly became uncomfortable that the interview was being recorded on tape. After the tape recorder was turned off, he called the evaluation of alternative placement options "an unusually poor piece of work." If time pressure is as critical to the quality of the evaluation of the placement options as this Task Force member indicates, it is puzzling that four to five months are allowed to pass from the time it is decided that the evaluations must be carried out until the actual memorandum—with three pages of text—is finished. Until this time the evaluation of the placement possibilities takes place at a leisurely pace. The argument regarding the existence of time pressure and its consequences for the evaluation of placement possibilities does not seem convincing.

In a relatively intensively utilized city center like that of Aalborg, one might expect so much competition for existing space that every application of space has a high opportunity cost and must be evaluated in relation to alternative uses. Such an assessment is not carried out. Considering, for instance, Nytorv-Østeraagade's historical function as a public gathering place and a market square for Aalborg, it could well be argued that the use of the area for a bus terminal would be a rupture with historical traditions. Alternative uses as parking space, street area, or possible recreational area also might seem realistic. A long-standing proposal with wide public support has been to reopen the "East River" which is presently covered by Østeraagade. This alternative is similarly not considered even though the construction of the bus terminal will have direct consequences for this proposal's likelihood of ever being realized.

That such evaluations of alternative utilizations of urban space are not considered in the placement of the bus terminal can be seen as yet another expression of the strong position of public transportation in the Aalborg Project and in Aalborg. The absence of these evaluations, however, is probably also related to a long-standing Aalborg tradition of expropriating marketplaces, squares, green areas, and other open spaces for building and transport purposes. Thus, several sites that the Aalborg city map identifies as "Square" (*torv* or *plads*) are now occupied by department stores, office buildings, banks, parking lots, and new streets. This tradition, too, can be seen as an expression of a power relation, in this case between a diffuse public interest in keeping the city open and green and the much more focused interest of establishing specific businesses and transport structures.

RATIONALITY AS JUSTIFICATION OF POWER

A short summary is relevant here. Aalborg's mayor, the alderman in charge of the Technical Department, and the management of the Aalborg Bus Company have both a desire and a strong expectation that a planned terminal for city buses be placed at Nytorv-Østeraagade. The desire has its background in Nytorv's large physical area and in Nytorv's central position in downtown Aalborg in relation to the network of pedestrian streets. Besides, Nytorv has historically functioned as a public space in downtown Aalborg and as the hub of Aalborg's city bus system. Last but not least, the construction of a bus street under the town's new civic center from Østerbro to Nytorv has led to a predisposition toward locating the bus terminal at Nytorv. If the terminal is not placed here, effective utilization of the bus street will be difficult. Several of the persons interviewed speak frankly about the bus street being a mistaken investment if the terminal is not located at Nytorv, even though this consideration does not explicitly enter into the formal evaluations of the terminal's site.

The consequence of the strong desire that the bus terminal be located at Nytorv is that several evaluations of alternative placement options for the terminal take on the character of technical rationalizations of a previously made decision. The evaluations of the alternatives were originally begun at the request of Aalborg's city architect, who was concerned about the possible negative aesthetic and environmental repercussions of building the bus terminal at Nytorv. With a power configuration consisting of Aalborg's mayor, the alderman for the Technical Department, and the Aalborg Bus Company on the one side, and the city architect on the other, the evaluations result in the clear-cut selection of Nytorv as the most suitable site for the terminal. This result does not reflect a balanced, neutral analysis, even though the attempt is made to lend it this kind of appearance. The result is due to the fact that in structural terms, with the choice of evaluation criteria and the mode in which they are applied to the individual placement possibilities, the evaluations recapitulate the pre-destined result: Nytorv inevitably becomes the logical choice. The chief planner for public transportation subsequently comments on what took place:

> I think that I had the view that the placement of the bus terminal at Nytorv was already settled upon . . . I viewed the City Architect's act as a pro forma act, he needed it for the purpose of indicating a professional attitude externally and internally. In this connection I should mention that it was the same City Architect who a few years previously had approved the destruction of Nytorv's north and south sides and the construction of the building complex located between the savings bank and the tourist bureau. And then approved the construction of the *Stiftstidende* [a large building complex with editorial offices and production plant for Aalborg's daily newspaper, *Aalborg Stiftstidende*] and *Salling* [the city's largest department store]. The aesthetic objection was difficult to take seriously.[8]

What emerges is a picture of technical expertise used as rationalization of policy, of rationality as the legitimation of power. Analyses of project documents support this interpretation, as do interviews with the highest political leaders—Aalborg's mayor and the alderman for the Technical Department—and with those staff members who carried out the evaluation studies of the bus terminal's placement possibilities. Another interpretation, however, can be found if one speaks with the leader of the Aalborg Project's Executive Committee, Aalborg's city engineer. He asserts that the evaluation work was carried out "neutrally and thoroughly:"

> It is clear enough that we who have been in the town for many years and have worked with the problem, with the issue, for many years, that we had a preliminary impression of how the bus terminal should be located. It is indisputable that we had such a view. But we can then go back and find several other things where we have had preconceived views and believed that they were correct, but where our analytical work showed that our preconceived views were wrong. So I would say that it was not a sham analysis. Even if deep down inside we believed that the analysis would point toward Nytorv-Østeraagade as the site for a bus terminal. I would also say that the analyses which were carried out were absolutely neutral and thorough, as they ought to be. In my view, the work itself does not bear the impression of a sham.

We may speculate as to whether the city engineer's views stem from a lack of insight into what has actually been going on. He did not originate the politically preconceived attitude about the terminal's placement, nor was he immediately responsible for the concrete technical evaluations. Perhaps his view derives from the fact that the work which was carried out under his formal direction, in principle—after generally accepted professional ethical criteria—*ought* to be "neutral and thorough," and that he is therefore unreflectively presenting the work as such: this is the way it ought to be, and therefore it *is* this way. Support for this interpretation is seen in the city engineer's use of the subjunctive mode in explaining that the analyses are "as they ought to be." Finally, it could be that the city engineer, consciously or not, is trying to hide a problematic piece of work, or that due to the time interval between the time of the interview and the actual events he has simply forgotten what really happened.[9]

POWER IS KNOWLEDGE

Regardless of the background for the city engineer's view, the string of events leading up to the decision on the bus terminal's placement is a clear example of a rationality-power relation at work. The rationality produced is actively formed by the power relations which are themselves grounded and expressed in processes that are social-structural, conjunctural, organizational, and actor related. Conversely, these power relations are supported by the rationality generated.

This is the situation in the preliminary phase of the Aalborg Project, even before formal objectives and an actual project design have been formulated and before politicians and the general public know about the project. And, as we shall see, this situation reemerges repeatedly through the entire life of the project, from genesis and design to approval, implementation, and operation. This type of rationality-power relations and their dynamic interplay are characteristic of the kinds of issues discussed here. It is a far cry from the kind of disinterested "neutrality and thoroughness" that Aalborg's city engineer talks about.

In the introduction to this book I mentioned Francis Bacon's famous words, "Knowledge is power." According to Bacon's dictum, which lies at the core of modernity, the Enlightenment, and rationalism, the more knowledge the better. In this and the previous chapter we have seen that the *verita effettuale* of rationality and power in the Aalborg Project stands Bacon on his head. In Aalborg, "power is knowledge." Power does not *seek* knowledge out of a Baconian imperative. Rather, power *defines* what counts as knowledge and rationality, and ultimately, as we shall see, what counts as reality. In Aalborg, the Baconian worldview thus yields to a Nietzschean question: "*What* in us really wants 'truth'? . . . *why not rather* untruth? and uncertainty? even ignorance?" (italics in original).[10]

Four

POWER DEFINES REALITY

> The possession of power unavoidably spoils the free use of reason.
> *Immanuel Kant*

There is more to the non–Baconian relationship between power and knowledge in the Aalborg Project. Much more. Barely a year has passed since the project was begun. The draft designs of the bus terminal at Nytorv are proceeding, and the project's path to implementation should be clear. Things, however, are not running smoothly in the Technical Department. Not everyone believes that the decision about the bus terminal is correct, and dissatisfaction creates friction in the project machinery. There are those who believe that the terminal is too large, considering that it will be located in the heart of Aalborg's historical center. For these people the question now becomes, "Can the terminal be made smaller?"

FROM TECHNICAL TO POLITICAL ARGUMENT

As mentioned earlier, one of the demands made by the Aalborg Bus Company was that the terminal should contain twenty parking spaces for buses. Even though it can be problematic to compare public transportation in various cities, it is nevertheless instructive regarding this particular demand that the Town Hall Square in the Danish capital of Copenhagen, the hub of a bus network serving a population ten times that of Aalborg, contains only twenty-nine bus parking spaces. The demand for twenty parking places in Aalborg derived from the previously mentioned "correspondence model," in which the buses from various lines stop at the terminal simultaneously, allowing passengers to transfer between lines. To allow for passenger transfer, however, the correspondence model requires space for the simultaneous parking of all the buses, which makes it especially land extensive.

In contrast to the correspondence model, a so-called frequency model allows a high frequency of buses on the most important routes through the city center. The frequency model gives low correspondence, whereas the correspondence model gives low frequency. In the frequency model, the buses' arrival times at the terminal are staggered, yielding a high frequency of arrival and departure. The frequency model would no longer require the buses to stop and wait at the hub point. The drivers' rest breaks could take place at the end stations, so that through passengers would not be delayed. Hence, the frequency model would significantly reduce the required size of a bus terminal, if not eliminate the need for it entirely.

In the decision about where to place the bus terminal, no considerations were made regarding the relative advantages and disadvantages of the two models. The correspondence model and the demand for the twenty bus parking spaces were taken as a given. After the decision about the location had been made, however, several members of the Aalborg Project's Task Force and Executive Committee began to discuss the advantages of the frequency model and the disadvantages of the correspondence model. A member of the Task Force comments:

> How much can the physical spaces [squares, streets, etc.] in the town really take? We clearly pointed out that the best solution seen from our point of view [the Office of the City Architect] for achieving good city spaces and not destroying them with those giant traffic machines was really the frequency model because you could actually be satisfied—if it was on Nytorv for example—with two bus parking places in each direction [on the T-intersection making up Nytorv Østeraagade], that is, six stops . . . The problem would have been solved much better with the frequency model. This is completely clear. The frequency model was our favorite . . . We could see that regardless of how one wanted to place [the bus terminal], it would be very hard [on the city center]. That is, if it was [placed] on the Railroad Station Square, then there would be no Railroad Station Square left; it would become one giant transit center. And it was also very hard on Nytorv.

Aalborg's city engineer now calls for yet another memorandum from the municipality's planning consultants, who are asked to evaluate the frequency model in relation to the correspondence model.[1] The consultants conclude that the correspondence model will benefit the 4% of Aalborg's bus passengers who (1) travel from a stop on a bus line with low frequency to a stop on another line, *and* (2) who transfer at the city center. The memorandum concludes that the frequency model partially "discriminates" against such passengers, but that some of the disadvantages can possibly be reduced via a careful planning of routes and driving schedules. On the other hand, application of the frequency model actually improves conditions for nearly 50% of the bus passengers: those who (1) travel through the city center without transferring, and (2) those who travel within the parts of the city where buses will run more frequently. Other transferring passengers obtain the same conditions in both models.

The Aalborg Bus Company reacts promptly to the consultant's memorandum, which can be interpreted as favoring the frequency model, and which is interpreted as such by those who desire a smaller bus terminal. Five days after receiving the memorandum, the bus company responds with a "Comment."[2] The company does not discuss the concrete passenger statistics mentioned in the consultant's memorandum but presents the problem as a case of two contrasting assertions. Distinctions are blurred by the company's argument that a combination of the correspondence and frequency models is already operating, in that at a given minute—fifteen and forty-five minutes after the hour, for example—a correspondence is achieved between one set of city bus lines, and at another point, ten and fifty minutes after the hour, for example, there exists a correspondence between another set of lines:

> It therefore seems that the "frequency model's" high frequency is already present, and that the frequency improvements which are additionally obtainable on the inner part of the main access roads are not significant. The *assertion* [italics added] that the buses drive in "clusters" [as pointed out in the consultant's memorandum] is thus not in accordance with the actual situation, and it goes without saying that efforts to retain this high frequency will be kept in the further planning of schedules. Aalborg Bus Company therefore believes that there is no basis to alter the existing planning basis for the city bus terminal.[3]

What is interesting in relation to power and knowledge is not whether the consultants' or the bus company's respective assertions are correct. Rather, it is the undocumented way in which the Aalborg Bus Company constructs and executes its argumentation. A member of the project's Task Force comments that an evaluation of the bus company's view versus the consulting firm's view "was never investigated thoroughly" and that the bus company "was not interested in having it investigated." By structuring the discussion in terms of two contrasting assertions, the principle of what Jürgen Habermas calls the force of the better argument is replaced by mere force. Instead of rational argument, one gets *Realpolitik,* and the bus company wins out because of its aforementioned political and organizational dominance.

In addition, after more than a year of planning and designing, time is now becoming a factor. The deadline for finishing the overall project design approaches and passes, and the Task Force is still discussing location and size of the bus terminal. Finally the project's Executive Committee decides in favor of the bus company. The considerations regarding the frequency model are simply dismissed, and the planning basis for the bus terminal remains unaltered. A member of the Task Force comments:

> [The "frequency" and "correspondence" models] are analyzed very late, as you can see, and [the consultants] write the memorandum, and [the chief planner for public transportation] writes another memorandum. Then all this is examined at a meeting of the Executive Committee. I do not know whether this is in the minutes. There was a—I don't know if you could say "big"—in any case some discussion of the two views. One view was that we hold on to the correspondence principle on the grounds of the consulting firm's memo and the remarks made by [the chief planner for public transportation], because he hints that in practice [the bus company] cannot live with the frequency principle. It has such great disadvantages. We came to the conclusion that in reality the time schedule [for the Aalborg Project] would collapse if we were to carry out a systematic analysis of this. So there were two main points of view which were discussed at the Executive Committee meeting, where we decided on the correspondence model.

WILL TO KNOWLEDGE, WILL TO IGNORANCE

Like the decision about the placement of the bus terminal, the decision about its size reflects the interaction between technical rationality and power. The documentation not produced is just as interesting as that which is produced. The decision to resolve a clear-cut controversy over arguments by simply refusing to investigate it further is "political" by any sense of the term. We can see that the closer one sits to political power, the less use one apparently has for technical documentation, and the less rational one is in this sense.

For example, a thorough analysis of the correspondence and frequency models would certainly involve an evaluation of whether the existing correspondences actually function in practice. Bus traffic in Aalborg was presumably already operating on the correspondence model, and it would have been relatively simple to investigate whether the correspondence between buses at the transfer points was in fact achieved, which is a necessary prerequisite for operating with the model at all. A subsequent study, conducted two years later, showed that about 30% of the arrivals in the peak hours were delayed and that the scheduled correspondence did not exist for these arrivals. For passengers arriving on delayed buses, transfer time is maximized instead of minimized: the passengers typically see the back of the bus pulling away just as they arrive at the bus stop with the delayed bus. A 30% chance of this happening means that the bus system is not particularly effective for transferring commuters and others who have to meet a certain time. This would seem a strong argument for abandoning the correspondence model. The correspondence study was carried out by the bus company under pressure from the Office of the City Engineer, who wanted the documentation. The correspondence model was, in fact, subsequently abandoned in favor of the frequency model during weekday working hours. At the start of the Aalborg Project, however, this information does not exist, and what it is more important, the bus company is not interested in this knowledge being produced. Instead, the choice of the correspondence model and the decision about the bus terminal's size are made *as if* correspondence is actually achieved. The end—a large centrally placed bus terminal—apparently justifies the means.

It also seems self-evident that the size of the bus terminal must be evaluated in the context of the evaluation of the terminal's location and not after this evaluation. The location possibilities are dependent on the size, and size is affected by location. Such an association, however, is not made explicit in either the consultants' or the bus company's memoranda. On the contrary, four out of the eight placement options are excluded from evaluation, solely due to their lack of holding capacity for buses. All four options would have had adequate capacity according to the frequency model, but they have already been eliminated and are not reintroduced, as they logically should have been, when the frequency model and terminal size are discussed.

It is interesting to note the difference in how the various parties involved in the Aalborg Project see and use technical documentation, and especially the difference between the Office of the City Engineer and the Aalborg Bus Company. It is a difference in attitude about the necessity of documenting one's objectives and projects. The different views seem to generate friction between the two parties, as can be seen from my interview with Aalborg's chief planner for public transportation:

> *Interviewer:* I believe I observe a difference in the ways which the Office of the City Engineer and the Planning Office for Public Transportation elaborate their documentation. It seems like the Office of the City Engineer places greater emphasis on documentation.
>
> *Chief planner for public transportation:* We carried out the documentation which we in the Task Force agreed had to be done. So that may be why there is no more [documentation] from this end [the Aalborg Bus Company]. If we

had decided that more [documentation] was needed, then we would have produced it . . .

Interviewer: When you sit here as a planner, and there is something you want to get through [the political process], what kinds of levers do you have to pull? Is it documentation? I mean, is it important for you that you can say, "Those are the figures, and therefore I want to have this and that?" Or are there other levers, like getting hold of the right persons and convincing them that this is the right thing to do?

Chief planner for public transportation: Today our situation is that we have only one path to follow, that is via the alderman [for the Fifth Department, i.e., public utilities].[4] If we are to get something done about which he is not convinced already, a strong documentation will be necessary. If it is something which we know he supports, then we in fact do not need to have very much documentation. Perhaps this may well have been the case with some of what we talked about before with the planning of the city center. It had already been decided that a bus terminal was to be built at Nytorv. To document its necessity, we probably regarded it as being less important.

Other members of the Aalborg Project's Task Force do not think that the bus company has always produced the documentation one could want. One Task Force member makes the following comments:

I think that [the bus company's powerful position in the Mayor's Office] has at times influenced—how should I say it—their willingness to carry out analyses meant to document the need for or effect of some of the measures taken concerning public transportation. They had no tradition for this . . . We in the Technical Department, and perhaps especially here in the Office of the City Engineer, tend to analyze things almost completely before they go any further. It doesn't happen every time, but we do it to a much greater degree [than the bus company] . . . If we proposed something, then it was often fantastically well-documented. There is no tradition for this at the Aalborg Bus Company, or at the Planning Office for Public Transportation. We have experienced, perhaps more in other contexts, that they certainly do not feel that there is a need for this kind of thing [documentation]. If they say that they cannot live with one or another proposal which we come up with, or [if they have] a proposal which they cannot get through, then we have certainly seen—at least when they were under the Mayor's Office, but it is partly still the case—that they do not document very well what the problem really is. They say that it just *is* this or that way.

On some occasions it has also been our experience—this applies to completely different matters—that they propose something where we might say,

"We are just not sure that we agree." Then they start saying that they can't live without it, or with it [whichever applies in the specific case]. Where we then say, "Well, then you must document that," and where [the proposal] then disappears. You know, they do not have the same tradition, and personally I think that this is due to the fact that during that phase [in the Mayor's Office] . . . the mayor was very enthusiastic about ensuring that public transportation had good conditions. So they did not need to document through and through. The Social Democrats held the majority [in the City Council] and the mayor had a very big influence [in the City Council and the Municipal Administration]. This means that if the mayor agreed with an idea, then you didn't really need to waste your energy on documenting it in every detail.

The bus company management seems to operate from the Nietzschean "doctrine of Hamlet": "Knowledge kills action; action requires the veils of illusion."[5] "Illusion" is produced through the manipulated evaluation of the location and size of the bus terminal. Better knowledge about the physical-aesthetic impact, about correspondence between buses, and—as we shall see later—about environmental consequences, when combined with a more balanced evaluation, might destroy the illusion and might "kill" the action the bus company wants: a large bus terminal in the center of town.

In summarizing this section, it is important to note that both the Technical Department as well as the consulting firm who elaborates the first design for the Aalborg Project initially desire a more complete and balanced evaluation of the bus terminal's location and size. Yet when they fail to succeed in getting their way against the bus company's pressure for placing the terminal at Nytorv-Østeraagade, the Technical Department proceeds to actively participate in the manipulated evaluation. The Technical Department actually lends its name to the evaluation by publishing it in the department's series of reports on the Aalborg Project, which they were not required to do.[6]

THE MAYOR'S MEMORIAL

In the decision-making process about the placement and size of the bus terminal, the Aalborg Bus Company utilizes a strategy I will call "defining reality." The bus company is not just, or primarily, preoccupied with the interpretation and social construction of certain concepts central to politics and planning in Aalborg. Rather, it seeks to directly influence the physical layout and functioning of the city itself. So, instead of spending—or wasting, as the bus company would see it—its time on investigating how the city and its transportation systems function, the bus company tries, with substantial success at this point in the life of the Aalborg Project, to define this functioning. This strategy can be employed because the entity doing the defining has a key position—politically, organizationally, and structurally—in the Aalborg Project. We will encounter the "defining reality" strategy again later among other strong parties in the project.

A truly balanced evaluation of alternative location options for the bus terminal would have included an evaluation of the terminal's size, an analysis of the relative benefits and drawbacks of each of the alternative locations, and a comparative evaluation of utilizing each location option for other potential uses. Instead of this kind of evaluation, the Aalborg Bus Company gradually pushes through an evaluation which (1) builds upon a set of evaluative criteria predisposed to the desired placement of the terminal at Nytorv-Østeraagade, and (2) emphasizes the benefits of the desired location while emphasizing only the drawbacks of the competitors. The result of the evaluation is a foregone conclusion: it serves to rationalize a prior political decision. Analysis, instead of acting as a foundation for intelligent policy making, becomes a manipulated instrument of politics.

As for the question of the bus terminal's size, the reverse tactics are used. When the bus company can no longer control the technical evaluations, and when the consulting firm's analysis calls into question the bus company's need for a terminal with twenty bus parking spaces in the very center of Aalborg, the bus company transforms the problem from a technical one to a political one by constructing it as two competing assertions. At the political level, the company is strongly allied with Aalborg's influential mayor, and it benefits from the upswing in public transportation in Denmark at this point in time. As a result, the bus company also wins the struggle over the size of the terminal. The data which speak against a large terminal is suppressed, and further study of the advantages and disadvantages of a large terminal is hindered. This is how one constructs a reality called a "large, centrally placed bus terminal."

In the controversy over the terminal's location, analysis is used to rationalize politics. For the question of the terminal's size, analysis is preempted by use of politics. *Techne* and rationality are thus clearly subordinated to and used as an integral part of politics and power in the decisions about the Aalborg Project's largest subproject. Documentation is not produced "neutrally and thoroughly," as textbooks and Aalborg's city engineer would have us believe. Efforts to analyze and document are made more in order to rationalize and legitimate established attitudes and prior decisions than to produce a balanced, documentary basis for making decisions. Where there is disagreement regarding the decisions, the documentation is manipulated or left out in order to strengthen one's own positions or weaken that of opponents. Analysis and knowledge are an integral part of the political-administrative power struggle.

The power balance in this struggle now proceeds to the design table for detailed drafting on its way to finding its physical-spatial expression: a monument to Aalborg's mayor and his buses. In this way a power-based political decision is given the appearance of having been technical-rational and democratic. Not only is the general public manipulated and ignored in this procedure, but so is the Danish Environmental Protection Agency, which subsequently finds the bus terminal's expected environmental impacts to be "unacceptable" and demands a renewed study of alternative location options for the terminal. In reality, the alternative locations and sizes for the bus terminal have never been evaluated neutrally, and today the bus terminal—popularly called the "Marius Memorial" (*Marius Minde*) after the mayor—is located precisely where a monument to power should be: in the historical core of Aalborg. The bus terminal has become yet another expression of a more than century-long tradition for brutalistic urban politics and planning in Aalborg, a politics the Aalborg Project was otherwise intended to halt.

With these considerations, however, we are getting ahead of our story. So far, we can provisionally conclude that power does not limit itself to defining a specific kind of knowledge, conception, or discourse of reality. Rather, power defines physical, economic, ecological, and social reality itself. Power is more concerned with defining a specific reality than with understanding what reality is. Thus, power seeks change, not knowledge. And power may very well see knowledge as an obstacle to the change power wants. This, I will argue, is the most important single characteristic of the rationality of power, that is, of the strategies and tactics of power in relation to rationality. Power, quite simply, produces that knowledge and that rationality which is conducive to the reality it wants. Conversely, power suppresses that knowledge and rationality for which it has no use. In modern societies the ability to facilitate or suppress knowledge is in large part what makes one party more powerful than another.

TO PRESERVE A MOMENT

So far in the Aalborg Project, the relationship between rationality and power can best be summarized in the following proposition: "Power defines rationality and power defines reality." This phenomenology of power and rationality is related to that most fundamental aspect of will to power, the will to survival. Will to power is manifested in the ability to make one's own view of the world the very world in which others live.[7] The Aalborg "transit lobby" clearly has this ability. Will to survival is Nietzsche's message when he speaks of people as "clever animals" who "invented knowledge," calling this invention both "arrogant" and "untruthful" but at the same time "a help . . . to preserve [man] a moment in . . . existence."[8] At the most basic level this is what the "Marius Memorial" is about.

According to Kant, "The possession of power unavoidably spoils the free use of reason."[9] On the basis of the case of the Aalborg bus terminal, we may expand on Kant by observing that the possession of more power appears to spoil reason even more. One of the privileges of power, and an integral part of its rationality, is the freedom to define reality. The greater the power, the greater the freedom in this respect, and the less need for power to understand how reality is constructed. The absence of rational arguments and factual documentation in support of certain actions may be just as important indicators of power as the arguments and documentation produced. A party's unwillingness to present rational argument or documentation may quite simply indicate the freedom to define reality.

As will be shown, rational argument is one of the few forms of power that those without much influence still possess; rationality is part of the power of the weak. This mechanism in part explains the enormous appeal of the Enlightenment project to those outside power. Machiavelli, however, does not put much trust in rational persuasion. "We must distinguish," he says in *The Prince*, "between . . . those who to achieve their purpose can force the issue and those who must use persuasion. In the second case, they always come to grief."[10] "Always" may be somewhat exaggerated, and much has happened in terms of Enlightenment and modernity since Machiavelli wrote these words. Nevertheless, at this stage Machiavelli's analysis certainly applies in the case of the Aalborg Project, which is premodern in this sense.

Nietzsche puts an interesting twist on the proposition "the greater the power, the less the rationality" by directly linking power and stupidity: "Coming to power is a costly business: power *makes stupid*," Nietzsche says, adding that "politics devours all seriousness for really intellectual things" (emphasis in original).[11] In a critique of Charles Darwin, Nietzsche further points out that for human beings the outcome of the struggle for survival will be the opposite of that "desired" by Darwinism, because "Darwin forgot the mind," and because "He who possesses strength divests himself of mind."[12] Nietzsche saw that the marginalization of mind and intellect by power was a central problem for the German *Reich,* and on this basis he predicted—correctly, we now know—the fall of the *Reich.*[13] The marginalization of mind by power will also become a problem for Aalborg's mayor, and it will eventually cost him his political life. Will to power is a will to life, but it may well lead to self-destruction.

In sum, what we see in Aalborg is not only, and not primarily, a general "will to knowledge" but also "a far more powerful will: the will to ignorance, to the uncertain, to the untrue! Not as its [will to knowledge's] opposite but—as its refinement!"[14] Power, quite simply, often finds ignorance, deception, self-deception, rationalizations, and lies more useful for its purposes than truth and rationality, despite all costs. But Nietzsche is wrong when he says, "Who alone has good reason to lie his way out of reality? He who suffers from it. But to suffer from reality is to be a piece of reality that has come to grief."[15] What makes Nietzsche wrong here is the "alone" in the first sentence of the quote. In Aalborg, we will encounter individuals and groups that have good reasons to rationalize and lie, individuals and groups that neither suffer from reality nor come to grief by it. These are individuals and groups that stand to gain from reality—or from certain interpretations, rationalizations, and lies about it—and that use politics to create the reality they want. When it comes to politics, even Plato—the ultimate defender of rationality—recommended the "noble lie," that is, the lie which would be told to the citizens of his model state in order to support its moral and political order.[16]

Five

RATIONALITY AS FROZEN POLITICS

Things are always at their best in their beginning.
Blaise Pascal

"HE WHO CONTROLS THE BUDGET HAS THE POWER"

The original intent of the Aalborg Project was to comprehensively regulate four main elements in urban development: (1) urban renewal, (2) land use, (3) traffic, and (4) environment. Early in the life of the project, however, it became obvious that urban renewal was falling behind the other activities in the project, and later on the same fate began to affect land use. The result has become a bias in the overall project design: traffic and environment tend to dominate the other elements. This chapter examines the relations between power and rationality in the genesis and design of the whole project.

Besides time pressures, one factor causing urban renewal to recede into the background of the Aalborg Project is that it is more complicated to implement than either land use or especially traffic planning. The municipality often does not own the properties or lands which are to be the objects of urban renewal schemes. Both private and public interests are involved, as are private invest ment and public funds. Urban renewal may be contrasted with planning for streets, malls, squares, bicycle paths, and highways, where the municipality owns the property or right-of-way, has the right of expropriation, and controls significant sums for capital construction and operations. A staff member from the Office of the City Engineer explains:

> If [land use planners and urban renewal officials] decide that some section of pri-
> vately-owned land must be changed to this or that, they have many more inter-
> ested parties whom they not only have to inform—we don't have to do that but

we normally do it anyway—they also have to make agreements with them because the land does not belong to them . . . Things are much simpler with us
since we deal with the roads. We deal with publicly-owned land. It is the public
sector which has the money. It is the public sector which decides. You have control over the whole affair, from when you first go out and look at things, to someone saying, "The construction is now finished . . ." And this makes some
difference in the strength of the planning, I would say.

In the same way, the municipality owns the city's bus company and has full
right to control investments and operations. Finally, with the Aalborg Project
management of planning activities for the city center, from having previously
been headed by the chief of city planning in the Planning Office, was moved
to the Office of the City Engineer. Aalborg's chief of city planning comments:

Chief of city planning: We ran out of steam. We were not awake, and perhaps we
did not have the necessary influence to be able to maintain the initiative. So it
became the city engineer's resources, it became the city engineer's money,
which was to be used. It was the city engineer's analytical machinery which had
to be put into operation. And we have no power over this. We have no influence
over how it functions, no knowledge about it. So in a way we were handicapped
from the start . . . In reality, as city planners we regret that the urban renewal
component has receded into the background. And I might as well admit that this
is because of a lack of initiative on the part of the planners, on our part. The city
engineer headed a far stronger organization. An organization which was well established, which had the tradition, which had much greater resources at its disposal. So the city engineer took the initiative and controlled planning, not in any
malicious way. He was the one who came up with the new proposals, and we
joined in and said, "Goddamnit, you just can't go any further until we have considered land use." So we kind of trailed behind. We could not keep up with the
pace with which he was moving. And we could not live up to the contribution
he was making.

Interviewer: How come you don't have the same resources?

Chief of city planning: He had a budget of several hundred million [Danish
kroner], while we had a budget of five million. He also had the task of designing
the projects. He had to execute the work. He did the negotiations with the police. He controlled the capital construction budgets. We have no capital construction budget. And it is a thesis I have that he who controls the capital
construction budget has the power. If you control the construction budget, then
you can promote a cause or you can scuttle it . . . City planning will always be dependent on sectoral planning, and sectoral planning is the planning which controls the budget. In all other areas as well, like recreation, schools, and everything

else. It is sector planning which determines when things are implemented, not us . . . We have only persuasion, only argument and persuasion, as a weapon.

Taken together, these factors generate a fundamental difference between sectoral planning and city planning, with the latter being often less directly action oriented and more complex, "slower off the mark," and more unpredictable than the former.

Besides these more structural factors, at the level of the individual actors two events tend to further weaken city planning, here understood as land use planning and urban renewal. First, an experienced and dynamic key member of the urban renewal staff resigns. Second, the Task Force member from the Planning Office, responsible for urban renewal, takes maternity leave. This combination of structural factors and changes in personnel leads one Task Force member to conclude that "the Planning Office was simply not equipped to carry out a real urban renewal plan for the city center."[1] In this way there occurs a fragmentation, already in the Aalborg Project's start-up phase so that the project becomes less comprehensive than planned.

If we next examine the power relations emanating from the project's two types of traffic planning—that is, the general traffic planning carried out by the Technical Department, and the public transportation planning executed under the aegis of the Aalborg Bus Company—it is the case that both organizations occupy strong positions as independent sectoral authorities with large budgets in the Municipal Administration. We have already seen, however, that structural, organizational, and personal factors allow public transportation planning to occupy an especially strong position in the project organization (see Chapter 2). This position is now further strengthened by the second oil crisis in 1979, in which Danish gasoline prices doubled in two years, leading to sharp increases in public transportation patronage and a decline in auto traffic. Aside from the chief of city planning's dictum that those who control the budget have the power, it is also true that, other things being equal, a budget and an activity in a growth phase generate more power than a budget and an activity in stagnation.

In contrast, the second oil crisis weakens the position of the Technical Department, since the reduction in construction and construction-related activities continues with the crisis. Compared with the aforementioned tenfold increase in subsidies to public transportation and the more than tripling of gross expenditures on this activity during the four years from initiation to inauguration of the Aalborg Project, the Technical Department's budget for construction and maintenance of roads, malls, squares, and parking areas increases by only 65% (current prices). Most of the latter increase occurs at the end of the period and is largely attributable to costs related to the Aalborg Project.

At the level of personal influence, Aalborg's mayor remains as strong as ever, and as supportive of public transportation. Organizationally, public transportation remains under the direct political and administrative control of the mayor. These were the factors which made it possible for the "transit lobby" to construct—figuratively and literally—a monumental reality like the "Marius Memorial," that is, the bus terminal discussed in the previous chapters. And it is these factors which now generate a pattern of project design whereby greatest weight is accorded to the public transportation component, followed by components for other forms of transport, environmental planning, land use planning, and urban renewal, in that order. Here, again, we are speaking of power relations which define a specific type of rationality and reality: the rationality of the project design and, subsequently, the reality of downtown Aalborg.

DESIGNING AALBORG'S FUTURE

After well over a year of work, the overall project design is starting to take shape. It consists of two main parts: (1) a plan for land use, responsibility for which lies with the Planning Office; and (2) a traffic, transportation, and environmental plan elaborated by the Office of the City Engineer. Urban renewal, originally conceived as a central component of the project, has now been reduced to a "Catalogue of Ideas" (Idékatalog) for specific isolated actions to be undertaken in the city center.

The Aalborg Project's land use plan includes the following objectives: (1) the total square footage of housing in the city center should be maintained and improved; (2) urban renewal activities should be strengthened; (3) the center's geographic limits should be maintained; (4) commercial, administrative, and regional functions should be located in secondary centers outside the city center; (5) extension of square footage for industry, workshops, and wholesale commerce should be avoided; (6) green areas should be expanded and upgraded; (7) open spaces in the residential zones should be upgraded.[2] Based on these objectives, a plan is formulated for land use in the form of indications for the location of various city center activities. In addition, a plan is elaborated for the specific use of floor space along the most important shopping streets and areas in the center of Aalborg.

The land use plan is not especially concrete or action oriented. It is summarily described together with other components in one of the eight reports that comprise the initial documentation for the Aalborg Project.[3] In several instances the report refers to "a later report" entitled "Downtown Aalborg: Proposals for Land Use Planning" (*Aalborg bykerne: Forslag til arealanvendelses-plan*), which will fully describe the land use plan.[4] This report, however, is never written. Altogether, the planning of land use, as mentioned, tends to fade away in much the same way as did urban renewal activities, even though land use does not recede quite as far into the background.

Traffic and environmental planning receive much more comprehensive treatment. A separate report provides more than a hundred pages of detailed descriptions of objectives, problems, plans, and strategies for traffic and environment in downtown Aalborg. Subsequently, after the implementation of the Aalborg Project, the chief of city planning concludes: "One could, in fact, have executed this city center planning . . . without having occupied oneself with land use at all." In my judgment, the chief of city planning is too modest here. And he is clearly mistaken as regards the original intentions of the Aalborg Project. Nevertheless, he is correct when he notes that traffic and environmental concerns dominate the Aalborg Project.

The Aalborg Project's plan for traffic and environment takes its point of departure in

> a political desire to accord increased priority to the urban environment, the more vulnerable road users [i.e. pedestrians and bicyclists] and public transportation, and to downgrade automobile traffic—especially commuting between home and work—to the extent that it causes conflict with the other types of transport.[5]

On the basis of this "political desire," a set of priorities is elaborated for environment and transportation which function as guidelines for developing a plan for traffic and environment. The order of priorities is as follows: (1) environment, (2) pedestrians, (3) bus passengers, (4) bicyclists and those driving mopeds (small motorbikes are a common form of transport in Denmark and Europe, especially for young people), (5) handicapped drivers, (6) commercial traffic, (7) shoppers coming into the center by car, (8) others coming by car to public offices and other enterprises, (9) residential parking, (10) home-workplace commuters using their private cars.[6]

Central to the plan for traffic and environment is a "traffic zone solution," to be introduced in Aalborg as the first town in Denmark to have this. Following the plan, downtown Aalborg will be divided into four zones having barriers which prevent their being traversed by cars. The objective is to make it more difficult to drive through the city center by car, thereby removing what is considered "unnecessary" auto traffic from downtown streets, estimated at 35% of total vehicular traffic. At the same time, a "ring road" encircling the city center and its four traffic zones is created by linking several streets, giving direct access to each of the four traffic zones from some point on the ring. In each zone a balance is created between the supply and demand for parking, with parking concentrated into fewer and larger areas along the ring road; parking places in smaller parking zones will disappear in order to reduce the number of cars searching for parking.

The street areas thus made free from cars will be revamped so as to improve conditions for the other types of transportation in the following ways: conditions for public transportation will be improved by the building of the above-mentioned bus terminal at Nytorv-Østeraagade and with the establishment of an "integrated bus stop," that is, another bus terminal at Vingaardsgade for transfer between city buses and suburban and regional buses. In addition, bus priorities are introduced, including "buses only" streets, "buses only" traffic lanes, and traffic lights which allow buses first priority. Conditions for bicycles and mopeds are improved by constructing a wholly new comprehensive network of bicycle paths. Pedestrians will be provided with more pedestrian streets and malls, overpasses, paths, steps, broader sidewalks, and "slowdown streets" (*stillegader*) which have barriers and speed bumps and give priority to pedestrians and bicyclists.

As a consequence of the traffic plan, it is expected that car traffic volume will decrease by 20–85% in the city center and increase by 40–70% on the streets comprising the ring road. However, Vesterbro—located on the ring road and one of the busiest and most hazardous downtown streets—will see a decline in auto traffic of roughly 30% due to reduced capacity, in that it will be given bicycle paths and more space for public transportation.[7]

The restructuring of automobile traffic per se is expected to reduce the number of accidents involving personal injury by 5%. At this time, a bicyclist or moped driver traveling one kilometer in the city center is fourteen times more likely than a car driver to end up injured in a traffic accident. Therefore, a comprehensive network of bicycle paths is planned with an expected 30–40% reduction in the number of accidents with injury for bicyclists and moped drivers. For all of downtown Aalborg, a 30% decline in accidents with personal injury is expected.

Noise levels, too, will drop: for Vesterbro and streets in the city center the reduction will be 2–5 dB(A), while the increase in traffic on the streets making up the ring road will lead to a 1–2 dB(A) increase in noise levels on these streets.

The plan reduces the number of public parking spaces by 15%, though only in the northern and southeastern zones, where there is an overcapacity. In the two western zones with a shortage of parking area, the number of parking spaces is to be increased by a good 20%. According to the plan, most of the parking will consist of metered spaces with time restrictions. The number of centrally located short-term metered parking spaces for shoppers in private cars will be increased, while the number of free, long-term parking spaces will be reduced by a third.

In sum, with the planned substantial reductions of car traffic in the city center and with the planned improvements for public transportation, bicyclists, and pedestrians and, finally, with the planned reductions in accidents, air pollution, and noise, Aalborg will be the first town in Denmark to make environmental issues the focus of town and traffic planning. And Aalborg will be the first town to seriously challenge that doctrine which more than any other has shaped post–World War II urban development in Denmark, Western Europe, and North America: the unhindered mobility and accessibility by car to all parts of the city. On both counts Aalborg appears to be a good decade ahead of all other towns in Denmark and most towns in Europe and America.

The fifth report in the series which documents the Aalborg project is the "Catalogue of Ideas" (*Idékatalog*) for urban renewal.[8] The catalogue is elaborated by a consulting firm hired by the Technical Department. Page three of the catalogue lists the objectives as helping to contribute to: (1) a better linkage of the central shopping zones of downtown Aalborg; (2) an improvement of the quality of the city center's public spaces, that is, streets, squares, and recreational areas; (3) an improvement in the city center's residential areas. The catalogue of ideas contains measures for achieving these objectives in terms of several specific projects at the level of particular streets, squares, or courtyards, with each individual project being depicted with "before" and "after" drawings to show how it could be implemented. Yet even in this early design phase the catalogue of ideas explicitly obtains the status of "material which will [not] be approved politically."[9] Neither at this time nor later on does the document have any real impact on the total Aalborg Project, again demonstrating the marginal position of urban renewal in the project as a whole.

THE CITY ENGINEER'S *ANGST*

The Aalborg Project's Task Force and the Copenhagen consulting firm which helps design the project's traffic plan conceive of the plan as being implemented in its entirety and all at once. Their inspiration derives from the Swedish town of Gothenburg, whose city council had previously implemented a similar type of traffic zone plan. In Gothenburg, emphasis was placed on implementing the plan in a single step, "overnight" (*över natten*) as the Swedes put it.[10]

When the Aalborg Project's Executive Committee is first presented with the Aalborg traffic zone proposal, a problem arises, as the committee members discover that the east-west zone boundaries will entail the closing of a main artery in the city center, namely Boulevarden/Østeraagade at Algade. This closing has been tried some years earlier and for the same purpose: to reduce automobile traffic in the city center. The closure at that time was strongly criticized by the Aalborg Chamber of Industry and Commerce (*Aalborg Handelstandsforening*) and by the local media. It resulted in a vigorous conflict over areas of competence between the Aalborg City Council, which had approved the closing of the street on the recommendation of the Technical Department, and the Aalborg Police Department, which together with the Chamber of Industry and Commerce and the local newspaper, the *Aalborg Stiftstidende,* sought to have the street reopened. The decision was appealed to the Danish Department of Justice and ended with the reopening of the street. The police, the Chamber of Industry and Commerce, and the *Stiftstidende* constitute a powerful troika in Aalborg politics. It is a troika we shall encounter again. The proposal to again close off Boulevarden/Østeraagade conjures up unpleasant memories for the alderman and other high level officials in the Technical Department.

In the minutes of the meeting in which the traffic zone system is first presented to the Executive Committee, we read: "The Executive Committee was in principle in agreement with the proposal but preferred that the possibility of perhaps dividing the proposal into stages be more closely examined."[11] In reality the meeting stirred a substantial amount of controversy because the Task Force members, who by that time had worked intensively on the design of the Aalborg Project for well over eighteen months, were reluctant to accept a "Stage One, Stage Two, Stage Three" approach to the project. A division into stages would in their view weaken the project and was itself seen as an expression of their superiors'—and especially the city engineer's—reservations about introducing restrictions on private cars in the city center. A Task Force member who attended the meeting of the Executive Committee comments:

> It was a meeting of the Executive Committee that was a real pressure cooker, if I could say so. The discussion was no holds barred. And the city engineer in reality forced his views upon the others . . . I think that there is a clear reservation on his part in that he [earlier] had participated in demanding that Østeraagade be closed. This is the part of the zone system which he is very much against because he is familiar with the problems it gave.

The city engineer himself remarks upon his reservations about an overnight implementation of the plan:

City engineer: I must admit about our consultants' proposal, introduced to me in a sudden and overwhelming way without me having seen any kind of preparatory work, that it was extremely restrictive. It seemed too restrictive to be able to be introduced all at once.

Interviewer: Restrictive towards whom?

City engineer: Towards . . . yeah, towards whom? In reality it was restrictive towards those driving cars. But perhaps I thought less about the drivers than about the public reaction. I was afraid that such a restrictive traffic policy would generate resistance toward the plan right away . . . Deep inside I am anxious about implementing something which the public is too great an opponent of. As much as possible, you must first implement the very restrictive measures when there is a kind of desire or demand for it on the part of the population. If you do not pursue things this way, you will simply find that your plan is upset.

The city engineer writes to the alderman for the Technical Department and to the members of the Aalborg Project's Executive Committee: "On my part, approval of the proposal requires elaborating a division of the traffic plan into stages."[12] The alderman backs the city engineer, and the result is irrevocable: the request by the Task Force that the project be implemented in one step is rejected.

Besides the fear of going too far with restrictions on cars, it is also true that some of the project's individual measures, such as the bus terminal and the network of bike paths, will be expensive to implement. For economic motives, therefore, it may also be advantageous to divide the plan into stages.[13] The economic argument, however, does not apply to the establishing of the core element in the Aalborg Project, that is, the four traffic zones for cars. This requires only a few inexpensive traffic signs and regulations. Moreover, it is generally the case that financial considerations do not have much significance in the Aalborg Project at this point in time, even if such considerations are used ex-post facto to justify the division of the project into stages. The real reason behind this division is a desire to avoid conflicts over what is considered a controversial issue: restricting the mobility of cars in Aalborg's center.

Ultimately, the Aalborg Project's traffic plan is divided into three stages with a total of forty-one subprojects. Only Stage One, with fourteen subprojects, gets scheduled for implementation.[14] The east-west zone boundary for cars with the closing of Østeraagade/Boulevarden, the main reason behind the desire to divide the plan into stages, is not included in this first stage. Stage One therefore involves a two-zone solution instead of the simultaneous establishment of four zones as conceived by the Aalborg Project's Task Force.

The most important subprojects in Stage One are the following: (1) constructing the bus terminal at Nytorv-Østeraagade; (2) establishment of an integrated bus stop for city and regional buses at Vingaardsgade, in effect a second bus terminal; (3) restructuring the urban and regional bus network in the city center; (4) provisional reduction of traffic and the introduction of bicycle paths on the main traffic artery of Vesterbro; (5) an east-west bicycle path through the city center along the route Østerbro-Borgergade-Kastetvej; (6) making Borgergade one-way between Vesteraa and Vesterbro in order to reduce traffic and create space for the construction of a bicycle path; (7) reducing car traffic by creating a "slowdown" street (*stillegade*) on Danmarksgade-Løkkegade; (8) zone boundary on Danmarksgade; (9) pedestrian mall and bicycle path on the western section of Algade; (10) zone boundary at the western part of Nytorv; (11) closing of Østeraagade at Slotspladsen square; (12) opening of Ved Stranden to automobile traffic; (13) shorter time limits and the introduction of fees for public parking places; (14) closing of small parking lots and streets.

In Stage Two, which is not scheduled in any precise way, the following subprojects are included: (1) establishment of all four traffic zones, (2) expansion of the bicycle path network, (3) elimination of smaller parking areas, (4) restructuring of the Railroad Station Square, (5) reduction and restructuring of traffic patterns in residential areas, (6) conversion of Vesterbro to include a "buses-only" lane and bicycle paths, (7) conversion of Boulevarden-Østeraagade to include bicycle paths, (8) zone boundary at Østeraagade, (9) closing of Ved Stranden to private auto traffic, (10) possible elimination of traffic signals at the Østeraagade-Nytorv intersection, (11) bicycle path on Algade (from Jernbanegade to Boulevarden), (12) closing of Algade to cars east of Budolfi Plads, (13) making the western part of Danmarksgade a one-way street, (14) restructuring of the Danmarksgade-Prinsensgade intersection, (15) making Vingaardsgade two-way east of Budolfi Plads, (16) footpaths and bicycle paths through the Kildeparken Park, (17) tunnel for bicycles and pedestrians under Prinsensgade between Kildeparken and downtown Aalborg, (18) bicycle paths along Jyllandsgade, (19) bicycle paths along Kjellerupsgade.

Finally, Stage Three, which is not really a stage but a collection of the measures in the project's traffic plan with lowest priority, contains the following subprojects: (1) footpaths and bicycle paths over the railroad zone between downtown Aalborg and the Kærby residential area, (2) footpaths and bicycle paths over the harbor areas, (3) traffic lights for pedestrians and bicyclists at the intersection of Slotspladsen and Østeraagade, (4) establishment of parking areas at Sauers Plads, (5) establishment of parking areas at the western harbor area, (6) establishment of parking areas at the freight railway yard, (7) reserving of parking spaces in residential streets for residents, (8) continued traffic reductions on "slowdown" streets.

WHOSE PROJECT? King, public, crowd

After the division of the traffic plan into stages, and after a year and a half of intensive design work, the Aalborg Project is presented to the general public for public debate and political discussion. Right up to the project's publication, however, the city engineer's concern regarding the project spawns anxiety within the Technical Department as to which offices and which individuals should publicly take responsibility for the project vis-à-vis the public. During the design phase, the alderman for the Technical Department has explicitly emphasized that he will not yet take a political position on the project. The section heads in the project's Executive Committee, when they see the final proposal for the design, recommend that either the alderman or the Task Force should take responsibility for the project officially. And the Task Force staff members, who along with the consultants are the project's actual designers, want as much weight behind the project as possible, and therefore would like to see either the alderman or the Executive Committee sign their names to it. A Task Force member explains:

> A discussion emerges about who is really behind this plan. Whose plan is it? Whether it was a proposal from the Executive Committee, whether it was the alderman's plan, that is the Second [Technical] Department's plan? Then the alderman says, "It is not!" And we quickly agreed that maybe it would be a good idea for it to be a staff plan which of course the City Council members were oriented about . . . Then there were some heads in the Executive Committee who proposed that it should be the Task Force's proposal, that is, it should not even be the heads who were responsible, but only the Task Force . . . Here the alderman simply flat out refused. Absolutely not [he said]! [The office heads] had followed the work for over two years, or however many years it was then, and so it was their plan. It was the first time things really came to a head . . . In the division of tasks I think that perhaps things have been going on in such a way that the heads, they are—I don't know whether to call it "forced" or "tempted"—to approve and work for something [the Aalborg Project] which was perhaps more progressive than if each of them had individually received a recommendation from their respective staff members. I am convinced of this. It would have been another plan than what we now have achieved. We can discuss, of course, whether someone then thinks it would have been better, and there are some of us who think that presumably it would have been worse.

At an orientation meeting of the City Council in which the public was invited, the alderman for the Technical Department clarified the division of responsibility: "The plans presented here are approved by the technical heads in the Second [Technical] Department, but I have not yet taken a position on the plans."[15] The plans are thus defined as technical, not political.

The alderman's refusal to take a stand does not mean that he has had no influence on the design of the plans. His influence has been both direct and indirect. A planner on the Task Force explains:

> The [section] heads made a big deal about evaluating what they thought the alderman would like to have. When we had meetings of the Executive Committee, [the city engineer] made a big deal about assessing what he thought the alderman wanted from this plan. So that when it was presented to the alderman, the technicians had already discussed some of the political implications. Sometimes [the city engineer] was very surprised when the alderman still did not think what he thought he ought to think in this or that situation.

It should also be emphasized that the alderman's refusal to put his name to the Aalborg Project cannot be understood as an attempt to distance himself from it. It is simply his way of saying that the project at this time must be considered a purely technical and administrative proposal. It is also a maneuver to ensure that the alderman can act more independently in the coming political negotiations over the project in relation to his own staff members in the Technical Department which he heads, in relation to the public, and toward fellow members of the Aalborg City Council.

Nevertheless, Aalborg's city engineer is again anxious about the course of events and the alderman's position. The city engineer is disturbed that, as head of the Aalborg Project's Executive Committee, he will be sponsoring a project that he basically sees as too radical. The city engineer believes he has seen the writing on the wall: there will be conflict about the Aalborg Project, and he himself will probably become a target of criticism. Two months earlier, immediately before the final plans had been written up and sent to the printer, he had expressed his considerations and reservations in a memorandum which a member of the project's Task Force called an attempt to "cover himself." The city engineer writes:

> The high access allowed to cars and the good parking possibilities which exist in Aalborg [today] could mean that the proposal might encounter widespread resistance and thereby difficulties in political approval . . . The proposal is so radical that I expect changes—perhaps important changes—during the coming negotiations prior to making [the plan] public.[16]

Regardless of the city engineer's motives in writing the memorandum, he is correct. The Aalborg Project's proposal for traffic and environment meets resistance, at times bitter resistance. In the following chapters we shall investigate from whom, how, why, and what consequences this resistance has. First, however, we shall ask why the Aalborg Project does not contain any alternatives; why there was only *one* plan when it is increasingly common in Denmark and elsewhere to consider alternative plans. And we shall conclude this chapter by taking up the actors' distinction of what they call a "technical" and a "political" project. I will argue that the distinction, although rhetorically useful for politicians, is a spurious one if we are to understand how power and rationality operate.

THE "ABSOLUTELY BEST PLAN"

During the time that the Aalborg Project is formulated, the professional and political debate on planning in Denmark is pervaded by discussions about two issues: citizen participation and alternatives in planning. We will return to citizen participation later. Here, in view of Aalborg's tradition of being on the forefront of planning, we may ask why there are no alternative proposals contained in the Aalborg Project.

The participants in the project should be allowed to answer for themselves. The chief planner for public transportation declares:

> I guess we were in agreement that we had come up with the absolutely best plan. And when all the technicians agree on this, then—well—then we chose to present a single plan.

Similar views are voiced by a lower-ranking staff member on the project:

> I would think that if we had presented several alternatives, then we would not have gotten the plan implemented . . . I think that it would have been a poorer plan because you might be more tempted to give in to some of the special points of view [from interest groups] . . . If you present one alternative where there are no bicycle paths, then it is tempting to go over to that alternative if you are pressured a lot by an opinion which really is not so "objective" because it has no possibility to be so. [People] do not know all the detailed considerations, all of the analyses that are documented. They can't do that.

Finally, the alderman who heads the Technical Department:

> For the fourteen years I have occupied this position, I have participated in a flood of citizen meetings and a flood of appeals to citizens to participate in debates. And it is my experience, even though I know that in newspapers and other places they say that we are pulling something down over their eyes by coming with a single design for a plan, it is my experience that there should be a single basis for discussion; otherwise the discussion becomes too diffuse.

However, even though the alderman, the Executive Committee, and the technical staff agree on not presenting alternatives to the City Council and to the public, this does not mean that alternatives are avoided. As we will see later, alternatives are produced as counterplans to the Aalborg Project.

Is "the absolutely best plan" which is "documented" by "analyses" really a "technical plan" as represented to the City Council and to the public? Right up to the moment of its political approval by the City Council, the Aalborg Project is explicitly defined by all involved as a technical project, based upon technical-neutral considerations about the connections between environment, land use, traffic, and planning. Technical and administrative staff, mostly engineers and architects, have formulated the fundamental ideas for the project; they have executed the planning work and have now presented the finished design to the City Council and to the public. Thus far, no politicians have been involved.

In working on the Aalborg Project, the technicians had two major sources of inspiration: the Nordkolt Project carried out under the Nordic Council of Ministers and the aforementioned traffic planning scheme in Gothenburg.[17] The Nordkolt Project was a comprehensive research and development project for the improvement of environment and traffic safety in medium-sized cities via limitations on automobile traffic and via placing higher priority on public transportation, bicycling, and walking. Aalborg was one of eight Nordic "experimental towns" in this project, which, like the Aalborg Project itself, was formulated purely by experts; it was elaborated by a team of prominent urban, environmental, and transportation specialists from the Nordic countries.

Some of the participants from Aalborg in the Nordkolt Project have now become key actors in the current Aalborg Project. In addition, the Nordkolt Project used the same consulting firm which Aalborg Municipality subsequently hired to design its own project. The Aalborg Project was seen as a welcome opportunity to implement what all involved saw as the good ideas from the Nordkolt Project and from Gothenburg. In Gothenburg the plan's traffic zone solution dramatically succeeded in reducing traffic accidents and levels of noise and air pollution.[18] Both the Nordkolt and the Gothenburg projects are unusually well-documented. In building on results from these two projects, the Aalborg planners sought to achieve a technically well-founded, and in this sense rational, project in Aalborg. And as we have seen, this was how the project was presented to the City Council and to the public.

We also have seen, however, in this and the previous chapters, that power relations are active and decisive in the design phase of the project. Weak support for urban renewal and land use planning combined with a powerfully positioned public transportation sector have left their mark on the project design: in the size and location of the bus terminal, in the central role of transportation and environmental issues in the overall design, and in the weak role of urban renewal and land use planning. Moreover, we have seen that the rationality behind the division of the Aalborg Project into phases was the rationality of power, or fear of power, not the rationality of technical or economic argument.

The official view of the Aalborg Project as a rational project, as a project formulated primarily in terms of technically neutral considerations, does not stand scrutiny. From its very outset, the rationality in the project and in the project's design exists within a context of power and is marked by this context in both form and substance. The project's rationality and the project's design are what Richard Rorty, following Cornelius Castoriadis, has called "frozen politics."[19] Things will not stay frozen for long, however.

Philosopher   Power
Rationality
Frozen   Politics

Six

THE RATIONALITY OF RESISTANCE

There is nothing more difficult to handle, more doubtful of success,
and more dangerous to carry through than initiating changes.

Niccolò Machiavelli

After the initial presentation of the Aalborg Project to the City Council, the
project is put on public exhibition and emerges from behind the walls of
the Technical Department to face the citizens of Aalborg. This initial
meeting with the public, and especially with the local business community,
will be the focus of this chapter.

CITIZEN PARTICIPATION OR NOT?

The Technical Department had originally not even considered including a
phase where the project was to meet the public. No public hearings and no citizen participation was planned at first. The original schedule for the project
contains not a single reference to such activities. And the minutes of an early
meeting in the project's Task Force make the following statement concerning
the publicizing of the project:

> It is assumed that all relevant authorities and interest groups will be informed via
> the press. According to an earlier agreement, however, ongoing orientation will
> be provided to the police.[1]

Later the Task Force nevertheless begins discussing the possibility of some sort
of citizen participation in the project. From a meeting of the Task Force, held
two months after the earlier meeting, we read:

> There is no possibility of including a citizen participation phase [*offentligheds-*
> *fase*]. . . unless the date of completion for the bus terminal is postponed. Discus-

sion of this point is therefore referred to the Executive Committee's [next] meeting.[2]

At this next meeting, however, the project's Executive Committee decides:

> The Chamber of Industry and Commerce and those businesses most affected, as well as the police, will be oriented as much as possible on a continuing basis. Aside from this, there will be no publicity before the [legally required] public hearings as part of the local plan procedures.[3]

Despite this development, the alderman for the Technical Department decides two months later that there will "be citizen participation with the purpose of collecting comments before the proposals [for the entire project] are presented to the City Council for approval."[4]

Dealing with the public takes time, and the result is that the starting date for the physical implementation of the project is delayed a year. Five participants provide different responses to the questions of why the Technical Department suddenly decides to initiate citizen participation in the project and who takes the initiative.

> *Task Force member:* In fact, I thought the alderman did.
> *Alderman for the Technical Department:* If I tell you that it was me, I might be lying.
> *Task Force member:* I think that the Task Force did. I think that it was the Task Force who proposed that there be citizen participation.
> *Aalborg's city engineer:* I can't answer that, but I suppose it was absolutely self-evident that there was to be citizen participation . . . You can't go forward with such a case without participation. Now, whether so much has happened . . . since then up to today, whether my attitude is different, I cannot say . . . For me it is astounding to hear that . . . we simply did not consider it obvious that there was to be citizen participation.
> *Aalborg's chief of city planning:* It was kind of in the air along with the proposed law for municipal planning.[5] Whether it came up in the Executive Committee or in the Task Force, I can't really remember, but it probably came from Technical Department staff members.

Evidently the originator of the citizen participation initiative remains unclear. No one can remember, and the documents of the Aalborg Project fail to point to any specific party as being responsible. The failing memories may be due to the fact that the question of citizen participation was seen as neither significant nor problematic for those involved in the project. At the start of the Aalborg Project, public participation in planning was a much discussed issue. This is why the city engineer calls citizen participation "self-evident." For the first time, Danish counties were carrying out their regional planning with legally required citizen participation. And all future municipal planning also would have to meet this demand. The need for public involvement was advocated by influential voices in Danish and international planning circles. It was "in the air," as Aalborg's chief of city planning says, and once the issue had been discussed, the implementation of citizen participation in the Aalborg Project therefore took place so easily and subtly that today no one can actually remember how it happened.

Citizen participation in the Aalborg Project was not yet legally required, but as usual Aalborg was in the forefront of such activities in Denmark. This was the case both because Aalborg had a tradition for doing so, and because in this concrete case the city administration saw advantages in voluntarily following the citizen participation guidelines contained in the new Law of Municipal Planning. By executing the project in accord with this law, it was expected that the Aalborg Project could later enter directly—with legal consequences according to the new law, and without additional measures—into the new municipal planning scheduled to begin in Aalborg a few years after the start of the Aalborg Project.

"CRUSH THIS PLAN!"

Citizen participation for the Aalborg Project starts with the opening of the above-mentioned exhibition about the project, and with a reception whose invitees include the mayor, the politicians in the City Council's Technical Committee, the press, and several Aalborg notables. A few days previously, a press conference had been held and the project now receives its first mention in *Aalborg Stiftstidende,* the town's only daily newspaper. The banner headline reads: "Four Hermetically Closed Traffic Zones in Downtown Aalborg." In the accompanying article the alderman for the Technical Department tries to calm public concern: "Before people become all too frightened," he says, "we must make clear that this is not something to be done in the course of a few months . . . It is perhaps a 10-year plan we are talking about."[6]

The municipality's planning staff are present for some hours daily during the first two weeks of the exhibition to answer questions from visitors. The exhibition lasts four months. The public is also informed about the project by printed material and public orientation meetings. The print campaign includes advertisements in the press, in posters and the distribution of a brochure. The project's Task Force proposes that 70,000 copies of the brochure be printed and distributed to all households, but the Executive Committee reduces this to 10,000 and decides that distribution should take place via shops, banks, and public buildings only.

The Technical Department decides that orientation meetings about the project may be held but "only at the request from an outside party." A total of nine meetings take place: two with the Aalborg Chamber of Industry and Commerce, three with local high schools, and one each with the Conservative People's Party Voters' Association, the Kayerød Neighborhood Association, the local branch of the Danish Town Planning Association, and the Danish Cyclist Federation, the latter being an important lobbying group in many Danish towns for traffic safety, equal rights for bicyclists vis-à-vis motorists on Danish roads, and for construction of bicycle paths. The head of the Technical Department, a Conservative alderman, takes part in the meetings with the Chamber of Industry and Commerce and the Conservative Voters' Association. Staff from the Task Force attend the other meetings.

The first citizen reaction to the Aalborg Project, however, occurs three weeks before the public participation phase even begins. It consists of a protest that will prove indicative of the way in which important groups in Aalborg receive the project. A property and business owner telephones the Technical Department because he has heard that the project will entail more buses on the street where his business is located. Having recently renovated his property for a million kroner, he believes that it will be damaged by the vibrations from the heavy city buses. He is therefore against the project. Later on, several shop-owners conduct a protest on one of the pedestrian malls: they petition against a bicycle path which is planned to cross the mall. The intersection is part of the Aalborg Project's bicycle route network.

Dissatisfaction among Aalborg's business community begins to build, especially among the retail shopkeepers, and soon things become more serious. One evening, the Aalborg Chamber of Industry and Commerce conducts an orientation and discussion meeting about the Aalborg Project for its members. The Chamber of Industry and Commerce represents local shops, industrial enterprises, banks, and other businesses. The Chamber's chairman is an ex officio board member of the local branch of the Danish Employers' Association. Founded in 1431 as an association of merchants, the Aalborg Chamber of Industry and Commerce calls itself the oldest and largest Chamber of Commerce in Denmark. Experience shows that it is a force to be reckoned with in Aalborg politics. The Technical Department is invited to the Chamber's meeting, the topic of which is "The Downtown Aalborg Plan—Life or Death?" The meeting is scheduled to take place in the conference room of a large downtown bank but must be moved to the White House Hotel (*Hotel Hvide Hus*) due to "overwhelming attendance." In addition to the board, the alderman for the Technical Department, his chief administrators, and staff members, 225 members of the Chamber attend.

On the same day as the meeting, *Aalborg Stiftstidende* holds an interview with the chairman of the Chamber of Industry and Commerce. The headline is "Traffic Restructuring Strangles Downtown Retail Sales." In the interview the chairman declares:

> One touches something dangerous here, for it concerns the customers' possibility to get to the stores. And if you want to maintain downtown Aalborg as an active retail center, you have to be aware of the risk.[7]

The chairman of the Chamber of Industry and Commerce, like the alderman for the Technical Department, sits on the Aalborg City Council representing the Conservative party. Both are high-ranking members of the party. Moreover, the Chamber's chairman is a member of the City Council's Technical Committee, an advisory organ to the Technical Department and hence to the alderman. Besides, members of the Chamber of Industry and Commerce are considered hardcore Conservative party supporters. A conflict over the Aalborg Project between the Chamber and the Technical Department thus will bring two leading members of the same party in conflict with each other and may even bring the alderman in conflict with his own constituency. A subsequent chairman of the Chamber of Industry and Commerce states in an interview about "the Chamber's City Council member" (euphemism for the chairman cited above):

> We at the Chamber of Industry and Commerce decided that we wanted to have a man from the business world inside the City Council . . . So we worked on our members and said that we now have a chance to get a businessman in. And it certainly went well, too.

The local newspaper headline about business being "strangled" in the city center brings out the main theme of the evening's discussion at the meeting of the Chamber of Industry and Commerce.[8] Aalborg's merchants complain that the Aalborg Project is according too low a priority to customers in private cars. They believe that the traffic zone solution would make driving in the city center intolerable, as would a reduction in the number of parking spaces. It is at this meeting that for the first time in the project's history we encounter a rationality which will have decisive consequences for the project and for Aalborg's environmental, traffic, and urban policy and planning. The rationality used by the Chamber of Industry and Commerce toward the city administration can be summarized in the following syllogism: (1) what is good for business is good for Aalborg; (2) what is good for motorists is good for business; (3) therefore, what is good for motorists is good for Aalborg.

In reality, this rationality has already penetrated the Aalborg Project. It formed much of the basis for the city engineer's decision to divide the project into stages. This again is an example of how power defines rationality. A company executive and former chairman of the Chamber of Industry and Commerce summarizes the organization's attitude toward the project to great applause from the audience:

> In the business world we are against restrictions—we have to be able to serve our customers. Restrictions never disappear . . . Form committees or study circles to crush this plan.[9]

Ironically, the talk of restrictions brought another member of the Chamber to expand on the previous chairman's contribution, again to great applause; he called for a prohibition on the establishment of banks and savings and loans institutions in the most important shopping areas of the city center:

> If we fill the pedestrian streets with banks and such, we will get a dead city with dead storefronts. This is a pressing matter because there are several applications from banks. Couldn't there be a temporary prohibition?[10]

Later on we will return to the Chamber's attitude toward restrictions. For the moment, the alderman for the Technical Department tries to calm the assembled business community. Influenced perhaps by the strongly negative mood at the meeting, he declares that the ten-year time frame for the project he has previously mentioned to a reporter has been extended: "[T]his is a 20-year plan which must be negotiated," the alderman now says.[11]

Concluding the meeting at the White House Hotel, the Chamber's board proposes establishing a committee to formulate proposals for changing the Technical Department's project. The proposal is approved, and the alderman for the Technical Department attempts to stimulate cooperation instead of confrontation by offering the Chamber assistance from the Technical Department's staff in the activity of the new committee. The alderman's offer of assistance is made without any prior consultation with his staff in the Technical Department. A staff member who sits in the auditorium and hears herself being promised out to help in the Chamber's work describes her reaction:

> It simply came like a bomb. It shook all of us up when we heard it. It came right from the podium, and it changed everything. By the way, the meetings [with the Chamber of Industry and Commerce] were terrible.

The next day *Aalborg Stiftstidende* reports on the "life-and-death" meeting in a four-column article entitled "The Municipality Risks Destroying Aalborg's Identity as a Business Center."[12] A day later the project is also discussed in an editorial entitled "City-Pruning."

It is said that apple trees can be pruned so intensively—or mistakenly—that they do not bear fruit for several years afterwards. Pruning and other encroachments on the living tissue of an urban society also have an important effect, but knowledge of such results is not commonly known . . . [The] consolidation of Aalborg's future downtown development is of utmost importance, and in fact too important to leave to specialists and elected politicians to make the decisions! . . . It may well be that the Technical Department staff have formulated the right plans, but the town's citizens should not feel themselves obliged to take it for granted just because so much work has been done on it. They should and must get acquainted with it, discuss it, and form an opinion about it.[13]

In this instance, Aalborg's newspaper acts as a critic of the city government's representative democracy ("too important to leave to specialists and elected politicians") and, uncharacteristically, as spokesman for more direct participation in the political process. Is *Aalborg Stiftstidende* indeed on the side of the new democratization movements in this issue? Does the newspaper support increased public involvement and citizen participation? Or is there something else going on? For the moment, we will let the newspaper's treatment of the case speak for itself. Later, when more actions and effects can be traced, we will return to possible explanations behind the statements of *Aalborg Stiftstidende.*

The Aalborg Chamber of Industry and Commerce responds to the *Stiftstidende's* appeal for direct citizen involvement. In the days following the meeting, the Chamber forms a "City Center Committee." A Steering Committee is formed and five working groups constituted. The committee and groups are told to follow the maxim: "Point out errors and negative consequences of the plan," and are asked to elaborate a counterplan to that of the Technical Department.[14] For its part, the Technical Department selects five staff members who will assist the Chamber's working groups and its Steering Committee.[15] Altogether sixty to seventy people are active in these groups during the four months it takes the Chamber to produce its counterplan.

At the outset, the Chamber declares that the working groups are open to anyone who is interested; for example, ordinary residents living in downtown Aalborg. It quickly becomes apparent, however, that the business community totally dominates the groups both in number and amount of effort.[16] The work becomes an internal matter within the Chamber, to be executed by and for the Chamber's members. A member of the Kayerød Neighborhood Association (*Kvarterforeningen Kayerød*), who personally approaches the Chamber of Industry and Commerce to be admitted into one of the working groups, explains:

We heard at one time that the Chamber would set up a study group [the working group for the area in which the interviewed person lives] concerning the

[Aalborg Project]. And they invited everyone to participate. I was over there to talk with [the chairman of the Chamber's City Center Committee] about what they wanted, and I said that I was interested in participating in the work. He promised to send me an invitation to the next meeting. But I never got one . . . He did not know that I came from the residents' association. I didn't say anything about it. But we discussed the city center plan, and we did not agree at all. So it well might be that he dropped the matter.

COUNTERPOWER AND COUNTERPLANNING

The Aalborg Chamber of Industry and Commerce has high ambitions regarding its counterplan. The Chamber is well-organized and establishes a strong central management to lead the work. The management places great emphasis on the creation of internal consensus and on presenting a united front toward the outside world. Only the Steering Committee's chairman is allowed to speak to the press.[17] The chairman of the Chamber describes starting up the work:

> We decide that if we are going to come up with a counter-proposal, it has to be a good one. It can't just be a "No!" Perhaps we have to come up with an alternative solution. So we set up these groups, and there was a lot of excitement. Good organizers were heading them, and the work was divided up into groups with a Steering Committee and all the rest. Now [in the Chamber's secretariat] we also have a section head who is an old military man.

Besides being well-organized, the Chamber also knows what it wants: the Technical Department's plans must be forced off the agenda and replaced by something more congenial to the business community. In the minutes of the first meeting of the Chamber's Steering Committee, we read:

> No one can support the division [of downtown Aalborg] into zones . . . Retail trade cannot live off the local inhabitants . . . Lift the restrictions and make the town traffic-happy [*trafikglad*] and friendly to the public.[18]

Given the Chamber's enthusiasm, its massive support from members, and the many participants in the working groups, the municipality's staff do not have an easy job assisting at the Chamber's meetings. One staff member describes the experience this way:

> The Chamber of Industry and Commerce was very angry about the plan, and when we showed up for meetings we were verbally abused, quite simply . . . [They were angry about] what we really wanted with the plan. We certainly de-

stroyed everything for them and for their businesses and for the business community. People couldn't come into town, you know. [The Chamber] proceeded in a very vulgar way. It was nothing like, "Let's sit down and discuss it." We didn't even get permission to explain what the intentions were with it. They're the ones who ran the meetings, and so when we showed up, they practically shot at us with rude remarks. You didn't really get a chance to reply . . . It was like they were just pouring shit over our heads. They didn't ask us any concrete questions. We said [among ourselves] that we should have received a "dirty work" allowance [*smudstillæg*] then.

That the dissatisfaction expressed by the municipal staff member is reciprocated can be seen in an interview with the leader of the Chamber's City Center Committee. The chairman explains:

It was difficult to communicate with [the municipal staff] because they had closed themselves off about the plans and felt that it was their task to sit and argue for the proposals which had been presented. Instead of going in more and helping with alternative things . . . It didn't matter whatever the hell we came up with here, [the staff] just demolished it.

After a hectic initial period, however, the level of activity and participation in the Chamber's various working groups begins to decline. Fewer people come to the meetings, they are not prepared, the organization becomes less disciplined and the leadership weaker. The chairman of the Aalborg Chamber of Industry and Commerce explains what is happening:

Interviewer: It seems as if the farther along we get in the process the more the activity of the [Chamber's] working groups and [its] Steering Committee begins to disintegrate.

Chairman: Yes, you're right [laughing].

Interviewer: What is it that is happening?

Chairman: It's funny you mention this, for I myself have been a little bit disappointed about it. In fact, you're right on target. And I, too, have speculated about what is really happening. What I think happens is that the proposal which we are presented with from the municipality is a big mouthful. It was a big report [eight reports]. There are many things which must be changed, among them the division of the city into zones. [The reports] say that [the project] must be divided into stages, but there are some who forget this. They think the whole thing is going to be implemented right away. This leads to some protest. That is, some feelings come into play here, and a whole lot of people come to us in the Chamber, to those of us on the board, saying that now we just have to do something about this. [They say] it is incomprehensible, etc. . . . we begin to work with it, and we did so in a serious way. Much was made out of it. We read the reports from the municipality. So I think that when [our work] collapses a bit, it is because the more you delve into it, the more you really discover that [the Aalborg Project] is not so crazy. That's my view. So you quiet down, relax a bit.

"UNITY IS VERY, VERY IMPORTANT"

But this is not the whole story. It is not a case of everyone in the Chamber of Industry and Commerce gradually starting to accept the Technical Department's project as they begin to immerse themselves in it. Some do accept it, but others do not. Hence, there appear internal divisions within the Chamber.

Moreover, the leadership of the Chamber's city center activities takes the attitude that the Technical Department's representatives in the Chamber's working groups and in the Steering Committee are using their participation to influence the other participants toward accepting the Technical Department's project. The chairman of the Chamber's City Center Committee explains:

> Generally I think that [the municipal staff] worked to influence [the participants], so that the proposal which [the Technical Department] had presented would be considered the best, instead of helping [us to come up with] alternative [proposals] . . . I think that the municipality had an ulterior motive when they sent in their specialists. And it meant that ultimately, or at least after the clarification phase, the Steering Committee ended up working without the assistance of the specialists.

Besides the possibility of exerting influence, cooperation also allows the municipal staff to gain insight into the kinds of opinions and attitudes that exist within the Chamber of Industry and Commerce. And this insight starts to become problematic to the Chamber when it turns out that the Chamber's working groups do not agree on all questions. This might be another important reason why the leadership of the Chamber of Industry and Commerce gradually finds the specialists' participation in the Chamber's work increasingly problematic: they have no interest in seeing the Chamber's previously "united front" exposed by the Technical Department. For the chairman of the Chamber's City Center Committee, "Unity is very, very important, collective action is absolutely decisive."

More specifically, the merchants on Østeraagade declare themselves in disagreement with the Chamber's opposition to the proposed bus terminal at Nytorv. The Østeraagade Business Association wants the terminal as proposed by the Technical Department.[19] According to the proposal, a part of Østeraagade will be converted for use as a bus terminal. Thus the merchants will gain

access to a large, and at this time rapidly, growing number of potential customers, people brought by public transportation directly to the door of their
shops. From here the disagreements move directly into the Chamber's city
center groups. After having worked with the project for a time, the "North-
East" and "South-East" working groups conclude that they, too, support the
municipality's proposal for the bus terminal.[20] The North-East Group tells the
Chamber's Steering Committee:

> The group believes that the bus terminal at Nytorv-Østeraagade can be retained
> and expanded by the municipality as proposed [by the Technical Department],
> albeit with so few costly investments as possible, for a trial period of, for exam-
> ple, two years. Hereafter we will have gained experience as to the kinds of fur-
> ther investments which may be deemed necessary.[21]

The South-East Group agrees with the North-East Group's proposal but "under the condition that the driving of private cars can be retained unchanged."[22] In taking these positions, the two groups come into conflict with
the Chamber's leadership on one of the most central points of the entire project. A geographically based conflict of interest divides the Chamber. And it is
primarily this conflict that is the real reason for the decline of participation in
the Chamber's efforts to come up with a counterproposal.

Another factor that further contributes to the divisions in the Chamber,
and to the fact that its work begins to disintegrate, is a questionnaire survey the
Chamber conducts among retail businesses in downtown Aalborg at this time.
The survey is conducted with the explicit purpose of obtaining documentation for the Chamber's view that motorists are the most important group of
customers in downtown Aalborg and that restrictions on driving will harm retail business. The Chamber's Steering Committee, as a point of departure for
its survey, reiterates: "[The Aalborg Chamber of Industry and Commerce] desires to see cars [driving] all the way into the city center . . . [since] about 60%
of earnings derive from customers driving their private cars who come to Aalborg from outside the city."[23]

The problem here is that the results are assumed to be known beforehand
and that the Chamber simply desires to see them confirmed "scientifically." In
fact, the Chamber is seriously mistaken. It sends out 300 questionnaires, of
which only fifty, or 17%, are returned.[24] The credibility of the survey is thereby
so low that it cannot be utilized with any degree of accuracy. This fact in itself
weakens the Chamber's argument with the Technical Department: the Chamber is unable to obtain the documentation it needs and which it has said in public it will obtain. Moreover, the low response rate is problematic in a situation
where the Chamber has insisted time and again that this matter is of major
concern to all retailers in downtown Aalborg.

Aside from the low response rate, those questionnaires which are actually returned also pose a problem for the Chamber's leadership. The responses correspond neither to the expectations nor to the attitudes of the leadership. For example, in response to the question "Do you believe that Nytorv should be expanded into a bus terminal with 18 bus parking spaces and immediate transfer possibilities between all lines?" twenty retailers answer "Yes" and eighteen "No." The Chamber's board had expected a massive "No" on this question. Instead they see confirmed those divisions that had already revealed themselves in the board's relations to the North-East and South-East working groups within the Chamber.

Two other questions, both concerning whether it would be more appropriate to place the bus terminal in the harbor area, as desired by the Chamber, are answered in the negative by a majority of respondents. Finally, the respondents' answers regarding the distribution of customers by means of transport do not agree with the figures the board had previously announced to the public. Where the Chamber's Steering Committee had declared that about 60% of gross revenue derived from customers driving in their private cars from areas outside Aalborg, the questionnaire data indicates that those in private cars, coming from both beyond *and* within Aalborg, comprise but 50% of gross revenues, and that only 43% of gross revenues (comprising all means of transport) come from outside Aalborg. The data from the 17% sample further indicate that those using public transport, bicyclists, pedestrians, and those on mopeds together constitute a customer group of equal importance to those customers driving their own cars. The two groups each account for 50% of gross revenues according to the questionnaire. Yet, as will be shown later, these figures are not correct either.

Initially, the Chamber does not use the results of the survey, probably because of the low response rate and because the responses do not mesh with Chamber policy. However, since the survey has already been previously announced in the press, and since the Technical Department, via its staff members in the Chamber's Steering Committee and working groups, already knows the results, the survey becomes public knowledge. A staff member from the municipality comments:

> There is no doubt that [the Chamber's board] did not use [the questionnaire] as they originally had intended. They had planned it as the core around which they could build up their arguments . . . [The results] got in the news, they couldn't avoid that. If my memory is right, they had made a big deal about making this big survey because the municipality certainly wouldn't [make such a survey] or would do so only later. They send out 300 questionnaires and get back 44, or how ever many they got [there were in fact 50]. That is of course somewhat of a

defeat . . . And it also happened that in the Steering Committee under the Chamber of Industry and Commerce, where I was assisting, they were sorry about having me at the meeting where [the survey's results] were presented. Only 44 responses had been returned at that time, and I think that the time limit had run out . . . The thing is that I had received a copy [of the results]. You can't hold something like that back . . . They also had to come up with some kind of response after they had inconvenienced 300 retailers by asking them to fill something out . . . I had seen the questionnaire. I think I got it before we found out about the results, and I was also very dissatisfied with the way the questions had been phrased . . . They were leading questions, and I certainly would have done something about them, if there had been a problem, understood in the following way: let us say they had gotten back 250 questionnaires, and they were all in agreement with each other, and they pointed in the same direction as the questions had led them to. Then I would certainly have raised questions about the validity of the survey. But now [with such few and diverging responses] it wasn't necessary.

The most important consequence of the factionalization in the Aalborg Chamber of Industry and Commerce is that the Chamber's Steering Committee fails to utilize the material produced by the five working groups to the extent originally intended. The board still desires to have a united front toward the outside, without any divergent standpoints. In response to the North-East Group which wishes to present its divergent viewpoint, the Steering Committee underlines its "broad agreement that no minority opinions should be presented to the municipality, as this would weaken our argument."[25]

The German philosopher Jürgen Habermas has spoken of domination-free (*zwangslos*) communication. What we see here is the opposite of what Habermas talks about. The result is that the views of the Steering Committee come to dominate the Chamber's comments to the Aalborg Project. In this way the small group of retailers on the committee come to shape the Chamber's policy. Ultimately, the great amount of work begun by the Chamber, and the new information it produces, is neutralized by attitudes these members had before the work began. Here, too, power is more concerned with defining reality than with dealing with what reality "really" is.

A second consequence of the factionalization is that the Chamber becomes delayed in its work. Originally the Technical Department had decided that the public phase would last four months, ending with a deadline for comments and objections. The Chamber of Industry and Commerce, however, now decides to ask the alderman heading the Technical Department for a postponement of the deadline.[26] On the same day the request is submitted, the

Technical Department grants a one-month postponement in order to give the Chamber's various working groups "reasonable time to evaluate [the proposal] and to respond with comments."[27]

When this new deadline arrives, however, no comments from the Chamber have been received by the Technical Department. This "nonactivity," too, is indicative of the Chamber's importance: it can first have the deadline postponed and then not stick to it. The Chamber's City Center Committee is busy struggling with a report which goes through five drafts before internal agreement can be reached. Only after an additional two weeks beyond the deadline does the Chamber have enough control over the material and the different factions that they can again present a united front to the outside world.

As the only party in the public phase, the Chamber of Industry and Commerce now publishes a genuine counterplan to the Aalborg Project, entitled "Downtown Aalborg: An Alternative" (*Aalborg bykerne—et alternativ*).[28] As mentioned, the report is strongly critical of the Technical Department's project, and, as its title indicates, it contains a counterproposal. This proposal will be discussed in the next chapter.

TACTICS VERSUS CONSENSUS

In sum, two points are worth recalling in our examination of the reaction of the Chamber of Industry and Commerce to the Aalborg Project. The first point concerns the way power defines rationality. The Chamber's rationale, that what is good for motorists is good for the retailers and thereby good for Aalborg, has already entered the Aalborg Project before the Chamber begins to use it. It provided a basis for the city engineer's decision to divide the project into stages. Now the Aalborg Chamber of Industry and Commerce directly attempts to use this rationale to further define the rationality of the project.

The second point worth noting revolves around the Chamber's ability to mobilize a united front. The Chamber decides to reject the assistance offered by the alderman to help elaborate its counterplan. Both here as well as in other contexts, the Chamber emphasizes presenting a united front to the outside. "Collective action is absolutely decisive," as the chairman of the Chamber's City Center Committee said earlier. Thus, when the Chamber's members are internally divided as to the main questions about the project, and when the Chamber's retail survey fails due to the low response rate, and, finally, when the work on the counterplan begins to fall apart, it becomes problematic for the Chamber to cooperate with the city staff. It becomes problematic precisely because cooperation will shatter the image of a unified business community elaborating a well-documented counterplan. Instead, the Chamber chooses to stop inviting the city staff to their meetings and to reject the possible input the staff might provide in helping the Chamber elaborate a counterplan. Tactical considerations clearly dominate any desire to reach some form of rationally informed consensus. The Chamber of Industry and Commerce simply does not seek such a consensus, which would be based on demands for validity, what Jürgen Habermas calls "the force of the better argument."[29] They do not see it as being an effective means of achieving the Chamber's objectives. The behavior described here is found not only in the ranks of the Chamber of Industry and Commerce but also in the Aalborg Bus Company, the Technical Department, the Aalborg Police Department, and the *Aalborg Stiftstidende*. It can be summarized in the proposition mentioned earlier, "The greater the power, the less the rationality." The Aalborg Chamber of Industry and Commerce does more than simply prepare itself to argue with the Technical Department. It arms itself for a war. The agenda is set not by a will to knowledge but by the will to power.

Seven

THE WEAKNESS OF THE BETTER ARGUMENT

> Being unable to make what is just strong, we have made what is strong just.
>
> *Blaise Pascal*

A long with the Chamber of Industry and Commerce's counterplanning to the Aalborg Project, but at a considerably more modest level of ambition, several other organizations and individuals submit comments about the project. Unlike the Chamber's contribution, these comments are submitted to the Technical Department on time, that is, before the expiration date of the public phase.

A total of twenty-four letters and twenty-six notes with comments are received, the latter coming from a suggestion box located at the project exhibition. The submissions comprise both support and criticism of the project.

THE PROJECT HAILED . . . AND CRITICIZED

The most prominent support for the project comes from the Danish Cyclist Federation, the Kayerød Neighborhood Association, and the Socialist People's party (respectively, *Dansk Cyklistforbund, Kvarterforeningen Kayerød, Socialistisk Folkeparti*). It is certainly an interesting combination of grass roots and Socialist support, inasmuch as the person formally heading the project, the Technical Department's alderman, is from the Conservative party. Support from these quarters is exemplified by the following comments from the Kayerød Neighborhood Association:

> We believe it to be very positive that the municipality has elaborated a comprehensive proposal for planning the city center's future. We like the idea of making

69

our city center safer for the vulnerable groups in traffic [svage trafikanter, i.e., pedestrians and those riding bicycles and mopeds] . . . The total amount of traffic will also be limited by the zone divisions in the center . . . We find it very positive in this plan that public transportation has attained high priority, that smaller parking areas are removed . . . that the residential zones are maintained, that the residents obtain influence on establishing slowdown streets, that future wholesale and industrial enterprises are not permitted. We hope that the municipality will genuinely work on the basis of these intentions in the future.[1]

Behind the positive comments from the Kayerød Neighborhood Association, however, lies a skepticism about the Aalborg Project's evolution from being a holistic project containing urban renewal, land use, traffic, and the environment to largely a matter of traffic and environmental issues. The association figures that having a traffic and environment project, however, is better than having no project at all, and it decides not to openly criticize the lack of comprehensiveness. A representative from the neighborhood association explains:

As we saw the problem, the city center plan was in fact exclusively a traffic plan. At the time we were working a lot with housing problems, and we thought that if the goal was to make comprehensive planning for the residents who live in the city center, you could not be satisfied just talking about traffic . . . But if you looked at downtown Aalborg as it looked then, and what it would look like after the plan had been implemented, it was still a big step forward.

The comments of the Danish Cyclist Federation closely resemble those of the Kayerød Neighborhood Association:

The Danish Cyclist Federation's Aalborg chapter has with considerable and positive interest studied and discussed the reports from the city administration's Second [Technical] Department . . . We find that the intentions presented in the proposal for "Downtown Aalborg [volumes] 1–5" point in the same direction as our own ideas about a humane and vibrant city . . . We place very high priority on the City Council eventually making a principled decision about the plan in its entirety . . . in accord with the principles presented in "Downtown Aalborg 1–5" (emphasis in original).[2]

Finally, among those contributions supporting the Technical Department one finds a statement from the trade union movement: the local chapter of the Construction and Building Workers' Union (Anlægs-og Bygningsarbejdernes Fagforening), which is part of the Confederation of Semi-Skilled Workers (Special-arbejderforbundet or SID), makes the only official statement from the trade unions about the Aalborg Project in its entire history:

The proposal concerning a change in the center which can reduce unnecessary automobile traffic will improve the environment in both the residential areas and in the city's center with benefits for all the municipality's inhabitants and guests. We can therefore essentially support the municipality's plan proposal and point out that these proposals can generate a large amount of significant employment which at the same time will reduce the municipality's expenses for job creation.[3]

As mentioned, critique of the Aalborg Project comes primarily from the Aalborg Chamber of Industry and Commerce and can be generally summarized in three main points. First, the Chamber disagrees with the Technical Department's priorities regarding different types of traffic, in which motorists in private cars have lowest priority. Second, they oppose the traffic zone solution in which streets will be closed and drivers rerouted. And third, they believe that the shopping patterns in downtown Aalborg are too poorly known to justify any restructuring of the city center at the present time. The Chamber therefore calls for a new study of retail sales. In addition, the Chamber provides a more specific criticism of individual subprojects, as discussed below.

As an alternative to the Technical Department's priorities of traffic types, the Chamber of Industry and Commerce proposes its own set of priorities: (1) pedestrians, (2) cars, (3) bicyclists and moped users [svage trafikanter], (4) public transportation.[4] In contrast, the Technical Department's priorities have cars in fifth place after bicyclists, moped users, and public transportation.[5]

The second main point of criticism from the Chamber of Industry and Commerce concerns one of the central elements in the Aalborg Project: the traffic zone solution. Here the Chamber declares:

Traffic in the center currently proceeds sensibly and without substantial problems between the various forms of transport; thus, there seems not to be any foundation for the restrictive measures on traffic in the center such as called for by the municipality's plans . . . We must emphatically distance ourselves from the plans for a division of the city center into traffic zones which will prevent internal individual auto traffic in the center.[6]

While not explicitly mentioned in the Chamber's report, it appears from the internal preparatory work that the main reason behind opposition to restrictions on cars is the fear that restrictions will adversely affect retail earnings in downtown Aalborg. Hence, in an internal report from the Chamber's City Center Committee to its Retailer Committee, the following reason is given for its current activity:

The commercial center cannot survive if the customers are forced out to the suburban shopping centers because of traffic restrictions . . . The City Center

Committee has made a quick investigation which among other things shows that drivers of private cars account for 50% of sales, and that 84% of sales are due to customers who come from the hinterland . . . We must get [the Technical Department's] plan postponed. The Chamber's chairman has as of today promised to work for this goal by appealing to [the alderman for the Technical Department].[7]

It is significant that the "quick investigation" referred to in the quotation is the above-mentioned questionnaire survey with its 17% response rate. The survey is also referred to in the report on the Chamber's counterplan, "Downtown Aalborg: An Alternative" (*Aalborg bykerne—et alternativ*), where it is used to support the private-car argument. Nowhere is there any mention of the low response rate and the low validity of the numbers quoted. The numbers are, in fact, wrong. It is not, however, validity the Chamber of Industry and Commerce is pursuing here, of course. It is the rationalization of an already held view: namely, that those in private cars are the most important customer group for the shops in downtown Aalborg.

Despite—or perhaps because of—its own survey, the Chamber of Industry and Commerce concludes that too little is known about the population's shopping habits. The Chamber thus recommends additional surveys before the Aalborg Project is implemented. That high priority is placed on such surveys is illustrated by the fact that the need for them is mentioned with capital letters on the first page of the Chamber's counterplan report:

THE REPORT SHOWS WITH MUCH CLARITY THAT NEWER AND BETTER ANALYSES MUST BE UNDERTAKEN IN ORDER TO ELUCIDATE THE NORTH JUTLANDERS' TRANSPORTATION AND SHOPPING BEHAVIOR IN AALBORG *BEFORE* MEASURES ARE TAKEN WHICH ATTAIN DECISIVE CONSEQUENCES FOR THE STRUCTURE OF THE CITY CENTER.[8]

A closer look at the motives behind the Chamber's desire for a study of shopping behavior indicates that the Chamber of Industry and Commerce has a hidden agenda. It does not wish simply to obtain better knowledge about shopping conditions in downtown Aalborg, it also wants to delay the project. This strategy seems to originate in the Chamber's North-East working group and is described in a letter from the group's chairman—who is also chief executive officer, responsible for all noneditorial affairs, for the newspaper *Aalborg Stiftstidende*—to the Chamber's board:

In our working group (N-E) under the City Center committee we have sought information about where the downtown shoppers actually come from . . . By involving the municipality in the plans [for a study of shopping behavior] it is perhaps possible, by this means, to delay the implementation of the city center project.[9]

Is it coincidental that the head of Aalborg's only newspaper is part of a group seeking to delay the Aalborg Project? Or has the newspaper itself an interest in such a delay? Would this be an editorial interest? A financial one? A mixture of the two? We shall return to these questions later on.

THE STROKING STRATEGY

Let us examine how the Chamber's report is received by the Technical Department. Aalborg's chief of city planning explains:

> We were, perhaps, somewhat disappointed about the result because it was difficult to use for anything. This was because they wanted to include everything, to solve all the problems without accepting the consequences of the individual proposals they made, and what the effect a solution within one area would have on the solutions desired for other areas . . . They wanted to improve the conditions for all categories of traffic. They would not accept that if you improve conditions for, say, pedestrians, bicyclists, and bus passengers then you have to reduce free access by private car. They wouldn't accept this consequence. They *also* wanted to improve conditions for those who drive private cars, to increase the amount of parking. But you just *can't* do everything if you accept that you have only the road network which you have. You can't do it. It is simply illogical to expect that you can improve conditions for all the categories without it leading to any limitations at some point. So I think [the counter-plan] was utopian.

The staff in the Technical Department believes that the Chamber's counterplan is, professionally speaking, poor work. At first they feel tempted to make a devastating criticism of it. Perhaps they see a possibility to reciprocate the criticism and abuse they had felt themselves subjected to when they worked in the Chamber's Steering Committee and on the five working groups some months earlier. A staff member explains:

> The [Chamber's counterplan] was very easy to take apart when we finally received it. It was not at all worked out or well-argued or anything. Normally you cannot expect this from a piece of residents' work. But they had made such a big thing out of us having done such a lousy job and that it should, instead, be done in such and such a manner. When you do things in this way, well you have to put some arguments on the table explaining why what we had proposed was so bad and why theirs was so much better, about how their plan would operate. And it

wasn't there. They came up with cheap shots and we could argue against most of the points very easily.

But the city staff is not allowed to argue with the Chamber. The alderman for the Technical Department is beginning to see that getting the Aalborg Project accepted and implemented is not about producing better arguments; it is about strategies and tactics. In fact, the staff members in the Technical Department begin to thoroughly criticize the Chamber's counterplan. Their efforts, however, are abruptly halted by the alderman and the various section heads in the Executive Committee. These officials instead decide to utilize what might be called a "stroking strategy" toward the Chamber of Industry and Commerce: they maintain an air of being receptive and constructive rather than critical and aggressive, even though they believe the Chamber has done a poor job with the counterplan, and that its arguments against the Aalborg Project are not well-founded. The staff member continues:

> At a meeting of the Executive Committee, attended by the alderman, the working group presented a proposal for the evaluation of the [Chamber's counterplan], a proposal to deal with it separately and evaluate it. And it was stopped . . . We agreed that the Chamber's report should be treated like all the other submissions, meaning it would be evaluated by themes [together with other proposals for a particular theme]. Then you cannot give them as devastating a critique as you could if you treated it as one paper from end to end . . . If we do it separately, then we can really go into it fully. And we let this drop. It would not happen.

We will encounter the stroking strategy again later on, in relation to other parties besides the Aalborg Chamber of Industry and Commerce. It will prove to be central to an understanding of the relationship between rationality and power. For now, let us examine point by point the various kinds of reactions received during the public phase of the Aalborg Project, and particularly reactions to the project's first stage, as it is this part of the total project which is the most concrete and which has attracted the public's attention most.

"GOOD AND SENSITIVE PLANNING" AND A HIDDEN AGENDA

The individual elements in the project's first stage generates a variety of reactions from the public. These can be summarized in nine main points.

1. *Establishment of the bus terminal at Nytorv-Østeraagade.* From all sides comes broad opposition to placing the bus terminal at Nytorv-Østeraagade. Opponents include the Chamber of Industry and Commerce, the Danish Cyclist Federation, and the Socialist People's party, all of whom want the terminal

placed somewhere else. The Chamber of Industry and Commerce, for example, notes that

> [a] terminal as designed by the municipality on Nytorv/Østeraagade will entail that the driving of private cars must be eliminated in the long run. *There is agreement in all* [the Chamber's working] *groups that this must not occur* [emphasis in original].[10]

The Chamber declares that bus stops can be built at Nytorv but that the terminal function with coordination of arrival times and passenger transfers should be moved northward, to the harbor area.

For their parts, the Danish Cyclist Federation and the Socialist People's party point out that building the bus terminal at Nytorv-Østeraagade will entail long walking distances between buses and lack of transfer possibilities between city buses on the one hand and regional (intercity) buses and trains on the other. The Cyclist Federation also believes, like Aalborg's city architect, that the Nytorv site is unfortunate because so many pedestrians traverse the area. They propose that the terminal be moved southward, toward the railroad station and regional bus depot. The public phase brings forth no major opinions in support of the city administration's proposal to place the bus terminal at Nytorv.

Regarding the terminal's size, a prominent local architect discusses the Technical Department's proposal during the public phase in a guest editorial (*kronik*) in the newspaper. In particular he attacks the need for so many short-term bus stops where buses will pause for a few minutes, so that passengers can change lines.

> The city planning exhibition, if I recall correctly, showed 18 stops for buses. This *cannot* be right. Of course there should be bus stops in the center, but not waiting spots. In Odense they need only eight spaces. In Aarhus, at the railroad station, about the same. Make eight stops and put the other ten buses into the traffic system in order to improve the frequencies of departures instead of having the buses waiting at Nytorv. The city's traffic areas are much too expensive to be used for bus parking. Waiting places for buses must be at the end stations, not in the middle of town [emphasis in original].[11]

2. *Restructuring of the city bus and regional bus networks and establishment of an integrated bus stop for city and regional buses.* Establishment of a bus stop to be shared by city and regional buses on Vingaardsgade is criticized by the Chamber of Industry and Commerce, supplemented by a homeowners' association in that part of town.[12] Their argument is that the street and the surroundings will be strongly overburdened by an integrated bus stop, with adverse conse-

quences for the flow of traffic and the environment. On this basis, the Chamber concludes that the bus stop should not be established and that the city and regional bus networks function well enough as they are. The Chamber therefore desires that the "*linking together* [*sammenkobling*] of regional and city bus transportation in the downtown area be avoided" (emphasis in the original).[13]

3. *Reduction of traffic on Vesterbro street*. The Danish Cyclist Federation supports the proposal to reduce traffic on heavily traveled Vesterbro Street. They are interested in reducing the many accidents suffered by bicyclists which occur on this stretch of road. The Chamber of Industry and Commerce, however, is unenthusiastic about the proposal, which entails a reduction from four traffic lanes to two. They view Vesterbro as having vital importance for access to and exit from the city center. Making access to the center more difficult via reducing car flow on Vesterbro is thus viewed as a threat to the flow of customers into the center.

4. *Establishment of an east-west bicycle route on Østerbro-Borgergade-Kastetvej*. The Chamber of Industry and Commerce calls attention to the fact that they do not find bicycle paths necessary: "None [of the Chamber's working groups] find reason to separate bicycles and mopeds from other road users. But those driving cars must respect the conditions of the more vulnerable road users."[14] Only a few comments, however, refer to this aspect of the Aalborg Project. The east-west bike route along Østerbro-Borgergade-Kastetvej is that segment of the project's first stage which appears least controversial at the close of the public phase.

5. *Creating a zone border at Danmarksgade*. The Chamber is against closing off Danmarksgade to cars by means of a physical barrier. They will accede to speed reductions in the street, however, as long as parking is not affected.[15]

6. *Establishment of a pedestrian mall and "bicycles only" street in the western section of Algade*. The Chamber opposes the proposal to close Algade to automobile traffic. The street should be maintained, says the Chamber, as an exit for cars from the city center to Vesterbro Street.

7. *Closing the western part of Nytorv Square to car traffic (zone border)*. As mentioned, the Chamber opposes closing Nytorv to automobiles and notes that car traffic ought to have unaltered access; hence, the Chamber maintains that there should be no narrowing or closing of the street, which would be the result if the bus terminal and bicycle paths were built as planned.

8. *Closing of Østeraagade toward the Slotspladsen Square*. The Chamber indicates that automobile traffic should have unhindered access to Østeraagade, which therefore should not be closed at Slotspladsen.

9. *Parking*. The Chamber is against the Aalborg Project's parking proposal with its elimination of dispersed parking places, shorter time limits, and the in-

troduction of fees. The Chamber finds the proposal to be based upon "*a cata-strophic philosophy*" (emphasis in original).[16]

Let us summarize the situation at the end of the Aalborg Project's public phase. Excepting the proposal for the placement of the bus terminal, which meets resistance from all sides, the project is supported primarily by the Danish Cyclist Federation, the Kayerød Neighborhood Association, and by the Socialist People's party, while it meets massive resistance from the Aalborg Chamber of Industry and Commerce on all cardinal points. The *Aalborg Stift-stidende,* in its editorials and headlines, has also shown itself to be critical of the project, while the newspaper's reporting has been more neutral.

Despite the fact that the project's public phase has formally ended, the debate about the project continues. As a staff member puts it, "You can of course say that we had a public participation phase. But it just keeps going. It goes on and on." Or as the Social Democratic group in the City Council concludes two-and-a-half years later, when the group presents *its* version of an alternative to the Aalborg Project, "The protests seem . . . not to want to 'die' in this case."[17] Debate, protests, and attempts to exert influence continue.

It is therefore a godsend when, one month after the end of the public phase, the alderman for the Technical Department receives a letter from the Danish Town Planning Association informing him that he and the Technical Department will be awarded the association's prize for "good and sensitive planning" for their work with the Aalborg Project:

> As the Danish Town Planning Association during the past decade has not found reason to award the year's "mayoral baton," we would like to award you, via the Association's chairman, architect Kristian Larsen, this year's mayoral baton for a good and sensitive planning for downtown Aalborg.[18]

The official grounds for awarding the prize to the alderman are professional: the Aalborg Project is seen by the Danish Town Planning Association as planning at its best. Together with the professional considerations, however, the association, as most other "players" in the Aalborg Project, also has strategic and tactical considerations: they wish to help commit the city government to the project. The chairman of the association's Aalborg chapter explains the background for awarding the prize:

> At that time, the Municipality of Aalborg had done a great deal of work to achieve something we in fact thought was a reasonable solution for the city center and a means of ensuring better conditions for public transportation and for those not driving cars together with maintaining the housing stock in the city

center. At the same time, the plan was presented as the staff's plan; that is, the alderman and the politicians had not taken a principled position when we awarded the prize. [The award] should be seen as an attempt to keep the alderman, and with him the politicians, behind the plan which had been presented; it would be more difficult for them to abandon it when it had been presented as something good and professionally award-winning.

The awarding of the prize seems to have its intended effect. For Aalborg's chief of city planning, the prize

is certainly a *cadeau* to the politician [the alderman], that he dared to execute and had the ability to execute what in fact was a quite radical plan, which broke with the traditional norms for traffic flow in a city center . . . We found it amusing, and we also think that in this way we received some support and a feeling that planners in the rest of the country agreed with us about what was necessary to do in the city center.

During the award ceremony, the alderman for the Technical Department states for the first time that, although he has not formally approved the project, he is "in solidarity with the plans."[19]

A POLICY AND PLANNING SUMMIT

Like citizen participation elsewhere, citizen participation in the Aalborg Project reveals that interest in and, especially, resistance to a policy or plan appears in conjunction with certain specific measures. The traffic plan's first stage is the most concrete part of the project, and opposition to it is directed primarily toward the individual subprojects which are part of this first stage. One-and-a-half months after the public phase ends, the Technical Department therefore begins to elaborate what will later be called a "reduced first stage."[20] It is expected that a more modest first stage of the traffic plan, which takes into account some of the criticisms from the Aalborg Chamber of Industry and Commerce, can be implemented with support from the Chamber, or at least without its opposition.

The reduced first stage is the fourth step in what now begins to resemble a gradual but significant reduction of the project's level of ambition. The first step in the "down-sizing" process was taken when urban renewal was marginalized in the project. The second step occurred when land use planning and zoning receded into the background. The third step was the division of the project into stages, where it was decided not to implement it all at once. And now the fourth step is to reduce the extent of the first stage by altering four key aspects. (1) Only half of the bus terminal, the section to be placed at Nytorv, will be constructed; the Østeraagade section will be taken into use without any new construction, employing temporary measures. (2) Danmarksgade will not be closed to through automobile traffic as originally proposed. The street instead will be converted into a slowdown street for a six-month trial period; this will cause a gap in the north-south zone border in Danmarksgade. (3) The western part of Algade will not be permanently closed to through auto traffic as planned; instead, the closing will be done provisionally in the form of a six-month trial period. (4) No parking places will be eliminated in downtown Aalborg during the first stage.

Regarding the elimination of parking places, which is central to the overall success of the Aalborg Project, interviews with the key actors indicate that not only is it decided that no parking places will be eliminated during the first stage but that the entire parking scheme in the Aalborg Project, which also includes the introduction of parking fees and more time restrictions on parking, will be taken off the agenda. Furthermore, this would last not only for the first stage but indefinitely. The reason for this is that the alderman for the Technical Department, like the Chamber of Industry and Commerce, cannot support the parking scheme. A staff member explains:

> At the meetings where the plan had been presented, the alderman said that although we [the staff] might develop the parking scheme, it wouldn't be [executed] in his time. So we might as well pack the whole thing away. And that's the way things went, too.

We will return to the parking issue later.

After the proposal for the reduced first stage is finalized by the Technical Department, the alderman invites the Chamber of Industry and Commerce to a meeting which in both invitation and its subsequent minutes is termed a "negotiation" about the Aalborg Project.[21] The negotiation takes place at top level. Only the leadership of the two organizations is present. The secretary for the Aalborg Project's Executive Committee, who also heads the project's Task Force and who up to now has participated in all the project meetings, is not invited. This makes the secretary very anxious about what is to happen at the meeting and about the fate of the project in general. The secretary elaborates:

> Secretary: I was very anxious at that time and thought, "Now the whole damn thing is going to fall apart, this thing and that thing," because I wasn't allowed to participate. Of course, I didn't ask about it. That's not done . . . Normally, if the circle was limited, I participated as secretary. But here it was crystal clear that it

was something tactical, that it was only the bosses. They wanted to speak completely freely. Then they could always decide what got into the minutes of the meeting. You don't always write up minutes of those meetings.

Interviewer: Isn't it possible to speak freely when you are there?

Secretary: I don't know. Perhaps they feel that if they wheel and deal then I could perhaps begin to protest about something or other. They do not have the same constraints on themselves as they would if I sat there and said, "Okay, if we give away this here then perhaps we will have to let that go over there, too, because it is all interconnected in this and that way." Instead, they can say, "If the Chamber of Industry and Commerce is against this thing, shouldn't we just give it to them?"

Interviewer: Why are they not interested in having the interconnections made clear, which you can do?

Secretary: Maybe it's a matter of being able to stand independently in a negotiation situation . . . Perhaps it also has something to do with—well, I don't know—perhaps it was a reconciliation which they didn't want any witnesses to. I don't know. It is pure speculation and subjective perception on my part. I think that the only meetings where I have not participated at the executive level are perhaps those with the Chamber of Industry and Commerce . . .

Interviewer: One would think that professionally it would be an advantage to have you there to explain the interconnections.

Secretary: Perhaps they deceive themselves, for of course things are connected in this way anyway. But on several occasions it has been my experience, also in those negotiations where I, too, participate . . . that the boss tends to make some general tactical considerations. Where you then sometimes see that they have staff members who go in and chirp, "Now we all should just keep in mind this and that," where [the boss] then simply brushes them aside. You know, it is easier to be entirely free of this kind of chirping. Then you deal with the clamor [from the staff] when you get home.

There is no clamor this time, however, and the anxious premonitions of the secretary are not realized, at least not yet.

The exclusion from this and other "summit meetings" of those who have designed the Aalborg Project is yet another expression of the weakness of the better argument and "the greater the power, the less the rationality." Why concern oneself with how reality really is when one has the privilege of defining it? Why use the force of the better argument when force alone will suffice? Power knows its privilege and knows how to use it. At the same time, the exclusion of the staff from such negotiations also reveals a key mechanism of how the Aalborg Project becomes more and more fragmented. The project is con-

structed precisely around the kind of interconnections the leader of the Task
force describes here, where changes in one place trigger consequences somewhere else. A mundane example: if a street that is closed to cars in the plan is left
open in reality, this may lead to more cars than planned on another street, thus
making it impossible to build a planned bicycle path or improve public transportation on that street. By not placing enough emphasis on interconnections
like this in the "summit meetings" between the Technical Department and
the Chamber of Industry and Commerce—by excluding, for example, precisely those experts who have detailed insight into such connections—the
functional coherence of the project becomes, as we shall see, more and more
neglected. An integrated plan becomes a fragmented reality. In more general terms, the problem can be expressed like this: that which ought to be a
rationality-to-power relation, if the relevant technical-functional linkages in
the project are to be ensured, instead becomes a power-to-power relation,
where functional considerations become subordinated to tactical ones.

At their meeting, the Technical Department and the Chamber agree that
the reduced first stage of the project can be implemented as suggested by the
Technical Department. The Technical Department's minutes of the meeting
read:

> Representatives of the board of the Chamber of Industry and Commerce and
> the entire Steering Committee of the [Chamber's] five city center groups
> agreed that the first stage be implemented . . . completely as described by the al
> derman.[22]

For its part, the Chamber's minutes conclude:

> The Technical Department accepts that . . . Danmarksgade will not be closed,
> and there will be no further zone divisions. Østeraagade will not be closed in the
> first stage . . . the bus terminal at Nytorv is to be built as planned . . . Nytorv is to
> be closed to private cars from Braskensgade street to Østeraagade, but loading
> and unloading will be permitted . . . [The Chamber's chairman] expressed his
> thanks for our having achieved some influence. The municipality's plans are
> causing uncertainty and are inhibiting the desire to invest. There are still certain
> things which [the Chamber] wishes to see resolved. [We] hope that the first stage
> provides experience, but the second stage must not begin before the need ap-
> pears. A slow development is preferred.[23]

Worth noting here is the choice of words in these minutes. The meeting is a
"negotiation," the Chamber "agreed," and the Technical Department "accepts." These words, and the content of the minutes generally, draw a picture
of a meeting which is a genuine discussion between equal parties, each of

which presumes to have the right to influence the final form of the project. This interpretation is supported by the fact that both parties to the negotiations move their positions substantially in relation to their original standpoints. The Technical Department accepts yet another set of reductions to its project, while the Chamber of Industry and Commerce accepts a project which far from meets their initial desires for changes. The meeting, and the general relationship between the Technical Department and the Chamber, has become a prototypical example of a stable power relation.

It is also worth noting that the Chamber of Industry and Commerce is the only outside interest group invited to negotiations with the Technical Department. And finally, it should be emphasized that the negotiations between the Technical Department and the Chamber occur prior to any review of the project by the City Council's Technical Committee, by the municipal Administration (*Magistraten*), or by the City Council itself. Here we may speak of *Realpolitik* in the prereview of the project before it is taken under consideration by the relevant popularly elected bodies.

These events lead us to conclude, if only provisionally, that the Chamber of Industry and Commerce has a special status and exerts special influence on the political process in relation to other parties.

POLITICAL RATIFICATION

After the Technical Department and the Chamber of Industry and Commerce have agreed on the content of the reduced first stage, the final design of the bus terminal at Nytorv begins, and the total project is sent for review to Aalborg City Council. First the council holds a three-and-a-half-hour orientation meeting about the project. During the meeting, the chairman of the Chamber of Industry and Commerce who, as mentioned, is also a Conservative City Council member and a member of the council's Technical Committee, describes the agreement reached between the Chamber and the Technical Department. He concludes: "The Aalborg Chamber of Industry and Commerce is in agreement with the Second [Technical] Department regarding the implementation of the revised first stage."[24]

Outside the City Council meeting hall, *Aalborg Stiftstidende* issues a warning. In an editorial the newspaper emphasizes the dangers inherent in intervening in the existing traffic patterns together with the necessity to carry out a study of the population's shopping habits. The paper's views are again identical with those of the Chamber:

> This modest first stage can be the introduction to a revolutionizing development which deprives our town of its utility for anyone other than those living in

the center . . . The question the city council members must deal with is: How much should one tamper with that living organism which the town is? How many arteries does one dare to convert into pedestrian malls or "slowdown" streets or "buses-only" streets, before the organism collapses from anemia?[25]

A few weeks after the orientation meeting, the Aalborg Project is again on the City Council's agenda, this time for final ratification. However, the council members from the Social Democratic party are not yet prepared to give the project their final approval. The Social Democrats want more information about various questions. The council votes to postpone ratification.[26]

A month later another attempt is made, and the project is now ratified with twenty-five votes for and only one vote opposed (cast by a City Council member representing the populist Progress party, *Fremskridtspartiet*). There are no abstentions.[27] Two-and-a-half years into the Aalborg Project, the Technical Department is finally given the go-ahead to implement the first stage of the project.

In sum, the image that emerges from the Aalborg Project at the time of ratification is of an innovative, comprehensive, and award-winning project. Leading Danish city, transportation, and environmental planners have synthesized the most progressive ideas about environmental improvements and traffic safety into a concrete project. But the image also reveals a project which on central points is manipulated and rationalized, even before it reaches the stage of political consideration. In addition, it is a project which already in its design phase begins to fragment. Manipulation, rationalization, and fragmentation all take place prior to the formal political treatment of the project. The activities of the formal political organs are so far overshadowed by the *Realpolitik* which goes on within the Technical Department, the Mayor's Office, the Aalborg Bus Company, and the Chamber of Industry and Commerce. It is the preliminary, backstage power play, not the plan's rubber-stamping by the City Council, which is the real politics of planning in Aalborg.

GREAT
PARAGRAPHS

Eight

THE *LONGUE DURÉE* OF POWER

> [N]othing is more incomprehensible than how an honest and pure
> desire for truth could arise among men.
>
> *Friedrich Nietzsche*

T he negotiations between the Technical Department and the Chamber of
Industry and Commerce described in the previous chapter cannot be understood as an isolated, unique event. These and similar negotiations will
later reveal themselves to be decisive for the Aalborg Project's fate, and they are
indicative of a well-maintained, well-functioning power relation. The real significance of this relation first becomes fully clear when analyzing the association between the department and the Chamber in the time perspective of
several decades or even several centuries, using the kind of historical perspective that Anthony Giddens—from Fernand Braudel and the French *Annales*
School—calls "*The Longue Durée* of institutions which creates the overall
framework of social positioning."[1]

THE "CONTRACT"

The negotiations between the Technical Department and the Chamber of Industry and Commerce take place in the context of the most important and
longest existing power constellation in the project, the cooperation between
these two organs. It turns out that the two parties have agreed on a "contract"
according to which not only the Aalborg Project but all matters under the
Technical Department which might be of interest to the Chamber will be subject to negotiation between them. The contract is not a mechanical result
agreed upon at one historical moment, once and for all. Rather, it is an ongo-
ing agreement intermittently renewed, renegotiated, and reconfirmed, typi-

cally on the initiative of the Chamber, which presses to obtain information and influence, followed by acceptance from the leadership of the Technical Department. As with other power relations, this relation is not static but is constantly being reproduced.

The current contract can be traced back to the period immediately after a major municipal administrative reform in 1970 (*kommunalreformen*), in which new municipalities were established in Denmark with increased administrative autonomy. The Chamber of Industry and Commerce was disturbed when the new municipality undertook to close a main downtown street without consulting the Chamber. In minutes of a meeting between the Technical Department and the Chamber during this period, we read that

> [t]he Chamber of Industry and Commerce strongly expresses its regret that the closing of Østeraa [street] occurred without previous consultation with the Chamber and urges that it be consulted in such cases in the future. The alderman regretted what had transpired, but he had tried to come into telephone contact with the individual board members of the Chamber of Industry and Commerce.[2]

The Chamber eventually succeeded in reopening Østeraagade, in cooperation with the Police Department and *Aalborg Stiftstidende*, which also opposed the closing. Hence, immediately after the municipal reform we already find the triumvirate in action which will subsequently reveal itself to exert decisive influence on the Aalborg Project. With this experience in mind, the Chamber decided that the possibility to exert influence on important decisions cannot depend on such factors as whether or not board members could be reached by phone. Therefore, the Chamber soon proposed another meeting with the Technical Department in which a more systematic cooperation between the department and the Chamber be established. The Technical Department's minutes of this meeting read:

> [The chairman of the Chamber] proposed that [the Technical Department] in the future take up closer contact with representatives of the retailers in the ongoing planning, especially regarding the city center. The alderman promised this on the condition that such an advisory committee of retailers be represented by the board of the Chamber of Industry and Commerce.[3]

Worth noting here is that the proposed cooperative organ is from the start termed an "advisory committee" (*rådgivende udvalg*). Thus, the committee is informally given the same status as that of the formal Technical Committee under Aalborg's City Council, a practice reflected in the Technical Department's subsequent treatment of the Chamber.

SEPARATION OF POWERS À LA AALBORG

One example pregnant with metaphor involves the planning of a major new thoroughfare in the city center in the mid-1970s. In the minutes of a Technical Department meeting, where it was decided who should be kept informed about the work, the external parties were listed as follows: "(a) the [City Council] Technical Committee; (b) the Chamber of Industry and Commerce; (c) the Police."[4] No more, no less, and in that order. Such is the separation of powers à la Aalborg. Here, as well as later, the Chamber of Industry and Commerce appears alongside the constitutionally determined *political power* on the one hand, that is, the City Council's Technical Committee, and with the equally constitutionally determined *executive power* on the other, that is, the police. Seen from the standpoint of general democratic standards, one must inevitably pose the following questions: What is a special interest group doing in such company? Does its inclusion here not constitute a deeply problematic deviation from democratic standards?

Moreover, by paying consistent attention to the established cooperative relationship, the Chamber of Industry and Commerce succeeds in obtaining more influence on the decisions in the Technical Department than both the Technical Committee and the Aalborg Police Department.[5] As shown, the minutes of the internal meetings of the Technical Department and the Chamber of Industry and Commerce gradually begin to mention "negotiations" and "influence" instead of "advising." It is this influence which provides the context for the statement by one of the Chamber's chairmen that

> our city government in several situations will not make a decision without having heard the Chamber's opinion, and one can well imagine some major issue that the city administration would be very hesitant about instituting against our expressed desire, accompanied by strong argumentation. It is extremely rare that things get so out of hand, and we must always remind ourselves that we certainly are not any supreme city council [*overbyråd*].[6]

Despite the last invocation, one might ask whether the Chamber of Industry and Commerce is not actually functioning as such a supreme city council in relation to the Technical Department. A subsequent chairman of the Chamber describes in an interview how cooperation with the Technical Department actually takes place:

> You know, we had the possibility to change the proposals they came up with in the Second [Technical] Department before they reached the Technical Committee [and the City Council]. For it has turned out that if [the proposals] first

reach the Technical Committee, and are presented there and are to be discussed in the City Council, then it is almost impossible to get them changed. In that case we have to go the other way around, by the political route, via the city council members.

More concretely, the cooperative relationship between the Technical Department and the Chamber of Industry and Commerce is maintained through a number of activities. First, regular meetings are held between the leaders of the two organizations, in addition to ad hoc meetings when specific issues make it necessary. Second, the Chamber invites more Technical Department representatives than other municipal personnel to its annual meetings where the annual report is presented. Third, there is the aforementioned permanent agreement between the two parties about orientation and negotiation.[7] Fourth, and perhaps most important, the Chamber of Industry and Commerce, as part of their "power maintenance" in relation to the Technical Department, is actively involved in ensuring that the alderman's post in the Technical Department is occupied by a person sympathetic to business interests and oriented toward cooperation with the business community. For instance, during the Aalborg Project "goal oriented business people in Aalborg" sponsored an advertising campaign for a Conservative candidate running for the City Council. This candidate, explicitly described as "the business community's man," went on to become the alderman for the Technical Department after the elections.[8] In fact, this has happened with every election in the twenty-five-year history of the Greater Aalborg Municipality, with the result that the alderman for the Technical Department has always been a Conservative, even during periods of Social Democratic majority in the City Council. It is interesting also to note that the post as alderman for the Technical Department is the only one of the four alderman positions that has not been held by a woman throughout the history of the municipality. According to a former chairman of the Chamber, 80% of the members of the Chamber are hard-core Conservative voters, and an unequivocal overlap exists between the Chamber's interests and the Conservative party platform.[9] Add to this the fact that during the Aalborg Project's design, ratification, and early implementation—the decisive period of the project—both the Chamber's chairman and the Technical Department alderman were City Council members from the Conservative party, and we certainly have the ingredients to secure stable cooperation between the Chamber of Industry and Commerce and the Technical Department.

The Conservative party's persistent choice of occupying the Technical Department alderman post can be seen as the choice of the business community as such. The choice reflects the efforts of business and conservatives to influence the development of infrastructure, zoning, environmental regulation, and other important conditions for the economic development of the city. In contrast, the Social Democratic party and the trade unions, while placing the mayoralty at the top of their list, tend to pursue alderman posts in the social or cultural departments. In this way a rough division in the political life of Aalborg has occurred, in which business and conservatives—via the alderman for the Technical Department—influence the local material conditions for production and commerce, while the Social Democrats and trade unions focus their energies on the conditions for social reproduction, that is, leisure time, sports, social welfare, culture, etc.

FROM THE BRASS CHANDELIER
TO THE "MOSS-GREEN BATHROOM"

A deeper understanding of the close cooperation between the Technical Department and the Chamber of Industry and Commerce requires us to go much farther back in time than the administrative reform of 1970. A time perspective of more than half a millennium is more suitable for exposing the historical roots of the cooperation.

The first mercantile legislation in Denmark goes back to Erik of Pommerania, whose decree of 1422 laid the groundwork for the Danish laws on trading towns (*købstæder*).[10] At that time trade was the basic occupation of these towns, and local government was dominated by the merchants. The typical form of government was a "magistrate" (*magistrat*) consisting of two mayors and five to twelve aldermen. The mayors were appointed by the king and were nearly always chosen from among the men in the magistrate. The magistrate typically supplemented itself, even though the aldermen in some towns were formally chosen by the local burghers (*borgere*).

According to Erik of Pommerania's decree, mayors and aldermen were not to be elected from among the ranks of higher officials and artisans but could come only from among merchants and burghers. By the 1500s, artisans also obtained the right to be elected to the magistrate. According to the Danish historian C. Klitgaard, however, even at this time it was "certainly very exceptional that anyone other than merchants, in addition to, possibly, brewers, goldsmiths, tanners, and others carrying out more reputable mercantile occupations, could obtain seats in the [magistrate], in any case in the larger trading towns."[11] Klitgaard finds the situation important to "remember if one wants to understand what from the viewpoint of the contemporary observer will be regarded as a strange mixture of the town's (municipality's) affairs and the merchant guilds' affairs, which again and again appears in the city archives preserved from the 15th and 16th centuries."[12]

As illustrated in this and the preceding chapters, one need not, however, go to the city archives from the fifteenth and sixteenth centuries in order to find the kind of "strange mixture" of municipal and business affairs Klitgaard describes. It exists in the city archives for twentieth-century cases, and it recurs in interviews with the people involved in these cases.

In the fifteenth and sixteenth centuries the merchants in the trading towns began to form guilds and other associations for the protection of their members' interests. Klitgaard explains that

> each town—and within the town those practicing each trade—came to create a small community for themselves, which kept close watch on preventing unauthorized people from penetrating their trade, and they continually sought to achieve as many advantages as possible for their own members, even if this somehow involved attacks on other classes or other towns.[13]

In this way class interests were established that still mark political life in many Danish towns. Nine years after Erik of Pommerania's decree, in 1431, the forerunner of the Aalborg Chamber of Industry and Commerce, the merchants' guild *Guds Ligoms Lagh* (Guild of God's Body), was formed on the initiative of Mayor Peder Ilfarsen of Aalborg. The town's mayors and aldermen, that is, the *magistrat*, was the guild's highest authority, but

> [t]he towns magistrate [consisted] of merchants and (now and then) of prominent citizens, and as the magistrate was also the guild's board, to whom, for example, accounts had to be presented, it thereby followed that the affairs of the town and those of the guild were often mixed in what on a superficial consideration seems to be a highly inexplicable degree, hence, when in 1608 a man presented the guild with a brass chandelier having a value of 30 *daler* [from which derives the American term "dollar"] he was in turn freed from all municipal burdens . . . and at guild meetings regulations were often passed which were to apply to all the town's inhabitants.[14]

Through the entire seventeenth century the number of merchants in Aalborg, the second largest town in Denmark, hardly ever exceeded 100, or about 2% of the total population. Nevertheless, the merchants completely dominated the town's life, politically and in other ways.[15]

Centuries from now, when Aalborg's history is written for our era, it will not be a brass chandelier that will pique the interest of historians, as in the quotation above, but perhaps instead a "moss-green bathroom," a gift to Aalborg's mayor from a local businessman and the cause of the so-called Aalborg Scandal, a major corruption scandal which led to jail sentences for both of them.[16] Where the receipt of the brass chandelier was not a problem for the city fathers in the beginning of the seventeenth century, historians will conclude that in the twentieth century a modern creation called "democracy" had appeared, and that the giver and taker of the moss-green bathroom were so unfortunate, or so ignorant, as not to take the rules of democracy into consideration.

Neither the brass chandelier nor the moss-green bathroom are unique in Aalborg's history. In 1682, in a case of misuse of public funds and of a stipend intended for the town's poor, Aalborg's mayor died in circumstances the town's sheriff said looked like suicide.[17] Later on the entire magistrate was suspended by the king in the same case, one of several scandals involving Aalborg's government that historians like to emphasize when recounting the town's history.[18]

The purpose of describing the *magistrat* form of government as growing out of a long tradition of identity between the city government and the business community, and to compare this tradition of class or "estate" (*stand*) government with today's situation, is to show that cooperation between the Technical Department and the Chamber of Industry and Commerce has long historical roots. Originally, the magistrate *was* the board of government for both the city and the business community. More important, when seen from the perspective of the *longue durée,* modern institutions and phenomena such as rationality and administrative neutrality show themselves to be both young and fragile in relation to the "estate" (*stand*) traditions which have consolidated themselves via centuries of daily practice. These premodern traditions, and the power relations that go with them, have penetrated into the forging of modern institutions. This is in spite of the fact that the very raison d'être of modernity is ideally to eliminate or balance the meaning of *stand* and tradition, and despite the fact that the process of modernization has been going on for more than two centuries. The rationality of power turns out to have substantially deeper historical roots than the power of rationality.

Modern institutions, therefore, remain partly unrealized, formal ideals. Or more precisely, they become ideals that are not and cannot be realized once and for all, but whose realization must be constantly fought for, strategically and tactically, in a power relation vis-à-vis the old traditions. It is out of this struggle that new traditions appear. Modern institutions, rationality, and neutrality can, in this sense, be seen as forms of power, not as end points of power. Modernity and democracy do not "liberate man in his own being," nor do they free individuals from being governed. Modernity and democracy compel man to face what Michel Foucault calls "the task of producing himself," and of generating practices of government that will not obstruct, but will instead advance, "the undefined"—and never-ending—"work of freedom."[19]

In the Aalborg Project, the century-old traditions of magistrate government and the associated practices of power maintenance demonstrate that it
may be immensely more difficult to effect change than was imagined by the
city administration's policy and planning staff when they launched the Aalborg
Project.[20]

Nine

RATIONALITY IN THE CONTEXT OF POWER

What is truth? a mobile army of metaphors.
Friedrich Nietzsche

The 25–1 ratification vote for the Aalborg Project indicates broad, political support behind the project on the part of the Aalborg City Council. Following ratification, the project moves into a relatively calm period. Highest on the project's agenda are now preparations for implementation, in the form of detailed planning, drafting, and actual construction of the individual subprojects in the first stage.

DECEIVING THE ENVIRONMENTAL PROTECTION AGENCY

Despite its reduction to half its original size, the bus terminal at Nytorv Square continues to be the largest subproject. In conjunction with the planning of the bus terminal, a more detailed "local plan" (*lokalplan*) is drafted following the stipulations of the Municipal Planning Law (*kommuneplanloven*). All "local plans," for example, must be prominently displayed and publicized for comment concerning their economic, social, and environmental consequences.

The local plan for the bus terminal receives eight letters of protest when publicized, including one from *Aalborg Stiftstidende* and four from other businesses located on Nytorv. In addition, the Office of Public Health for North Jutland County objects to the plan citing insufficient information about its effects on air pollution and noise. Finally, letters objecting to the plan also arrive from the committee for Historical Preservation (*Fredningsnævnet*), the administration of North Jutland County, and the Danish Cyclist Federation.

The Technical Department has its doubts about whether building the bus terminal will require certification according to the Environmental Protection Law. Hence, when the City Council, on ratifying the Aalborg Project, decides that the citizens of Aalborg must be informed of possible environmental hazards, the council decides to elaborate a series of environmental impact studies of the bus terminal.[1] These impact studies, together with the "local plan" proposal, are sent for comment to the Danish Environmental Protection Agency (*Miljøstyrelsen,* hereafter referred to by the familiar abbreviation EPA).[2] At the same time, the material is also sent to the National Planning Commission (*Planstyrelsen*), which is the certifying authority specified by the Municipal Planning Law. This procedure is followed with the intention of ensuring that eventual protests or demands for treatment of the matter according to the stipulations of the Environmental Protection Law will not delay project implementation.

The EPA, however, turns out to have misgivings about the project and about the environmental impact studies furnished by a Copenhagen consulting company working on the case. The agency finds the expected noise levels at the terminal to be "unacceptable."[3] Noise levels of 66–72 dB(A) at Nytorv and 68–70 dB(A) on Østeraagade[4] exceed both the 65 dB(A) maximum acceptable for street-facing building facades proposed by the Danish Road Noise Committee in 1978 and an established planning goal of 55 dB(A).[5]

As for air pollution, it is expected that nitrous oxides will be a problem. On the southern part of Østeraagade the annual average of nitrous oxides is expected to reach 194μg/m³ during the first stage of the Aalborg Project. This is nearly twice the existing German maximum acceptable limit of 100μg/m³.[6]

The Environmental Protection Agency also questions the methods of calculation and the assumptions used.[7] One problem, for example, is that both noise and air pollution are calculated as averages over longer time periods than the actual time intervals in which the buses will wait in the terminal with their motors running. The EPA thus concludes that the impact studies do not adequately account for peak effects when all the buses are parked in the terminal, motors running, while passengers transfer from one line to another. The actual air pollution levels in fact can be expected to be much greater than those calculated in the impact studies. Finally, the EPA considers as inadequate the validity of the models used in the impact studies for air pollution; hence, the validity of results is also deemed inadequate.

In brief, the Environmental Protection Agency views the bus terminal project as an environmental hazard. For the EPA it makes no difference that Nytorv and Østeraagade are already heavily burdened by air pollution and that other areas in downtown Aalborg are also polluted. The EPA seeks an improvement in the situation. And the bus terminal will certainly not improve air quality; on the contrary, air quality will deteriorate, according to the EPA.[8]

On this basis, the EPA suggests—like Aalborg's city architect, the Aalborg Chamber of Industry and Commerce, the Socialist People's party, and the Danish Cyclist Federation before it—a feasibility study of possible alternative sites for the bus terminal. The Technical Department informs the EPA that this question has already been studied and that the studies showed that there were no other possibilities than Nytorv-Østeraagade. The studies the Technical Department refers to here are the same as those discussed above in Chapters 2–4. Here the studies were shown to be manipulated rationalizations of a previous decision, and it was pointed out that there exist other possible sites for the terminal. The Environmental Protection Agency, however, accepts the explanation from the Technical Department, apparently without evaluating the validity of the siting studies in the same way as the agency has evaluated the validity of the environmental impact studies. Thus, the EPA accepts Nytorv as the only possible site for the bus terminal on a false basis.[9]

For the EPA, the problem now becomes one of trying to reduce the harmful environmental effects around Nytorv. In solving this problem, the agency recommends that the municipality implement the following measures: (1) existing and new buses should be equipped with more effective muffler systems, (2) bus motors should be turned off if buses stop for over three minutes at the terminal (the buses will typically park three to five minutes), (3) the bus drivers should be instructed to drive so as to minimize noise and air pollution, (4) the buses themselves are to be maintained so that they operate with optimum antipollution efficiency.[10]

The EPA puts muscle behind its recommendations by asking the North Jutland County administration to carry out a more detailed assessment of actual pollution in the bus terminal. It is suggested that the assessment take place a year after the bus terminal is put into operation. Its purpose will be to determine whether further antipollution measures must be implemented as part of the operation of the terminal. The Environmental Protection Agency's recommendations gain further weight by the agency stating that a structure such as the bus terminal is in principle subordinated to the Environmental Protection Law's stipulations on environmental certification, and the EPA will only forego the certification procedure on condition that they gain influence via negotiations.[11] The influence of the Environmental Protection Agency via this channel is agreed upon by Aalborg Municipality, the National Planning Commission, and the EPA.

The Technical Department views the Environmental Protection Agency's procedures as "certainly somewhat untraditional."[12] The department is not used to genuine quality control over its planning activities, and the city engineer, in an internal memorandum, discreetly asks his colleagues "how seriously we should take the Environmental Protection Agency's recommendations."[13] Publicly, however, the Technical Department declares that it will follow the recommendations of the EPA. In this manner the way is cleared for the construction of the bus terminal at Nytorv.

RATIONALITY IN "LITTLE TOWN"

One month later, the ground is broken for the bus terminal, and the debate about the terminal's location comes out of the shadows. A general experience regarding project implementation is confirmed in Aalborg: the more concrete a project becomes on its way from concept to reality, the more concrete and the stronger the reactions to the project. As mentioned earlier, the placement of the bus terminal was the most controversial question in the Aalborg Project's first stage. The proposal for placing the terminal at Nytorv-Østeraagade was met with resistance and protests across the board in the public participation phase. Not one voice was raised in support of the proposal. The protests, however, were discounted by the Technical Department in the final revision prior to ratification of the Aalborg Project, and the protesting parties had apparently reconciled themselves to the situation. But a few days after the ground is broken for the terminal, protests reemerge from a new corner. A four-column double headline on the front page of *Aalborg Stiftstidende* now reads, "Aalborg's City Bus Terminal Is Located Completely Wrong."

The county supervisor (*amtsborgmester*) for North Jutland County emerges as one of the many opponents of the Nytorv bus terminal.[14] North Jutland's county supervisor, like Aalborg's mayor, is a social democrat. He is also chairman of the newly created North Jutland Transit Authority, which has obvious interests in Aalborg's public transportation. The supervisor, quoted in *Aalborg Stiftstidende,* declares:

> It would have been much better if [the bus terminal] had been located near the Regional Bus Depot and the railroad station. Then there would have been a real connection between long distance traffic, regional transportation, and the city buses . . . The people of northern Jutland will come to suffer because of this mistaken location.[15]

Three days later the *Stiftstidende,* under the headline "City Council Member Demands That New Bus Terminal Be Stopped," can report that the matter will again be raised in the City Council by the Progress party (*Fremskridtspartiet*), the intent being to "stop this mistake before it becomes much too big."[16] For the first time, criticism of the project is so strong that Aalborg's mayor must come forward to defend it, especially when the criticism touches his "baby" and area of responsibility, the city buses. The situation of the mayor and the county supervisor disagreeing, although both are Social Democrats, is one every political party seeks to avoid: two high party figures in open confrontation. The fact that Aalborg's mayor comes forward, and that he does so in open confrontation with a prominent fellow party member, emphasizes how acutely the municipality views the situation.

The power relation between the mayor and the county supervisor, and between the municipality and the county, however, allows Aalborg's mayor to emerge victorious. Neither North Jutland County nor the North Jutland Transit Authority has the possibility to sanction Aalborg Municipality because the municipality had ensured itself total decision-making competence over the Aalborg Bus Company when the North Jutland Transit Authority, of which the bus company is a part, was created. And Aalborg's mayor, with the largest number of personal votes of any Danish local politician, stands so strong in the Social Democratic party and in the City Council that he can simply reject the criticism outright. Negotiation and creation of consensus over the issue is seen as irrelevant. The documents and interviews reveal not a single meeting or exchange of formal correspondence between the two parties about the case. Communication takes place via the press, something characteristic of open confrontations, the mayor now telling *Aalborg Stiftstidende,* and the county, in no uncertain terms, "No one should interfere in where Aalborg Municipality builds terminals for the city buses."[17]

Yet even though rejecting the criticism of the bus terminal's location is a pure power move, the municipal administration nevertheless seeks to legitimate its decision with some apparently analytic considerations. One of the formal arguments publicized by the Technical Department and the Bus Company in the debate about the terminal's location is that the vast majority of bus passengers enter and exit the buses at Nytorv and that Nytorv is therefore the natural location for a terminal. For example, Aalborg's chief of city planning is cited in a local weekly newspaper:

> It is a fact that each day about 10,000 transfers occur to and from the city buses at Nytorv-Østeraagade, and that most of the passengers also have errands in the center . . . However, a few hundred—perhaps a thousand—transfers from regional to city buses and from city buses to regional buses take place at the [regional] bus depot and the railroad station. The location of the city bus terminal at Nytorv-Østeraagade is the right choice for Aalborg . . .[18]

Nevertheless, entries, exits, and transfers within any public transportation system must take place where they are feasible, and this is where individual lines meet each other. In Aalborg this is primarily at Nytorv. If the feasibility of transfers were altered because of changes in the network—for example, by placing the main intersection of the bus lines somewhere else—the figures would change accordingly. Even though it is correct that a large number of the passengers' final destinations, that is, shops, offices, etc., are located around Nytorv as compared with the railroad station and bus depot, from a transportation planning perspective this does not in itself constitute an argument for placing the bus terminal at Nytorv. That the destinations around Nytorv are important for bus passengers means only that the buses ought to pass by Nytorv.

The rhetorical and circular quality of the Technical Department's argument regarding transfers is indicative of how difficult it is to provide an analytic argument for the bus terminal's location. Aalborg's chief of city planning is apparently clear about this himself when he explains in an interview:

> We believe that we could document that [the bus terminal should be located at Nytorv]. There was the weakness in the argument, however, or in the documentation, that the bus system already looked this way [having its intersection at Nytorv]. We *had* the transfers at Nytorv. So the conclusion was given.

And in direct extension of this quotation, the chief of city planning tells a story which contains perhaps the most telling metaphor for how rationality is used in the Aalborg Project:

> It's like the story of Little Town, where the bell ringer calls up the telephone exchange because he has to set the church clock. So he calls the telephone exchange and asks what time it is, and the telephone operator looks out the window towards the church clock and says, "It's five o'clock." "Good," says the bell ringer, "then my clock is correct."

POWER THROUGH RATIONALIZATION

Yes, the clock is correct—and the bus terminal survives yet another round of attacks on its way to finally materializing at Nytorv.[19] But the rationality of the decision is just as imaginary as the time in "Little Town," its consequences as real as twenty diesel buses, all with their motors running, parked in a downtown square heavily traversed by pedestrians and bicyclists. The assertion of Harold Garfinkel and other ethnomethodologists, that the rationality of a given activity is produced "in action" by those who participate in this activity, holds true in this case.[20] Rationality is context-dependent; the context of rationality is power; and power blurs the dividing line between rationality and rationalization.

We see that when powerful actors require rationalization and not rationality, the rationalization is miraculously produced. The freedom to interpret and use "rationality" and "rationalization" in the service of power is a key element in enabling power to define reality. It is this freedom that structures the rationality of power. The relationship between rationality and rationalization becomes what Erving Goffman calls a frontstage-backstage relationship.[21] On stage rationality dominates, if nothing else as rationalization presented as rationality. Backstage, hidden from public view, it is power and rationalization that dominate. The project's staff are quite aware that they rationalize, aware that they present rationalization as rationality. Their rationalization is more sophisticated, for they are aware that rationalization violates accepted codes of professional ethics.[22]

Power

Rationality vs. rationalization

Politics

Democracy

Interests

Resistance

Knowledge

Expertise

Problem Definition

Agenda Setting

2-3
15
16 ff
22-23
36
58
53
78
83
87
95

Ten

INTERPRETATION OVER TRUTH

> [W]hatever exists, having somehow come into being, is again and again
> reinterpreted to new ends, taken over, transformed, and redirected by
> some power superior to it . . . [A]ll subduing and becoming master
> involves a fresh interpretation.
>
> *Friedrich Nietzsche*

"BEAUTIFULLY WASTED EFFORTS"

Parallel with the work on the local plan for the Nytorv bus terminal, Aalborg Municipality submits a formal request for environmental certification for the second bus terminal in the Aalborg Project, the integrated bus stop for both city and regional buses on Vingaardsgade. The bus stop contains eleven bus stopping places and an expected traffic flow of 1,150 buses per day.[1] The stop will be located in a residential area. This will make environmental conflicts more acute than at Nytorv, which lies in a business district. The municipality therefore chooses to apply for official certification of the city and regional bus stop in accordance with the stipulations of the Environmental Protection Law.

In the meantime, members of a law firm whose offices are on Vingaardsgade hear of the plans for the bus stop on their street and of the environmental impact statement being prepared in connection with the application for environmental certification.[2] The lawyers address the City Council, saying that the bus stop will cause environmental damage on Vingaardsgade. In addition, the lawyers are dissatisfied that the bus stop is being subjected to an environmental certification process instead of being part of a more rigorous "local plan" procedure with obligatory public hearings:

> We believe that this is not fair to those persons affected by this process, who can obtain no concrete influence on their future situation. The [environmental certification procedure] is certainly in accord with the letter of the law, but certainly not in accord with the Municipal Planning Law's intent; namely, that

citizens should have influence on factors which have significance for their physical surroundings. By elaborating a local plan, there is also the possibility that the City Council could be presented with proposals for changes in the project, which would entail a better solution as seen from various viewpoints.[3]

The law firm, however, obtains nothing from its complaint. No local plan is executed for the bus stop at Vingaardsgade, only the application for certification according to the Environmental Protection Law which is submitted to the county Environmental Department.

Six months later, the county responds, saying there is a conflict of interest in the case: the county operates the newly created North Jutland Transit Authority, whose chairman is none other than the county supervisor, and the authority wants to utilize the integrated bus stop on Vingaardsgade. The case therefore is sent onward to Copenhagen, to the Environmental Protection Agency, which is the responsible authority at the national level. The alderman for the Technical Department in Aalborg, provoked by the county's delaying tactics and the meager results obtained thus far, scribbles across the county's reply to the municipality: "Oh, well, the beautifully wasted efforts of North Jutland County."[4] Commenting to me on the situation, Aalborg's chief planner for public transportation remarks:

> The county's shelving of the bus stop at Vingaardsgade . . . must be seen in connection with the fact that the chairman of the county's Technical Committee . . . was also director for the Aalborg bus depot. [He] was an opponent of the bus stop because it would take passengers away from the bus depot and thereby worsen its economic situation.[5]

The county's delaying tactics, which also may be its revenge for the city's decision to locate the city bus terminal at Nytorv, generate a domino effect which will show itself to have devastating consequences for the entire Aalborg Project. In the first place, it becomes necessary to abandon the implementation of the city and regional bus stop on Vingaardsgade as part of the first stage of the project. This means that parts of the city and regional bus network cannot be changed as planned, including the moving of the existing city bus lines on Algade to Vingaardsgade. This, in turn, means that bus traffic must still be permitted in the western part of Algade, which therefore cannot be converted into the planned pedestrian mall and "bicycles only" street. Once again the Aalborg Project is truncated.

AMBIVALENT FEELINGS ABOUT BANKS

Besides the two detailed plans for the bus terminal at Nytorv and the integrated bus stop on Vingaardsgade, the Technical Department, as part of its preparations for putting into operation the Aalborg Project, also draws up two other related subprojects: a "Plan for Building Use and Preservation for Downtown Aalborg" (*Etageanvendelses og bevaringsplan for Aalborg bykerne*) and a survey of shopping patterns. Let us examine each of these in turn.

As concerns land use planning, the plan for building use and preservation is the most important single measure in the Aalborg Project. The objective of the plan is to prevent banks, savings-and-loan associations, insurance companies, offices, and similar nonretail businesses from occupying the ground floor of buildings, that is, at street level, in the most important shopping streets of the city center. The intention of the plan is to preserve these areas as genuine shopping streets. Technically, the plan is designated a "local plan" (*lokalplan*) and therefore has immediate legal consequences for the individual properties within the areas affected.[6]

It is unclear who actually originated the idea to prohibit more financial institutions on Aalborg's shopping streets. A Social Democratic member of the City Council Technical Committee believes that he had the idea:

> I came up with it back then, I'll take credit for that. It happens when the SDS Savings Bank [now known as Unibank] wanted to buy the corner property on Gravensgade [and Bispensgade]. I have read in "News from the National Planning Commission" [*Nyt fra Planstyrelsen*] that one could use what's called a Paragraph 17 prohibition.[7] And I try to get it on the agenda of the Technical Committee.

The chairman of the City Center Committee under the Aalborg Chamber of Industry and Commerce, however, has his side of the story:

> We [the Chamber] demand it. The idea probably comes from the pedestrian street associations via the Retailer Committee [*detailhandlerudvalget*] . . . A lot of things are happening in the banking world and in the insurance world at this time. So we very quickly make sure that something happens. The pressure comes from us . . . It was SDS's [bank] branch which gave the impetus, and a reasonable solution was found.

Finally, a staff member from the Aalborg Project Task Force has her version of the prohibition's origin:

> I can't remember . . . It was at a time when one bank after another was opening up all over the place. The pressure was on in the banking community. And then I can remember that I talked with [the above-mentioned Social Democratic member of the Technical Committee] that it was foolish, and that we could instead impose [the prohibition]. I had seen this someplace else, in Horsens or some other small town farther south. He also thought that it sounded like a very good idea. He would back [the proposal]. So some time went by, and then I think

it was really he who took it up in the Technical Committee, I think so. And then it got through by that route.

The documentary evidence confirms that the above-mentioned Social Democratic member of the Technical Committee is the first to formally take up the proposed building use and preservation plan within the city government. In a letter to fellow members of the Technical Committee, he proposes an investigation of the possibilities of retaining shops and avoiding financial institutions in the center of Aalborg.[8] It is not until a year later, however, when the Chamber of Industry and Commerce gets interested in the matter, that the proposal starts to move. The problem is then raised at the "life and death meeting" of the Chamber discussed in Chapter 6. At the meeting, the shopowners appeal to the alderman for the Technical Department for a temporary prohibition.[9]

Just a week prior to the meeting, the head of the Chamber's Retailer Committee had explained to the local press why the committee was opposed to more banks in the center:

> We are doing it, quite simply, out of love for downtown Aalborg . . . We conceive of a local plan which states that banks and insurance companies cannot establish themselves in the center of town without permission, but with possibilities for dispensation, of course. Some people will perhaps assert that we are going against our own ideas about free development. But we don't feel this way.[10]

With the Chamber of Industry and Commerce now backing the prohibition, a broad base of political support is established, ranging from Socialists to Conservatives. The elaboration of the local plan, legally confirming the prohibition, can therefore begin.

Internal conflicts might have been expected within the Chamber of Industry and Commerce in reaching agreement on the bank prohibition. After all, the Chamber officially presents itself as the main voice of free market enterprise, including competition and the right to set up business without hindrances. On several occasions the Chamber has declared that "restrictions are evil" and has made the rationality of free enterprise its own rationality—at least officially. In practice, the actual operation of the free market often proves to be in contradiction to members' interests. This is the case, for example, when new outside enterprises establish themselves in Aalborg and gain a market share at the expense of local firms, or when banking institutions and insurance companies, which also often come from outside, are able to offer higher rents for prime commercial space than local enterprises.

In these kinds of situations, free-market ideology gives way to local pragmatism: the Chamber finds it useful to have the Technical Department and the
planning laws control market forces to the advantage of the Chamber's members. The end justifies the means, and the means are, again, rationalizations
which here too show themselves to be a fundamental tactical weapon in the rationality of power. In the case of the prohibition on banks, the difference between what the Chamber of Industry and Commerce says and what they
actually do is so obvious that the Chamber itself is painfully aware that its image
could be construed as one of inconsistency and hypocrisy. Hence the Chamber's statement to the press, cited above, in which the retailers' representative ad-
dresses the problem of "going against our own ideas" and proclaims the
Chamber's support for the prohibition "out of love for downtown Aalborg."

Yet it is not only because of ideological inconsistency that there might
arise disagreement among the Chamber's members about a prohibition on
banks. A more immediate reason is that representatives of banks, savings-and-
loans, and insurance companies are present within the Chamber itself. It turns
out, however, that the financial institutions have only limited influence. According to the chairman of the Chamber's City Center Committee, banks may
not occupy seats on the Chamber's board. The chairman explains:

> We have *very* ambivalent feelings about banks. We do not have any bankers on
> our board. It is because if we first get a banker in, then he sits there for 50 years.
> He won't leave. Because—how shall I say it—it is a good PR-platform to have
> for a bank, right? . . . We dare not take bankers [on our board], we just don't. In
> any case I am against [banks] and we have been absolutely consistent in main-
> taining this line: that we will not accept the banks. We want to cooperate with
> the banks and we do cooperate with them. But we don't want to have them run-
> ning the Chamber of Industry and Commerce.

Besides the public relations argument, by which banks may use the Chamber's
board as a PR platform, an additional reason behind the lack of banks on the
Chamber's board is that the local business community has an interest in keeping outside businesses from exerting undue influence in the Chamber. Aalborg's financial institutions tend to be branches of outside firms. Hence, the
absence of banks on the Chamber's board also seems to reflect local efforts to
prevent the entry of outside capital and influence.

Finally, an additional explanation for why the Chamber was able to agree
upon a prohibition for banks might be that those banks which already *have*
branches in downtown Aalborg, and who *are* members of the Chamber, would
have an interest in preventing outside competition from entering "their back-
yard." In the case cited above, it is the Copenhagen-based SDS Savings Bank,

Denmark's largest, which becomes the test case for the new prohibition on nonretail storefronts. When SDS requests permission to establish its first branch in Aalborg, a member of the City Council Technical Committee hints that immediately before denying the request to the outside competition (SDS), the city government grants permission to a local bank, Provinsbanken, because it funds local sports activities:

> The problem was [that] Provinsbanken . . . wanted to expand their Slotsgade branch and they almost did not get permission. But since Provinsbanken donates a lot of money to [local] sports activities, you can well see that suddenly we had a whole lot of discussions, also inside our group [the Social Democrats on the City Council]. [Provinsbanken] was therefore allowed to hurry up and establish their branch. But SDS, that we could agree on. They were a new competitor coming in. All the other [politicians] sat on [the board of] North Jutland Savings Bank [*Sparekassen Nordjylland*] and other banks. And in this way we could agree that now [the prohibition] had to be enacted.

A subsequent chairman of the Chamber talks about the same case:

> SDS had purchased [a prime downtown business corner] and wanted to have the bank all the way around it. They applied [to the Technical Department] and the department asked us. We said that we thought it would be enough if they got a storefront up on Gravensgade [away from the corner inside a gateway]. We wanted a real store on the corner. We got one, too.

When the local plan, with its prohibition on banks, is published and comments and objections solicited, the municipal planning office is surprised by the reaction. A staff member explains in an interview: "We received simply a stack of objections which we practically had never had before, I mean serious objections." A total of twenty-one objections are registered at the Technical Department, mostly from property owners unwilling to accept the consequences of the plan for their properties, including what they see as a risk of a decrease in property values. One typical objection reads:

> The undersigned . . . owner of the property at [address] . . . hereby objects . . .
> The possibility is being taken from me to sell to a whole range of buyers, namely those with money, i.e., the banks, insurance companies, etc. This cannot avoid affecting the property's commercial value in a negative way, and in the worst case making it altogether impossible to sell at a sensible price.[11]

Among the more substantive objections we find a letter from the Chamber of Industry and Commerce. The Chamber now objects to the very plan they themselves had helped to propose and implement just one year before:

The local plan's very strict regulation regarding a total prohibition on the establishment of banks and insurance companies on the street level in the entire local plan area in all situations can harm both the urban community as well as the further development of business.[12]

The Chamber's letter goes on to explain that the local plan's restrictions are too inflexible, and it is proposed that the prohibition be softened by allowing the possibility of dispensations.

It is possible that the Chamber's objection should be taken at face value and that they actually believe that the prohibition they themselves had called for has become too restrictive in the Technical Department's proposal. It may be also that the Chamber's protest to the Technical Department is simply a face saving measure in order to mollify those banks and insurance companies who are among their members.

While the Chamber's motivations will remain unclear, the Technical Department rejects the Chamber's protest with reference to the Municipal Planning Law, which already allows for the dispensation provisions proposed by the Chamber. The remaining letters of objection cause only minor adjustments in the local plan's regulations. The revised plan is then ratified by the City Council and later finally approved by the National Planning Commission in Copenhagen. The free market in Aalborg has become less free, at the request of the major proponent for free market regulation, the Aalborg Chamber of Industry and Commerce.

PRESS AS WATCHDOG . . . OR LAPDOG?

As mentioned previously, the Chamber of Industry and Commerce has on several occasions asked the municipality to carry out a comprehensive study of shopping patterns in downtown Aalborg. The Chamber wishes to obtain more knowledge about the size of purchases, where the customers come from, what kinds of transportation they use, etc. The need for a shopping survey is strongly emphasized in the Chamber's counterplan and repeatedly has been mentioned in its on-going negotiations with the Technical Department. The Technical Department, however, earlier informed the Chamber that it has no funds to carry out such a survey. Nevertheless, negotiations between the two parties lead to a resolution—that were such a survey to be done, it would be executed in cooperation between the two parties.[13] The Chamber also agrees to help finance a possible survey.

In an interview, the chairman of the Chamber's City Center Committee explains why the Chamber continues to press for a shopping survey:

[The Technical Department] just did not want to believe our arguments, especially as concerns closing off [of downtown Aalborg to car traffic] and where the shoppers were coming from. And we must be the first to know something about this, right? But they referred to some old studies in another situation and asserted that there had been the oil crises, and the number of cars was declining and things like that. But no one can say this is a static situation. It would have *become* a static situation if the plan had been implemented. Then it could not have been changed. Then we would have been deadlocked and the city maybe destroyed. This is what we had to have some arguments about [via a survey]. The intention is also to make the city a better place to do business in, and to be in. And here we agreed entirely [with the Technical Department]. But we could just not convince them that it was the driving of private cars [*bilismen,* "car-ism"] which contributed to a *very, very, very* big part of the more important revenue. It is this [revenue] which maintains the 200 specialty stores. *This* is the argument where we say, "We must have this analysis."

At a City Council meeting about the Aalborg Project, the Chamber's chairman once again emphasizes the need for a shopping survey. He is backed by the *Aalborg Stiftstidende.* The newspaper publishes an editorial on the same day as the City Council meeting:

It is praiseworthy that the municipal administration has presented its plans, among other things at a prolonged public exhibit. From residents have come a certain amount of comments. Also in the form of readers' contributions to the newspaper. But it is a big question whether the extent of citizen comments can provide the City Council with adequate guidance about the mood in the town and the wisdom of the plans which have been drawn up. City planning is certainly a science, and a layman's objections can be held back for fear of "scientific" rejection. It therefore seems appropriate that there must also be a consumer analysis like that proposed by the Aalborg Chamber of Industry and Commerce.[14]

Worth noting here is the reduced importance the newspaper now attaches to "citizen comments" and the designation of city planning as a "science." This view represents a 180-degree turn in relation to the view the paper had expressed—in its coverage and in its editorials—during the public phase just nine months previously. At that time, the *Stiftstidende* had insisted that the Aalborg Project was "too important to allow it to remain in the hands of professionals and elected officials to make the decisions." Aalborg's citizens, the paper had intoned, "should and must immerse themselves in [the project], discuss it, and take a position on it."[15] At that time, the paper was supporting the actions of the Chamber's working groups. Now it is the Chamber's call for a shopping survey which they are backing.

The incompatibility of these two forms of argumentation—that is, first against and then for city planning as an expert activity, first for and then against city planning based on citizen participation—again reveals that the end justifies the means; it is an excellent example of what Michel Foucault calls "the tactical polyvalence of discourses."[16] We are dealing with yet another expression of the rationalizations of prior interests, desires, decisions, attitudes, assumptions, theories, prejudices, and myths which permeate the Aalborg Project. Such rationalizations occur not only in the editorials of the *Aalborg Stiftstidende* but also in the upper echelons of the municipal administration and within the ranks of the Chamber of Industry and Commerce. Rationality once again shows itself to be context-dependent, the context being power. And in the context of power the line between rationality and rationalization, if not lacking altogether, is certainly vague.

As for the *Aalborg Stiftstidende,* a systematic review of more than a decade of the newspaper's coverage of the Aalborg Project reveals a distinctive congruence between, on the one hand, the newspaper's views and the timing of their publication and, on the other hand, the Chamber's views and the timing of their being made public. We will see additional examples of this below. It should be emphasized that this conclusion applies primarily to the newspaper's editorials and headlines. The main texts of *Aalborg Stiftstidende's* daily reporting on the project are more balanced, even though they usually lack the depth of investigative and analytical journalism; this means that the most extensive coverage tends to be given to the viewpoints that are most conspicuous to the journalists. Here the journalistic approach results in an emphasis on the views of the business community, whose statements are consciously and tactically repeated so as to attract more press coverage. It is these factors which cause the alderman for the Technical Department, in an interview with me, to conclude that "I don't think that the [*Aalborg Stiftstidende's*] contribution in the city center debate was neutral."

An obvious question regarding the *Aalborg Stiftstidende's* handling of the Aalborg Project and the newspaper's support for the Chamber's views is whether the paper itself may have had an independent interest in supporting these views. In fact, there is considerable evidence that the *Stiftstidende's* support for the positions taken by the Chamber is closely related to its own immediate interests. *Aalborg Stiftstidende* has both its editorial offices and printing facilities on the Nytorv Square and thus has a clear financial interest in free access to and from the paper's property as part of its daily operations. Moreover, free access is a selling point for anyone owning the property, and it so happens that the paper is planning to sell and to move to new, larger facilities outside the city center. Any restrictions on the kind of buyer or the buyer's use of the old buildings would certainly detract from the value of the property, and decreased property value is not in the interests of the paper's owners.

The *Stiftstidende*'s chief executive officer explained to me in an interview that the paper's management views the Aalborg Project as harming the paper's operations in several respects: the restrictions on automobile traffic, the siting of the bus terminal at Nytorv directly up against the paper's buildings, and the project's prohibition on banks and insurance companies occupying the ground floor of the paper's buildings. The executive elaborates:

> Since we continued to have production in the *Stiftstidende*'s building on Nytorv, we certainly had to be interested in being able to get to the building by car . . . and it is, of course, clearly an increased value for the property if it could be used for banking activities on the ground floor. Then more buyers would be interested in it. So we had an interest in seeing to it that the [bank prohibition] clause was not applied.

Aalborg Stiftstidende is a member of the Chamber of Industry and Commerce, and the paper's chief executive officer headed one of the working groups that participated in elaborating the counterplan to the Aalborg Project. The chief executive officer is responsible for all noneditorial affairs for the paper. In fact, it was the chief executive officer and his working group who originated the idea of carrying out a survey of shopping patterns in downtown Aalborg, so as, "by this means, to delay the implementation of the city center project," as he stated in a letter to the Chamber. The letter was written on *Aalborg Stiftstidende*'s letterhead.[17]

From the perspective of journalistic ethics and in terms of our discussion of rationality and rationalization, we may ponder whether *Aalborg Stiftstidende*'s specific economic interests in the project had an influence on the paper's coverage. It is beyond doubt, however, that there exists an overlap between the views of the *Aalborg Stiftstidende*'s editors, as expressed in its editorials, and the paper's financial interests. A causal association between the paper's editorial line and its financial interests can be neither confirmed nor rejected, however, as no one in the paper's editorial or financial management with whom I conducted interviews desired to clarify this question for me. A former journalist at *Aalborg Stiftstidende*, however, has no doubt that there was a connection between the paper's financial interests and its press coverage:

> Of course the management [of the paper] talked with the editors, of course they did. And this is why the editorials [about the Aalborg Project] appear as they do.

Given the fact that *Aalborg Stiftstidende,* being Aalborg's only daily newspaper, has a virtual monopoly on the town's printed media, and given the fact that at this time there was no local TV or local radio stations, the paper's coverage of the Aalborg Project must be viewed as problematic. According to accepted standards of journalistic ethics, a monopoly situation imposes special requirements as to balance and neutrality. As far as the Aalborg Project is concerned, *Aalborg Stiftstidende* cannot be said to have lived up to these standards. The paper has not been a public interest watchdog in this case but, instead, a watchdog for private business interests, notably its own and those of the Chamber of Industry and Commerce.

THE "HIDDEN JUNTA"

Following the *Aalborg Stiftstidende*'s and the Chamber's widely publicized demands for a consumer survey, the Technical Department, despite its claims a few weeks earlier that no funds were available, suddenly finds the money for a study. The Chamber holds an ad hoc meeting with the Technical Department, in which they propose that the "AIM" market research and polling institute carry out the survey. According to the Chamber's minutes of the meeting,

> AIM's proposal for a method is approved. As the survey is undertaken on our initiative, we have promised to support it on the order of 25,000 [Danish kroner] maximum. This money, however, must be raised among the merchants' associations, who must be interested in the subsequent analysis of traffic and shopping habits. (Addition: discussed in the Retailer Committee . . . associations outside the city will not participate. Others do not have money for it).[18]

For its part, the Technical Department notes, "The Chamber of Industry and Commerce has approved the revised program [for the shopping survey] and will pay part of the costs, which are expected to be around 250–300,000 kr."[19] The actual expenses will be 300,000 kroner, of which the Chamber of Industry and Commerce will actually pay less than 10%.

 With an acute sense of timing on the part of the Technical Department, the results of the survey are published immediately prior to the implementation of the first stage of the Aalborg Project.[20] According to the AIM survey, total purchases in downtown Aalborg amount to 1.1 billion kroner annually. The Technical Department focuses primarily on the fact that the survey contradicts the Chamber's figures and assumptions regarding the distribution of revenues by form of transport. Whereas the Chamber of Industry and Commerce, in its critique of the project, has repeatedly stressed that 50–60% of gross revenues, if not more, stem from customers driving cars, and that planning hostile to drivers would thereby lead to a reduction in retail earnings, the survey now shows that each of the three groups—(1) motorists; (2) pedestrians, bicyclists, and moped drivers; and (3) users of public transportation—accounts for equal shares of gross revenue. Since those customers who drive their own cars shop less frequently, and for a larger amount per transaction, they account for the lowest proportion of the total number of shopping trips: 22%, versus 33% for those in public transport and 43% for pedestrians, bicyclists, and moped drivers.

Aalborg Stiftstidende, interviewing the chairman of the Chamber's City Center Committee, tells its readers that the chairman "acknowledges being astonished as to how many customers use public transportation."[21] At the same time, however, the chairman points out that one should not look at total gross revenues alone but should examine the share of specialty goods (*udvalgsvarer,* literally "choice goods" or premium goods, including luxury goods) as compared to the share of sales of staples, etc. (*dagligvarer,* literally "everyday goods"). According to the chairman, who owns a specialty shop himself, this is because (1) it is the specialty shops which distinguish a center more than the sales of groceries, and (2) specialty goods generate the largest share of earnings. Specialty goods are thus more important for the retailers and for the downtown economy than other types of goods.

The chairman of the City Center Committee also cites these factors in my interview with him, in which he comments on my interpretation of the survey results as rendered above:

> *Chairman:* Well, it shows that you, too, have not understood the [results of the] report. Because what counts for the city's retailers is not the giant sales which lie in the supermarkets' food sections. If you subtract them, you will obtain other percentages. And the purchases made by those driving their cars have a *much, much* higher average. It is the specialty goods which create the gross earnings, the profits. It is the specialty goods which create a center at all. If the specialty goods are not found in a center, then you get an American-style situation. Slums. Food products make up a very large part of sales. Try and subtract them and then analyze where the earnings come from.
>
> *Interviewer:* Has the Chamber tried to do that?
>
> *Chairman:* Oh yes, yes. We also presented it to the municipality. I think that we reach a figure where those driving cars make up far more than 50% of the specialty goods trade. Now specialty goods also include clothes, etc. It is hardly so marked for clothes. But as soon as you go over to genuine specialty goods [i.e., excluding clothes and other textiles], then the proportion of drivers gets very, very large. And there is one thing you shouldn't forget. If you put the whole thing together and say, "How much is sold in total?" then you're missing about

15%, which comes from customers outside Aalborg Municipality. And god-damnit, they all come in their cars. I'll guarantee you that 95% come to Aalborg municipality by car.

Interviewer: Are everyday goods not so important for a center?

Chairman: No, because it is only a question of supplying the local residents, right? It certainly has nothing to do with creating an atmosphere in a town. This is not what makes a town fun and nice to be in and interesting to walk around in. It's not [large supermarket chains such as] Føtex and Kvickly which give the town any kind of atmosphere. They are not what create the experience of being here. Then people can just as well drive out [of town] to [the suburban discount warehouse] Bilka, right?

While customers in cars do indeed account for a higher proportion of specialty goods sales than other groups, it does not necessarily follow that this particular clientele should have a special status in city politics and planning, and that shopping for conventional goods, being "only a question of supplying the lo-cal residents," should have lower priority. It might well be that planning should operate with a priority given to motorists, but such a policy option does not derive from social and economic laws for shopping, nor from the data collected in the survey. From a different perspective one might argue, as the municipal-ity does, that keeping local residents in the center is important for keeping the center alive and therefore that shopping for this group should have priority also. Whichever preference one holds, the political priority is only ostensibly grounded in facts.

Furthermore, the chairman of the Chamber's City Center Committee overestimates the significance of the drivers, even if we allow for the revamped categories he proposes. The share of motorists' purchases in downtown Aal-borg is not "much, much higher" or "far more than 50%." On subtracting both conventional goods and clothes and textiles from gross revenues and then ex-amining the remaining sector of pure specialty goods, as the chairman pro-poses, it appears that motorists account for 45% of the revenues in this group of goods. Since pure specialty goods constitute 33% of total earnings, the share of specialty goods purchased by drivers thus comprises but 15% of gross revenues (i.e., 45% of 33%). Were we to accept the chairman's argument, it would mean that city policy makers ought to accord highest priority to the specific activi-ties (specialty shopping) of a specific customer group (drivers) who contribute only 15% of the total sales in downtown Aalborg. Even when seen from a strictly sales point of view, such a policy seems problematic. Through a com-plicated web of influences and rationalizations, however, this is precisely what the actual policy becomes in Aalborg. Let us see how this happens.

The preference given to motorists who shop for specialty goods must be seen in the context of the fact that the City Center Committee, formed as part of the Chamber's Retailer Committee, is dominated by a small group of specialty shop owners.[22] A policy which places high priority on those driving private cars meets the interests of this group more than any other group in downtown Aalborg, because, as mentioned, the proportion of customers driving cars is higher for specialty goods than for any other type of goods. The specialty shop owners have succeeded in instituting their policy as Aalborg's policy by, as a first step, getting the policy approved in the Chamber's City Center Committee which they, as said, dominate themselves. The second step in the increasing rationalization of this special interest and its eventual metamorphosis into the status of "public interest" and "general welfare" is the approval by the Chamber's Retailer Committee, which ranks above the City Center Committee. In this way, the small group of specialty shop owners obtains a policy status by which they "speak for" all the Chamber's retailers. The third step is having the Retailer Committee's view approved as Chamber policy by the Board, and in the fourth step this becomes the policy of the entire Chamber. The fifth step consists of the Chamber's negotiations with and influence on the Technical Department; the specific interests of the specialty store owners penetrate the public system through these negotiations and obtain significant influence on the department's policy. In a sixth step, as we will see, the Chamber obtains endorsement for its policy from Aalborg's Municipal Administration (*magistraten*), which in a seventh step promotes the policy for approval by the City Council. The eighth and final step on the way from a special interest to a "public interest" policy is the City Council's approval of the policy as the city's own policy. In this way the 15% becomes 100%. Seen from a tactical point of view, keeping such a policy on the right track for years on end and through so many different organizational bodies requires clever and persistent lobbying. Such work demands people with organizational skills, and the Chamber of Industry and Commerce indeed contains many capable organizers. It also demands thorough maintenance of the power relations which are involved, not just from year to year but over decades, if not centuries, as we have seen. The "care of power relations" has high priority for the Chamber of Industry and Commerce. In modern organizational theory, groups such as the specialty goods retailers within the Chamber—small groups with great, though convoluted, influence—are called "hidden juntas."[23] This hidden junta has already exerted substantial influence on the Aalborg Project and will continue to do so.

THE POWER OF INTERPRETATION

In contrast to the Chamber of Industry and Commerce, the Technical Department views the results of the shoppers' survey as unavoidable evidence against the Chamber's views and in favor of their own strategy: the bicyclists, those on mopeds, pedestrians, and those using public transportation must be accorded higher priorities in downtown Aalborg, says the Technical Department, the interests of those driving private cars must be downgraded. It therefore seems strongly misleading and unusually provocative to the staff and the leadership of the Technical Department when *Aalborg Stiftstidende* chooses to report on the shopping survey with the following four-column headline: "Aalborg's Best Customers Come Driving in Cars."[24] Judging from the headline, it appears that myths die hard. The repetition of statements until they have an effect is a principal strategy in the rationality of power and in the way in which power defines reality. The myth that drivers are the most important customer group in the city center has been repeated again and again, even—or perhaps especially—when solid investigations reveal the myths for what they really are: political desiderata. Regardless of these investigations, the myths have had and still have unequivocal influence on the Aalborg Project's physical appearance and its possibilities of implementation. We must conclude that if a powerful party such as the Chamber of Industry and Commerce says that motorists are a much more important customer group than others, then other parties begin to act, and the project and physical reality come to appear as if this were the case, regardless of the empirical evidence.

It should be noted that myths about drivers are not necessarily incomprehensible prejudices. The life span of the myths hinges upon the Retailer Committee's ability to define the Chamber's policy with reference to the Aalborg Project, and on the fact that this committee is dominated by specialty goods retailers with an interest in depicting reality in this particular way. There is nothing mystical about the link between their interests and their interpretations: Those driving cars are the major customer group for the specialty shops. What is "mystical" is the way in which the specialty shop owners on the Chamber's Retailer Committee are able to turn their interests into city policy.

The headline in *Aalborg Stiftstidende* is formally correct, inasmuch as it applies to the fact that those in cars buy more per visit than do other customer groups, and because 35% of sales in downtown Aalborg stem from customers who come by car, while those using public transportation account for 31% of sales, and so-called light traffic, that is, bicyclists, pedestrians, and moped drivers also account for 31%. As regards the shopping survey's news value, however, the headline is strongly misleading, inasmuch as drivers are shown to be much less significant as a customer group than originally thought. After all, the text of the article makes clear that two-thirds of total sales are made to people who do *not* come by car. Headline and text thus convey two opposing messages, as if they were written by two different people—which they probably are, the text by a journalist and the headline by an editor. The Danish Press Committee's "Rules for Good Press-Habits" state that "in form and content *headlines* and subheads must *correspond to the article they introduce*" (emphasis in original).[25] This rule of journalistic ethics could not be said to have been respected in the case of *Aalborg Stiftstidende*'s coverage of the shopping survey.

For the Technical Department, this misleading headline is the straw that breaks the camel's back, and it is headlines like these, together with the newspaper's strongly critical editorials, which forces the alderman for the Technical Department to complain about lack of fairness in the paper's coverage of the project. The alderman explains:

> I think that I, not I but everyone here in the house [the Technical Department], hardly received a totally fair treatment [in the press]. I think that a line was already in place, coming from *Aalborg Stiftstidende* among others, that this [project] was garbage.

The chief of city planning now wants to strike back at both the *Aalborg Stiftstidende* and the Chamber of Industry and Commerce. He is fed up with both of them. Normally it is the official policy of the Technical Department not to reply to press criticism unless asked. A staff member explains the reaction:

> [The chief of city planning] was very upset about [the mention of the shoppers' survey in *Aalborg Stiftstidende*] and wanted to obtain permission from the alderman to submit a large piece in the paper. He had in fact written it. First the alderman said, "No," if I remember correctly. Then he tried again, and then the alderman said that if he absolutely wanted to, he could submit it, as long as it was his personal opinion. But he didn't do it anyway.

Here is an excerpt from the proposed commentary by the chief of city planning written for the *Aalborg Stiftstidende:*

> One cannot . . . talk about, for example, the purchases of drivers being dominant in relation to those of other road users, bus passengers, or pedestrians . . . It is just as important to plan for bus passengers, bicyclists, and pedestrians, who taken together make up 65% of the purchases. Parenthetically, it can be mentioned that [the chairman of the Chamber's City Center Committee] has stated to the *Stiftstidende* that public transportation is more important than what the Chamber of Industry and Commerce had expected, (which must logically imply that they have overestimated the importance of one or more of the other traffic forms [perhaps the driving of private cars]) [parentheses in original] . . . The City Council has resolved that major new roads and extensions of existing roads in the dense part of the city must be avoided, which accords well with many other tendencies in society, including the interest in maintaining the ur-

ban environment, improving traffic safety, and converting from private to public transportation.

The instruments of planning, as previously mentioned, therefore consist of regulating traffic within the possibilities accorded by the existing street area; that is, removing the unwanted through-traffic and other measures which can lead extraneous vehicles out to the main traffic arteries as directly as possible.

When the Chamber of Industry and Commerce, in its alternative to the city center project, calls attention to the fact that private cars should be able to drive unhindered through the downtown area, that parking conditions be improved, that public transportation be expanded, that bicycles and motorbikes have unhindered access everywhere (outside the pedestrian streets), that the conditions for "non-vehicular" road users be improved, that retail deliveries can operate without problems, that better conditions be created for pedestrians—all this together with the establishment of more green areas, expansion of housing, maintenance of downtown functions, more jobs and better public services, then it is a list of wishes which everyone could put their name to. The problem lies in fulfilling, within the existing framework, the often contradictory goals. Priorities must be set, and it must be accepted that it will entail restrictions on freedom within one domain to achieve important advantages in others . . . In my opinion, the report on shopping in the city center does not produce any need to propose changes in the planning objectives. On the contrary, I think that [these objectives] have been confirmed on many points.[26]

The chief of city planning never publishes his article. He explains why:

> *Chief of city planning.* It was a kind of self criticism, you know. It didn't promote the case, and now we had just received a certain amount of goodwill from the Chamber of Industry and Commerce. So there was no reason to dig [trenches] . . .
>
> *Interviewer:* But was it you yourself who decided that the article would not appear?
>
> *Chief of city planning:* Yes!

The decision of the chief of city planning again expresses the "stroking" strategy in which confrontation is actively avoided. The goodwill from the Chamber of Industry and Commerce that the chief talks about is due to the fact that the shopping survey has helped open the Chamber's eyes to the fact that there are other groups of customers going into Aalborg's shops than those driving private cars, groups that put significant amounts of cash into the shopkeepers' cash registers. This recognition is noted by the chairman of the Chamber's City Center Committee in an interview:

The chairman: We may also say, we learn to accept, that there are other customers than those in their cars. That is, the municipality gets something on us because we must acknowledge that there is a somewhat bigger—considerably bigger—share [of revenues] from other traffic groups . . . We must admit that we learned that there is a customer group—and it is larger than we thought—who come on their bicycles and who use public transportation.

Interviewer: What influence has it had on the Chamber's attitude, in more concrete terms?

Chairman: When we get farther along, we can better accept the way in which the bus terminal is located. Absolutely. And it has also shown itself later in that [the bus terminal] has had enormous consequences for business.

Apparently, the timing of the publication of the shoppers' survey played a role in this connection. The results were published two weeks prior to the start of the implementation of the first stage of the Aalborg Project, and the results appear to have helped soften significant opposition. However, the chief of city planning and the Technical Department are mistaken in their evaluation of the Chamber's goodwill. The Chamber in fact draws a fundamentally different conclusion from the shoppers' survey than does the Technical Department, a conclusion largely unnoticed by the Technical Department for a long time. The Chamber's leadership realizes that there are indeed other important customer groups than those who drive cars. And this causes the Chamber to reduce or withdraw their previous criticism of those subprojects aimed at improving conditions for bicyclists, public transportation, etc., such as the network of bicycle paths and the bus terminal at Nytorv. After the publication of the shopping survey, the previous harsh criticism of these projects simply ceases.

Nevertheless, the Chamber's view of reality is not structured by the same analytical rationality as that of the chief of city planning or the Technical Department. The Chamber therefore does not draw the same conclusions with regard to priorities as the planning chief and the department. The Chamber of Industry and Commerce wants "to have their cake and eat it, too," as the alderman will later express it.[27] In other words, there exists a single survey and two interpretations. The Technical Department's interpretation sees the survey as solid, analytical documentation for the Aalborg Project's downgrading of automobile traffic and its upgrading of public transportation and nonautomotive forms of transport in order to achieve environmental improvements and improved traffic safety. For the Chamber, however, the survey documents the possibility to increase earnings for the city's shops by improving conditions for nonautomotive and public transportation, but without at the same time giving lower priority to motorists. It is a classically clear example of an evaluation dependent on the eyes of the beholder. Empirically speaking, the survey results are not interesting in themselves. They may or may not reveal a single "reality," but that is not important. Rather, it is the interpretations of the survey results that are important. And the decisive aspect in relation to the fate of the Aalborg Project is not whether one or the other interpretation is "correct" or "true" but which party can put the greatest power behind its interpretation. The interpretation with the stronger power base becomes Aalborg's truth, understood as the actually realized physical, economic, ecological, and social reality. Here again, then, is an example of how power defines reality. The evidence from the Aalborg study confirms a basic Nietzschean insight: interpretation is not only commentary, as is often the view in academic settings, "interpretation is itself a means of becoming master of something"—here master of the Aalborg Project—and "all subduing and becoming master involves a fresh interpretation."[28]

City is organism— various parts have to relate well, & relating well, needs to have information.

Eleven

ANTAGONISTIC REACTIONS AT PLAY

[W]henever one finds outside forces called in by a party of men residing in a city, it may be taken for granted that this is due to a defect in its constitution.

Niccolò Machiavelli

There is a certain satisfaction in coming down to the lowest ground of politics, for we get rid of cant and hypocrisy.

Ralph Waldo Emerson

SEVEN ROUNDS OF PROJECT REDUCTIONS

Four years after it was begun, the Aalborg Project has undergone six "rounds" of progressive reductions from its original design. The first round occurred when urban renewal measures were virtually eliminated from the project agenda (see Chap. 5). The second reduction occurred when land use planning and zoning met largely the same fate as urban renewal. After this, the Aalborg Project is dominated by transportation and environmental issues: the urban environment will be improved primarily via changes in traffic and transport conditions. The third reduction occurred when the project's Executive Committee, led by Aalborg's city engineer, decided that it would be too radical to execute the total project all at once, as originally planned. Instead, the project was divided into three separate stages, with a schedule of implementation only for Stage One. The fourth reduction was the indefinite postponement of the project's parking policy. No fees would be implemented, nor would there be any new restrictions on time limits to regulate traffic and improve the environment in downtown Aalborg. The fifth reduction was the so-called reduced first stage which the Technical Department negotiated with the Chamber of Industry and Commerce in order to make the project more acceptable to the business community: half the city bus terminal was eliminated, and the closing of certain streets and sections of downtown to car traffic was abandoned. Also postponed were a pedestrian mall and bicycle paths (Chap. 7). Finally, the sixth reduction of the Aalborg Project was the postponement of the planned construction of the integrated bus stop for city and regional buses. This postponement made it necessary to maintain bus traffic on Algade, thus destroying the original plan to make Algade totally devoid of motor vehicle traffic (Chap. 10).

It now appears that a seventh round of project reduction is taking place: the plan to eliminate bus traffic from Danmarksgade in order to turn it into a residential traffic street and zone border is dropped. Under pressure from local merchants and residents, the bus line is restored on Danmarksgade after the street has been without buses for a brief period. The proposed traffic reduction on Danmarksgade will therefore have to be achieved by establishing a "buses only" street on a section of Danmarksgade, and a detour for cars by which they would have to maneuver their way around the bus street and an adjacent square. The latter causes the alderman for the Technical Department, whose first name is Hans, to be nicknamed "Rodeo Hans."

The already reduced and now further amputated first stage is cut down to eight subprojects in addition to the plan for building use and preservation mentioned in Chapter 10. This is a far cry from the forty-one subprojects, the comprehensive plan for urban renewal, and the comprehensive plan for zoning and land use originally planned. The eight remaining subprojects are the following: (1) construction of the bus terminal at Nytorv; (2) experimental traffic reductions on Vesterbro, including bus lanes and construction of north–south bike route; (3) construction of an east–west bike route at Østerbro-Borgergade-Kastetvej; (4) slow-down street at Danmarksgade-Løkkegade; (5) closing of the western part of Algade to automobile traffic; (6) establishing a zone border (prohibiting through traffic) for automobiles at the bus terminal area on the western part of Nytorv; (7) closing of Østeraagade at Slotspladsen Square; (8) Opening of Ved Stranden road to auto traffic.

"OH, MY GOD, THIS IS *TOTALLY* WRONG!"

In the final weeks before the first stage is to begin implementation, to be marked by the opening of the bus terminal, the business community decides to offer some positive support for the Aalborg Project. The Aalborg City Association (*Aalborg Cityforening*), a group of local merchants, takes on the task of arranging the opening festivities and contacts the alderman for the Technical Department to find out which local officials should receive formal invitations. At the same time, the association calls attention to the fact that "there exist as yet no finished plans, but we can promise that there will be sufficiently serious arrangements."[1] On the day of the terminal's official opening, Aalborg's mayor—"Bus-Marius"—heads the festivities by unveiling a cornerstone at the Nytorv bus terminal. For the additional entertainment of those in attendance, the Aalborg City Association holds a "City Yo-Yo Championship," doles out balloons and piggy banks, shows cartoons for the children, and plays music.

No sooner has the first stage of the Aalborg Project been inaugurated before the public debate again flares up. Numerous letters are sent to the *Aalborg Stiftstidende,* and the Technical Department also receives a number of letters and oral comments from organizations and individuals. Here are a few examples:

A letter from a condominium owners' association to the Technical Department: "At the general assembly of our homeowners' association . . . we have discussed the serious situation for our residents which has arisen following the closing to normal auto traffic—on a trial basis—of Algade's exit toward Vesterbro . . . There is now considerable through traffic down Jernbanegade toward Vester-bro . . . We understand the desire to reduce traffic on Vesterbro, but we must emphasize that this will not be achieved in this way . . . [We] must strongly request that the above-mentioned closure of Algade be taken up for renewed consideration."[2]

A letter to *Aalborg Stiftstidende:* "So we have come to one of Aalborg's days to remember: With a bit of paint on the streets, street barriers, and traffic signs, the Technical Department tries to cut down automobile traffic in downtown Aalborg. It was needed, too."[3]

A petition with 13 signatures received by the Technical Department: "The undersigned hereby protest against: the closing to normal individual transport in Algade from Gravensgade to Vesterbro, the detour on Danmarksgade at Frederiks Torv, the bus lane on Vesterbro."[4]

A letter addressed to the alderman for the Technical Department: "I cannot understand that there is not enough space on Nytorv for all kinds of vehicles in both directions . . . Excuse me for taking so much of your time, but the closing of Algade has especially irritated me, and after the experience yesterday [traffic jam] I had to vent my feelings."[5]

Another letter to *Aalborg Stiftstidende:* "Aalborg is certainly showing the way— but out of town. It will be a long time before we again dare to enter this maze!"[6]

A letter to the alderman for the Technical Department: "The traffic regulations executed on Vesterbro and on Danmarksgade are simply rubbish."[7]

Another letter to the alderman: "The bus lane on Vesterbro is an insult to drivers, an affront, as is the closing of Algade toward Vesterbro. It cannot be right that the mayor (for it is certainly he who is in on this) must have lanes reserved only for buses. In the big cities in Russia there are car lanes reserved for the fat-cat bureaucrats [*pampere*] so they can drive around easily. Should the buses be Aalborg's 'fat cats'? . . . Is there any town in Denmark which is more hostile to cars [*bilfjendtlig*] than Aalborg?"[8]

A statement to the Technical Department by the local chapter of "Falck," the Danish ambulance/car-towing service: "[We] want to express our unequivocal disapproval with the above-named traffic restructuring in the strongest possible terms."[9]

Finally, a satirical local affairs column in the newspaper: "[H]as the Boulevard not been forgotten in this game? Here traffic still functions largely without problems. If the reason is that there are not enough traffic planners in the current staff, then even during this period of economizing and elections we must find a way out of this problem and expand the staff. The traffic planners are so close to having created total chaos that it would be unreasonable that the wretched god of money should place obstacles in their way."[10]

In sum, three interrelated objections stand out: (1) the network of downtown streets has become all too complicated for motorists, (2) traffic flow and accessibility in the center has deteriorated for cars, (3) drivers in the downtown area are forced to make too many detours. These objections must be viewed in light of two factors. First, unfortunately for both the Aalborg Project and the Technical Department, the project is being implemented during a period when the downtown area is undergoing a great amount of regular street repairs. Resurfacing of the two most heavily traveled arteries in town, the Limfjord Bridge and Vesterbro, has resulted in traffic jams. The situation worsens when the Aalborg Theater undergoes a remodeling, blocking part of an adjacent street. Finally, an underground heating duct in another main artery begins to leak, and the excavation and repairs on the duct lead to temporary blockages of traffic. These events, although trivial when seen separately, all obtain considerable significance when taken together. And no distinction is made in the public debate between these problems and the problems created by the Aalborg Project. The project becomes a scapegoat for all of Aalborg's current traffic problems, including those of a clearly temporary nature.

The second factor behind the renewed protests against the project is that information from the city government to the public regarding the changes made in the city has been very limited. Two years earlier, when the project's public participation phase was taking place, people were informed about the project via pamphlets, posters, a reception, an exhibition, paid advertisements in the press, and by meetings. With the implementation of the project, the city is content with a few paid advertisements and some routine newspaper cover-

age. This proves to be a mistake. It turns out that precisely in the implementation phase, where the project becomes tangible reality to people, information
should have been especially intensive so as to avoid misunderstandings and to
achieve increased project acceptance. A Technical Department staff member
explains:

> *Staff member:* People couldn't find their way around when they came into the
> city, and there were some streets which were closed off. So they become angry:
> "What a bunch of shit, what's happening here?" And they go to the police and
> to the alderman. I think that in the end a big sign was placed on Vesterbro with a
> diagram of how to drive through. It was simply out of necessity. People couldn't
> figure it out at all. But it was too late. This was already fourteen days after [the first
> stage] had begun. A new traffic map should have been hanging in all the places
> where people came and one should have been able to get a pamphlet in the
> stores, the post office, and everywhere else. Much more should have been done
> about this.
>
> *Interviewer:* Why didn't you [i.e., the staff] do something about it?
>
> *Staff member:* I don't really think that we thought much about it at the time
> . . . only when things really got rolling did we discover, "Oh, my God, this is *to-
> tally* wrong!"

Those who designed what they called "the absolutely best plan" now state,
"We believed that the technically good plan would implement itself."[11] This
may seem rather naive, but it touches upon what has been identified as a general problem of planning. The president of the American Planning Association, for example, in a recent article about American city planning, described
the tradition of planning thusly: "If you believed in reform *hard enough,* it
was thought, reform would naturally come about" (emphasis in original).[12]
Machiavelli is clear in pointing out the problem with such an attitude: "[A]
man who neglects what is actually done for what should be done learns the way
to self-destruction."[13] Or as folk wisdom has it, "The road to hell is paved with
good intentions." Here we might add that so is the road traveled by the planners
in the Aalborg Project at this stage in the life of the project. Hans Magnus Enzensberger's "Postscript to Utopia" could just as well be an epitaph for planning, modernity, and the Aalborg Project. Enzensberger sees an alternative to
the attitude of the planners in Aalborg and similar modernists, that is, to believing and hoping that plans will work: "Instead of hoping for a redemption
via a clear and unambiguous idea," Enzensberger writes, "[one must] rather
rely on an infinitely complex . . . process, which not only understands progress
but also retreats, not only understands how to take initiatives but also how to
avoid something."[14] Currently, planners in Aalborg hope for redemption via

a clear and unambiguous idea—the idea manifest in the Aalborg Project—and they neglect the "infinitely complex process" of strategies and tactics that needs to be attended to if this idea is to move from belief to reality. "Where the planner proceeds, the revolution is completed," planners would sometimes jokingly remark. Maybe on paper, but not in reality, and certainly not in Aalborg. A revolution has been planned for Aalborg. Much has been made of telling the public about all the good things the revolution would achieve. But somebody has forgotten to communicate exactly what will happen on the day the revolution begins. What is lacking is a realist's sense of the practical, a realist's experience that power, effective communication, and day-by-day monitoring have to be used to sustain ideals, norms, plans, and rationalities when these proceed from the drawing board to reality. In this way, yet another obstacle is generated on the Aalborg Project's difficult path from idea to execution.

COOPERATION BECOMES CONFRONTATION

The situation with a public that does not understand the project and the resulting heavy criticism makes both staff and executives in the Technical Department uneasy. At a meeting in the City Council's Technical Committee almost eight weeks after inauguration of the Aalborg Project, committee members tell the Technical Department that "public information ought to be repeated regarding the traffic regulations."[15]

A few days later, the Technical Department contacts the Chamber of Industry and Commerce and asks for the Chamber's aid in writing an advertisement to help drivers find their way around Aalborg's restructured inner city and into the parking lots and shops. The Chamber, however, refuses to help. It has other plans.[16]

The Technical Department therefore executes the public advertising campaign by itself, but again misfortune strikes. The campaign is put together in a hurry, and a key diagram comes to direct cars the wrong way down a one-way street. *Aalborg Stiftstidende* cannot avoid making fun of this error the day after the diagram has appeared in the paper.[17] This is again one of the details that may substantially influence the success of the project.

The Technical Department is not the only one who is now worried. The Chamber of Industry and Commerce fears that the confusing traffic situation in the city center will have negative consequences for retail sales, especially during the coming highly lucrative Christmas shopping period. The Chamber therefore writes an open letter to the Technical Department's alderman to request that a number of key elements already implemented and put into operation be temporarily suspended. Simultaneous with sending the letter to the alderman, a copy also is sent to the press and to several other important "players" in the Aalborg Project. Parts of the letter read:

> At a board meeting of the Aalborg Chamber of Industry and Commerce today, the board has decided to request of the alderman that the following traffic restrictions be suspended immediately up to and including New Year's Day, and that via public announcements efforts be made to inform Aalborg's large suburban group of customers that Aalborg during this period is an "open city". . . . The Aalborg Chamber of Industry and Commerce has received expressions of open dissatisfaction with traffic conditions involving individual transport [i.e., cars], an increasing number of statements from dissatisfied customers, a decline in sales which goes beyond the declines caused by the current economic situation [i.e., the general recession] in the affected branches, and finally, a great anxiety regarding Christmas season revenues. We therefore propose and ask that restrictions be suspended for the following locations during the above-mentioned period: (1) *That the Nytorv bus terminal area be opened to automobile traffic* . . . It is precisely the closing of Nytorv, as we have previously pointed out, which to a very great degree has contributed to the traffic pattern becoming so confusing, especially for customers from outside the city and for tourists. (2) *That Algade be opened to automobile traffic* . . . (3) *That the end of Østeraagade* [at Slotspladsen] be opened in order to ease access to and exit from the city center . . . We are experiencing an extremely difficult period for businesses, and when considering at the same time the fact that many retail firms generate a disproportionately large portion of their yearly earnings precisely during the Christmas month, it is the view of the Aalborg Chamber of Industry and Commerce that we cannot allow ourselves to experiment during this period . . . We hope for the alderman's good will and prompt attention to this letter [emphasis in original].[18]

From the minutes of the board meeting when the Chamber's leadership decides to send and to publicize the letter, it also appears that the Chamber, with the help of an advertising agency, has produced a draft for "a large advertisement which can eventually be used if the Municipality does not lift the restrictions."[19] The slogan for the advertisement and the campaign it would introduce is written in language that leads one to think of war: "Make Aalborg into an open city."[20] And it is precisely in the direction of war that the Aalborg Project is evolving.

The letter from the Chamber hits the Technical Department like a bombshell and causes the Aalborg Project to move into a new phase with regard to the power relations that have shaped the project in its long journey from genesis to design to political ratification, implementation, and operation. Up to now, the project and the relation between the Technical Department and the

Chamber has been characterized by a stable power relation: there have been divergent views regarding ends and means for the project among the two parties, but the internal disagreements have been cleared up on a continuous basis via stable, informal, semi-institutionalized power mechanisms. These stable power mechanisms are now replaced by direct confrontation, or what Michel Foucault calls "the free play of antagonistic reactions."[21] It is the first time we see a complete change from stable power relations to open confrontation in the Aalborg Project. Let us therefore examine this shift in more detail.

The alderman's treatment of the Chamber's letter quickly meets the desires of the Chamber for "prompt attention," but the "good will" sought by the Chamber is clearly lacking. The antipathy to the Chamber's requests can be attributed to several factors. First, the Technical Department does not want to revise the already executed measures in the midst of what is considered a six-month trial period. The purpose of the trial period is to gain experience and to systematically collect data and evaluate the effects of the implemented measures. Various "before-and-after" studies are in the making. Changing the measures or eliminating them in midstream will remove the possibility of evaluating them. Only six weeks previously, the Technical Department had reiterated to the Aalborg Police Department that the "stipulated trial period for the traffic conditions in the city center will be executed as planned."[22]

Second, the Chamber's request is an indication that it has now abandoned its original acceptance of the reduced first stage in the Aalborg Project. This acceptance was the result of elaborate negotiations between the Technical Department and the Chamber of Industry and Commerce. The Chamber's letter therefore constitutes a violation of the results agreed upon in the negotiations.

Finally, the leadership of the Technical Department and especially the alderman are upset that the Chamber, besides sending the letter to him and to other Technical Department heads, has also distributed it to the press, to the police, and to the chairman of the City Council's Technical Committee. This procedure violates a written agreement and decade-long established practice between the Technical Department and Chamber of Industry and Commerce whereby they would orient each other in matters of common concern prior to informing the press and the public.

In an interview I conducted with him, the alderman for the Technical Department was hesitant about discussing the Chamber's violation of trust. The chairman of the Chamber of Industry and Commerce, however, had no such inhibitions. His side of the story:

> [The alderman] was really angry at us . . . He scolded me, saying, "If we're going to cooperate, if you want the Chamber to be informed about the proposals before they are presented, then you people must not betray us and stab us in the back."

The chairman of the Chamber's City Center Committee also commented:

> *Aalborg Stiftstidende* would certainly very much have wanted permission to write
> about what we had done. But then we had a completely clear agreement that we
> should first inform [the Technical Department]. It is only when we did not have
> good communication with the [Technical Department] that we go directly to
> the *Stiftstidende*. I have to admit this. It was purely in order to get our voice heard,
> when things were evolving in a bad direction. We could see that things were go-
> ing completely haywire up toward the Christmas shopping period . . . We could
> not get any communication going with the alderman at that time. We were
> fighting verbally over the telephone, I might just as well say.

BRINGING OUT THE HEAVY ARTILLERY

The alderman for the Technical Department, furious at the Chamber of Industry and Commerce, has no intention of giving in to the Chamber's requests. The Chamber thus brings its heavy artillery into the raw power struggle
which the implementation of the Aalborg Project has now become. The "big
guns" consist of two outside companies, F. Salling, Inc., and Dansk Supermarked, Inc., the latter a subsidiary of the A. P. Møller Corporation, one of
Denmark's largest and oldest shipping conglomerates. Dansk Supermarked
is one of Denmark's top 100 companies and is considered part of "the core
of Danish business."[23] Dansk Supermarked is owned jointly by F. Salling,
Inc., and by the A. P. Møller Corporation. Within the A. P. Møller group of
companies, Dansk Supermarked is the second largest subsidiary as measured in
sales, right behind the firm's shipping activities, which has always been its core
business. The president of Dansk Supermarked, who will later approach Aalborg's city engineer with a proposal for changes in the project, is considered
one of the Danish businesses' "many men of power."

Dansk Supermarked and F. Salling have direct interests in downtown Aalborg since they own the "Føtex" and "Salling" department stores. Both stores
are located in the city center and directly adjoin the newly constructed bus terminal and the pedestrian streets. The leadership of the Chamber, together with
the director of the Salling department store, contact the chief executives of the
two companies and obtain their support in the struggle with the Technical Department. The chairman of the Chamber's City Center Committee is a central
figure in this turn of events. He explains (names deleted, replaced by positions
in brackets):

> The Salling company is brought into it. The two of us, [the Chamber's chair-
> man] and myself, do it along with [the director of the Salling store in Aalborg]—

who can draw on the president down there [the president of Salling's main office in Aarhus] and on [the president of Dansk Supermarked] . . . We tell them that we simply have to have a decision. And we want it here and now. The problem concerns, among other things, [the reopening of] Algade and it concerns passage across Nytorv square up to the ramp [to the Salling store's parking lot, i.e., reopening the western part of Nytorv, including the bus terminal, to car traffic]. The road signs were poorly placed. They were laid out as prohibiting entry, and entry *was* prohibited because the sign was placed incorrectly [in the opinion of the Chamber] . . . One could not drive up [to Salling's parking lot from the west]. And we phone them from the Salling department store's office and say, "It *must* be now, or we will go to the press."

   We push it hard. I think it is I who talks to the alderman. Yes, I'm the one who calls there and says, "We must resolve this, and it is only a question of moving the sign. It cannot be any big problem." I cannot remember the conversation, but he was really pissed off because we had gone to the press first. "Why didn't we come to him?" [he demanded]. Then I say, "But we have been to you. [The chairman of the Chamber] has made a request and publicly said so. And nothing has happened, and something *must* happen." But damn it, he says, he will not accept being treated this way. Then I say, "Okay, it's a question of life and death for Christmas shopping, it means that much. Something *must* be done." Then I think he says, "We will try to take a look and investigate it." Then he calls back and says that it can be done anyway, that it is legal [to drive into Salling's parking lot from the west through the bus terminal]. It was not. But he said on the phone that it was legal . . . "Snap!" we said. And so they had to move the signs. And then it also got out to the public that it was now possible . . . This is what was important for us, that the traffic not be stopped.

We will return to what the "Snap!" means. In the meantime, after receiving the call from the Chamber and from Salling, and before returning the Chamber's call, the alderman contacts the person formally responsible for the Aalborg Project, the city engineer, in order to hear his opinion about what is happening. The city engineer recounts:

   The alderman, nice man that he is, says: "What would you say if right at this moment I decided that [Algade] be reopened?" And my answer was—I am just about to say naturally—that I would take it just nice and easy, as a fact. He asks directly, "What would you say if I reopen it immediately?" I said, "I would say nothing against it. You're the politician . . ." [But] I do not agree that it should have been reopened.

The city engineer informs the Task Force what is happening. A staff member comments:

> It spreads like a ball of fire through the entire house . . . We were really pissed off because first we [in the Task Force] fought against a trial period. Then when the six months are shortened to six weeks, and [the streets] are suddenly opened again, then it is clear, you say to yourself, "This is disgusting, he can't do that." But it happened anyway . . . [and] when the alderman has made a decision, then he's made a decision . . . and then not much more really happened.

As for the traffic prohibition on cars in the bus terminal, the heat of debate seems to create a confusion. It all occurs very quickly and with considerable resistance by the Technical Department. The Chamber of Industry and Commerce utilizes the confusion to restore automobile traffic in the bus terminal on the western part of Nytorv, as indicated in the quotation of the chairman of the Chamber's City Center Committee cited above. Aalborg's city engineer continues:

> *Interviewer:* Has Salling any influence on the "No Through Traffic" sign on Nytorv being moved so that cars can enter their parking lot [by making a short-cut through the bus terminal]?
> *City engineer:* Yes.
> *Interviewer:* How?
> *City engineer:* Oh man, I'm really sorry to say it, Oh man! Do you know?
> *Interviewer:* I have a hunch, but I don't know exactly.
> *City engineer:* Would *you* like to tell me why?
> *Interviewer:* No . . .
> *City engineer:* Okay. But I just have to say first that there is no pressure on this matter, none at all. There is no one here in this house who allows himself to be pressured, not by Salling either. It has nothing at all to do with that. Salling got the impression that the signs down there indicated that passage from Østeraagade was allowed up to and *including* Braskensgade, so that you could drive from Østeraagade over Nytorv [through the bus terminal] and up Braskensgade [thus reaching Salling's parking lot by a short-cut]. Salling got the impression that this is the way it is. By mistake they received confirmation of this. Then Salling announces, even over their public address system, that this is the case. So there is wild confusion, and politically it is decided that there is nothing else to do but move the sign.

Thus, the "Snap!" mentioned above by the chairman of the Chamber's City Center Committee refers to the Chamber's use of the confusion it has helped create. The "Snap!" is a trap for the Technical Department which consists of spreading, under cover of the confusion, the wrong message: that a short-cut through the bus terminal is allowed for cars. The message is diffused to so many people and so quickly that the Technical Department—given the amount of opposition already encountered—dare not try and correct it. The alderman for the Technical Department recounts the situation as follows:

> We were in a trial period and back then my people said: "You should *not* change it now." Then I got that strong pressure regarding Christmas shopping. And I said to the city engineer, after I had argued with the Chamber of Industry and Commerce and all kinds of other people: "Let us in God's name get some peace. If we can get the police with us, then we will change the arrangement." I think we said that we will include the January "sale" period and revoke [the temporary permission for automobile traffic on the western part of Nytorv] again on the first of February . . . But it is correct that I was on very hostile terms with the Chamber of Industry and Commerce, and it could get me to say that perhaps this has also contributed to . . . me having encountered much resistance elsewhere.

"DEEP THROAT"

On the day after the Chamber sends out its open letter, *Aalborg Stiftstidende* brings a long critical article about the Aalborg Project. Under a four-column headline, entitled "Mid-Town Has Become Confusing," the article brings quotes from the Chamber's chairman, the head of Aalborg's tourism office, a Police Department spokesperson, and the chief of the Aalborg Taxi Company, all of whom criticize the changes in Aalborg's traffic patterns. The article concludes that "despite certain positive tones, everyone is more or less critical, and the merchants are losing customers."[24] The following day, the alderman for the Technical Department begins the eighth round of reductions in the project, in what now starts to resemble an all out decimation of the entire plan. The alderman decides to temporarily reopen the western part of Algade to auto traffic. The street was planned as a pedestrian mall and bicycle street.

On the same day, the chairman of the Danish Cyclist Federation's Aalborg chapter, in a confidential letter to a member of the Technical Committee under Aalborg City Council, expresses his opinion that the above-mentioned article in *Aalborg Stiftstidende* is "commissioned work with reference to the conclusion."[25] When I asked the chairman of the Cyclist Federation what he meant, he mentioned a new player in the project, *Deep Throat*:[26]

> *Interviewer:* You write a letter about "commissioned work?"
> *Cyclist Federation chairman:* Yes, in December, a new person begins to appear; at the time we called him "Deep Throat." I don't know if you have seen the film, or heard about the Watergate case.
> *Interviewer:* Who was Deep Throat?
> *Chairman:* I don't know. Perhaps you should talk to NN [name of a city official] about whether he will agree to be quoted on this. But in any case, we talk to

each other on the phone. And all this with "commissioned work" is based on this . . . NN says to me that the *Stiftstidende* now wants to scuttle [the project], and they want to do this because this is what the Chamber of Industry and Commerce wants. There is a connection between them. Then things go fast. I think I said something about the [Technical] Department also utilizing us for their purposes, right? That is, at a time when they think that now they have done something beautiful with downtown Aalborg . . . then NN calls me and says that things are going horribly wrong, that goddamnit, they want to scuttle it again, and they want to do it fast. It is one of the few times when I really have gone out and said, "Now I have to get people going to write letters to the newspaper." So the remark about commissioned work, you know, it's that the Chamber of Industry and Commerce, through the *Stiftstidende,* presses NN or presses the department to get this off the agenda as quickly as possible . . . It was NN, then [who was Deep Throat], but at the time he said, "Hell, you must not tell anyone!" Perhaps it is somewhat ridiculous when looking back on it, but we [the leadership of the Cyclist Federation] were just sitting home in my living room having tea and sandwiches, and then NN calls one night and says, "Goddamnit, something's got to be done." And after the phone call I was very much in doubt about whether I should say it to the others—my buddies over there—that this was NN from the Technical Department who called to say that now you all have to get off your asses, but you must not say it is I who told you.

According to Deep Throat himself, a secret connection to the Cyclist Federation had been established a few years before, during the Aalborg Project's design phase, when some planned bicycle paths through downtown were being criticized by various parties. Deep Throat approached the Federation and called attention to the fact that they ought to mobilize in favor of the bike paths. The Federation followed Deep Throat's recommendation, and the bike paths were in fact constructed as planned.

The situation at this stage in the Aalborg Project is a metaphor for the relation between rationality and power in the project. On the one hand, symbolizing the rationality of the project, is the ordinary civil servant, all alone, the "Deep Throat," who in Aalborg as well as in Washington risks his career in order to mobilize public opinion and a sense of justice. On the other hand, as a symbol of power, sits A. P. Møller, one of the largest and most influential companies in Denmark. It is David against Goliath, with the important difference in relation to the ancient biblical tale that here Goliath wins over David. Perhaps this is one of the important functions of such tales: to present a reality different from that which we live. To give hope. For the Aalborg Project, the situation is currently hopeless.

Twelve

FAREWELL TO REASON

> We must distinguish between . . . those who to achieve their purpose
> can force the issue and those who must use persuasion. In the second
> case, they always come to grief.
>
> *Niccolò Machiavelli*

RATIONALITY YIELDS TO POWER

Four days after Deep Throat tries to mobilize the Danish Cyclist Federation in support of the Aalborg project, *Aalborg Stiftstidende* brings yet another extensive, critical article about the project. The next day the Technical Department alderman opens the western part of Nytorv Square, temporarily, to automobile traffic. The reopening of Nytorv occurs five days after the reopening of Algade and again after pressure from the Chamber of Industry and Commerce. With the opening of the western part of Nytorv, cars may now drive directly through the bus terminal, in clear contradiction to the project's objectives and design.

On the following day, the Danish Cyclist Federation sends an appeal to the alderman for the Technical Department to stand by the Aalborg Project and restore the first stage:

> We of the Cyclist Federation's Aalborg chapter have viewed with increasing anxiety the recent month's debate in the *Stiftstidende* regarding the implementation of the city center plan . . . We strongly urge the department to sustain the main objective of the plan. We are thus astonished that the trial period with the traffic plan's first stage has been discontinued after a very short time. We therefore appeal for a restoration of the first stage, despite protests from certain rush hour travelers . . . and from anxious merchants who blame the Technical Department for a possible stagnation in sales rather than blaming the general recession in our economy. We appeal to the alderman and to the department to also take upon themselves the interests of nonautomotive traffic, the bus passengers, and

the inner city residents by restoring the fulfillment of the city center plans. In the hope that reason will return to the department, we wish you a Happy New Year.[1]

The appeal for a "return to reason" comes from one of the least influential actors in the Aalborg Project. This underscores the point made earlier that the less power an actor has, the more emphasis is placed upon reason; and the more power, the less weight (see Chap. 4). Reason is one of the few forms of power which those without much influence still possess. This mechanism in part explains the enormous appeal of the Enlightenment project to those outside power. In Aalborg, however, reason, that is, the rationality which lies behind the project, does not return. In open confrontation, reason yields to power, in this case the power the Chamber of Industry and Commerce puts behind its desire for unrestricted movement of cars in downtown Aalborg. It is this difference in the ability to put power behind their arguments which Machiavelli refers to when he insists, "We must distinguish between . . . those who to achieve their purpose can force the issue and those who must use persuasion. In the second case, they always come to grief."[2] "Always" may be somewhat exaggerated, but it certainly applies in the case of Aalborg.

Inside "the house," that is, the Technical Department, following an initial period of shock, staff and executives begin to discuss what has happened. They are dissatisfied about the fact that the measures already implemented have been changed in the midst of the project's trial period. Staff members are asking themselves and each other not only if it is *proper* that the alderman has single-handedly decided the changes, but also if it is *legal:* if the Aalborg City Council is the organ that mandated the measures to be enacted, is it not the City Council, and only the council, which can legally eliminate them again? The alderman's actions are indicative of the marginal position of the City Council in the Aalborg Project and reflect the central importance of the power relation between the alderman and the Chamber of Industry and Commerce. Most of what passes for "politics" in the City Council consists of rubberstamping the *Realpolitik* conducted outside the council. In this case the council does not even get the opportunity to rubberstamp the alderman's decisions.

The questions of propriety and legality, however, are discussed by the managers and staff members only orally and only with each other as a kind of hidden, dissatisfied murmuring in the corridors of the Technical Department. Nobody takes up the issues with the alderman directly. Outside the department, however, the chief planner for public transportation writes an official letter objecting to the alderman's dispositions and sends it to the municipality's Financial Administration (*Økonomisk Sekretariat*):

> The city center plan is an expression of a forging together the desires of many interest groups, and we believe that it is unreasonable that the interests of some

groups [read: Aalborg Chamber of Industry and Commerce] be satisfied after the fact, without there having been undertaken a new and comprehensive assessment by the City Council.[3]

The chief planner also points out that the alderman's decisions now make it impossible to evaluate the effects of the project, that cars passing through the bus terminal will create problems for the buses driving to and from the terminal's bus parking spaces, and finally, that the planned establishment of the integrated bus stop for city and regional buses on Vingaardsgade is made more difficult. The chief planner for public transportation is the only member of the project's Executive Committee not employed by the Technical Department, and therefore the only one not directly or indirectly subordinate to the alderman. Besides submitting his letter of objection to Aalborg's Central Administration, the chief planner also drafts an internal memorandum to the staff members in his own department. Here he concludes that

it is unsatisfactory to participate in a task for 2–3 years with an infinite number of meetings, studies, memoranda and reports, and afterwards experience that a relatively undocumented polemic in the press and pressure from, among others, the Chamber of Industry and Commerce, which had been heard and involved in the approved plan, leads to a puncturing of a plan which had been approved by a nearly unanimous City Council. Generally speaking, this must entail that in the future we will closely assess the resources expended by our side in similar types of cooperation.[4]

The Technical Department does not change the implemented project for technical reasons. The assertions regarding massive traffic jams in downtown Aalborg put forward in the press are continuously investigated by the staff. After measuring the maximum time delay in the intersections with the heaviest traffic they find a maximum delay of three-and-a-half minutes, while the average delay in other zones of heavy traffic is usually less than two minutes.[5] The Technical Department finds this acceptable and concludes that there are no technical arguments for altering the Aalborg Project prior to the expiration of the trial period. That the implemented project is changed in the midst of the trial period is due, then, only to factors related to the power struggle between the Chamber and the Technical Department.

"THAT PLAN DIED DURING CHRISTMAS"

The managers and staff members in the project's Executive Committee and Task Force are not alone in their dissatisfaction, disappointment, and anger. The Technical Department alderman, too, is both embittered and indignant about what has occurred and about the treatment to which he has been subjected by the Chamber of Industry and Commerce. He publicly terms this treatment "pressure."[6] His bitterness emerges in the third major article about the Aalborg Project in the *Stiftstidende* within the same week. The article is a double interview which a former journalist at the paper regards as "excellent, really refreshing."[7] The interview, called by the paper a "traffic duel" (*trafikduel*) is, indeed, quite unusual. For the first time, the alderman now publicly acknowledges his fellow Conservative party and City Council member, the chairman of the Chamber of Industry and Commerce, as his adversary in the Aalborg Project. In the interview, the two exchange the following remarks:

> *Alderman for the Technical Department:* It is unreasonable the way people have allowed their emotions to run away with them in this case. I wouldn't be surprised if the traffic regulations were made the culprit for the outbreak of war in the Middle East.
>
> *Chairman of Aalborg Chamber of Industry and Commerce:* Doesn't it bother you that many of your supporters on this issue vote for the left-wing parties when there is a city council election?
>
> *Alderman:* Well, I can't administer just for those who drive cars or just for the merchants.
>
> *Chairman:* [I]t would make it much easier to find one's way around town if you opened Nytorv [permanently] again.[8]
>
> *Alderman:* Absolutely not. Nytorv will *not* be opened to through traffic . . . The merchants on Nytorv have their customers come by bus right to their doorsteps, but you obviously want to have your cake and eat it too.
>
> *Chairman:* [S]urely you must understand that the merchants become anxious and want conditions changed if they see their sales falling drastically because the customers cannot find their way to the shops. Many out-of-town customers are simply afraid to try to come into town.
>
> *Alderman:* If you are dissatisfied, you can ask for a meeting with me instead of running to the newspaper, which you did the other day.
>
> *Chairman:* It had become a pressing issue. We wanted to save the Christmas shopping season.
>
> *Alderman:* It was pressure. I understand well that the individual businessman has problems because of the falling purchasing power, but I am upset about the behavior of the Chamber of Industry and Commerce. They are not the ones with whom I will discuss future traffic regulations. It will be the users, the citizens.
>
> *Chairman:* If you mean the second stage in the city center plan, then we must immediately object. The proposed zoning divisions, with the mid-town area di-

vided up into four zones which drivers cannot cross, we will fight this. That plan died during Christmas . . .[9]

The fact that the chairman for an interest group can publicly and so self-confidently declare a plan "dead," a plan approved by the responsible and democratically elected City Council with a vote of 25–1, once again reveals where real power lies in Aalborg. Even to the alderman, with over a decade's experience of dealing with and adapting to the Chamber of Industry and Commerce, this behavior has now become too chauvinistic. He begins to see people in the Chamber the way Machiavelli does when he says, "One can make this generalization about men: they are ungrateful, fickle, liars, and deceivers, they shun danger and are greedy for profit."[10] The alderman is growing increasingly appalled by this type of behavior, and for the first time in the history of the Aalborg Project he now breaks with the Chamber. In the space of a few days, years of stable power relations have been transformed into an antagonistic confrontation. Both parts are now forced to behave in reaction to the acts of their adversary, ex post, while previously, in their "era of cooperation," they had coordinated their actions ex ante.

Though we are now witnessing a naked power struggle, attempts are still made to legitimate actions using rational argument. This time, however, the arguments come not from the Technical Department, which publicly declares itself a victim of pressure, but from the Chamber of Industry and Commerce. The Chamber justifies its actions by referring to factors such as traffic chaos and falling sales. According to the studies carried out by the Technical Department, however, there are no special traffic difficulties in downtown Aalborg at this time, aside from temporary problems related to road work, district heating repairs, etc. In addition, it is later documented that downtown retail revenues are increasing during precisely the same period when the Chamber of Industry and Commerce has been insisting that they are declining (see Chap. 16).

Altogether, it appears that the Chamber of Industry and Commerce, instead of waging a battle against declining sales, is trying to obtain what the alderman called "having your cake and eating it too." The Chamber's objective is to increase that portion of retail customers who bike, walk, or take public transportation but without a corresponding reduction in those customers who come by car. The arguments used by the Chamber are rationalizations of this objective, and here, too, rationality yields to power. Despite the imaginary foundation of these rationalizations, however, their consequences are tangible—as tangible as the money that flows into a cash register.

Besides the fact that the second stage in the Aalborg Project is killed off over Christmas, the first stage remains permanently crippled. The alderman's reopening of streets to cars, as mentioned, is initially a provisional measure, valid until New Year's Day. Yet the pressure on the Aalborg Project continues into the new year, and the project's opponents attempt to make the provisional changes permanent. Among others, the president of Dansk Supermarked, which owns the Føtex, Salling, and Bilka department stores, sends a letter in early January to Aalborg's city engineer, in which he argues that the reopening of the streets should remain permanent. During a visit to Aalborg, the company president and his chauffeur have apparently found it difficult to reach the Salling department store.

> [We] came from Bilka and were on our way to the store to visit [the director of Salling in Aalborg]. [The chauffeur] was very upset, as he had previously thought himself to be an experienced Aalborg driver . . . Half of Vesterbro had been converted into bus lanes, so there was a lot of bumper-to-bumper traffic, but one could at least get through. As usual, we turned down Vingaardsgade and drove down Østeraa in order to turn toward Nytorv along the store, in order to park at our own parking place. This is not possible any more, and instead we continued onward down Østeraagade turning left down Ved Stranden street. If one knows the town well, one probably ends in Nyhavnsgade and finds the way to Slots-gade, from which one can reach the parking lot. However, if one does not know the town so well, there is a big risk that one's irritation will gradually be so great that one gives up and instead drives home.[11]

STREET FIGHTING: THE POLICE REFUSE TO ENFORCE THE LAW

The pressure on the Technical Department increases when it appears that the Aalborg Police Department decides not to enforce the prohibition on through traffic in the bus terminal at Nytorv, even though the police, along with the Chamber of Industry and Commerce, have earlier accepted and approved this arrangement. As the Chamber abandons its part of the agreement, so does the Police Department. Because the western part of Nytorv has been reopened to auto traffic, enabling cars to reach the Salling parking lot, drivers are tempted to illegally traverse Nytorv, the border between the eastern and western zones of downtown. In fact, the Technical Department records 1,000 "illegal border crossings" per day, and eventually the level of auto traffic through the bus terminal will be equivalent to that before the terminal was built. In an interview with the author, a senior police officer explains the police's lack of interest in enforcing the law:

> *Police officer:* We [the Aalborg Police and the Technical Department] have had a minor disagreement as to whether one should be allowed to drive through [the

bus terminal at Nytorv]. The idea was certainly that it should be completely closed, and we did not agree. And it is indeed not the case today either. Even though there is a sign saying "No Through Traffic," it is used anyway.

Interviewer: Is it not the task of the police to enforce the prohibition?

Police officer: Yes, it is.

Interviewer: Are you enforcing it?

Police officer: No, we are not. We hope that together with the municipality we can reach agreement that the "No Through Traffic" signs can be taken down, because we believe that an area has been created where car traffic can be allowed because it will proceed while paying attention to the more vulnerable [nonvehicular] traffic. And the fact that there are buses which stop down there helps to lower the speed and other things. So it is still our view that there should be a possibility to drive through [by car]. . . We have used the period gone by to prove that it is possible. It *has* been possible with cars down there . . . [The prohibition] can certainly be enforced, but it demands a lot of work to obtain the evidence. And, as I said, we have not put much heart in doing it.

The police also argue in the same interview that there are tasks which are more important than enforcing the traffic regulations on Nytorv:

It would cost a lot of personnel, for we have to come up with the evidence that it has been the driver's intent to drive through. And we would get lots of lame excuses . . . That they realized that they had forgotten their wallet, and then they had to drive home and get it again . . . We all work with limited resources in one way or another, and if we have to think of traffic safety, which is one of our major tasks, then there are other places where our limited possibilities to contribute yield better results. It is not exactly at Nytorv that the traffic injuries and accidents happen.

In fact, the number of traffic accidents with personal injuries at Nytorv rises considerably following the implementation of the first stage, and there is much evidence that a major cause of the accidents may be the very cars which the police will not prevent from entering Nytorv (see Chaps. 18 and 19). Aalborg's city engineer does not agree with the police's assessment. In an interview he says:

I do not agree with the police, but the police have greater experience in this area than I do. I certainly think that the traffic prohibition [on Nytorv] should be enforced. It *can* be enforced, it is relatively simple. One can see from one end of the square to the other. The driver who drives straight through can be seen. That it can be enforced is absolutely certain. Whether it would hold up in court I don't know, but I think it would.

The Police Department and the Technical Department work with diametrically opposed objectives on this point, despite the fact that the police are formally supposed to enforce the traffic prohibition and thereby ensure that the Aalborg Project's intentions are realized. In relation to the original plans, the zone border in the city center is now perforated at both Danmarksgade and Nytorv Square. It therefore functions only sporadically as a barrier for both through and local traffic in the city center. The combination of the Police Department's "relaxed" attitude, the extremely critical coverage by *Aalborg Stiftstidende,* and the appeals from the Chamber and from Dansk Supermarked is powerful enough so that the reopening of Nytorv and Algade to cars, originally a provisional measure for the Christmas shopping period, is now extended and subsequently made permanent.

The Police Department's actions indicate that as power attempts to define rationality and reality, it can put even the law out of operation. Or more precisely: the law's interpretation and enforcement can be a central part of the rationality of power. The reopening of Nytorv to cars also shows that alliances give strength. This is not the only time that the triumvirate composed of the Chamber of Industry and Commerce, the Police Department, and the *Aalborg Stiftstidende* has exerted influence on the project. In the same manner, we have seen the effects of the Chamber's connections to big business. Alliances are an important part of the rationality of power, and the fact that the Technical Department has fewer and weaker allies than its counterparts in the Aalborg Project, and instead puts more trust in rational argument and consensus building, places the project in a weak position.

Before we leave the struggle over Aalborg's streets, we may note that immediately after Christmas *Aalborg Stiftstidende* reports "record Christmas sales."[12] The director of a major department store says, "Christmas sales far exceeded our expectations."[13] And the January "sale" is apparently going even better; the director of Salling states, "In the 18 years we have been here, there have never been so many people in the store. The best days from before Christmas are greatly surpassed." Later on, in January, the director informs the city engineer that sales during the first three months after the Aalborg Project was inaugurated exceeded those of the same period the year before.[14] There is an apparent lack of agreement between this information and the declarations of declining sales that the Chamber of Industry and Commerce had repeatedly made during the month of December. We will return to this issue later on, when it can be analyzed in more detail (see Chap. 16).

Despite the Aalborg Project's "amputation," the Technical Department alderman has apparently not lost his sense of humor. Immediately after the New Year, he sends the following clipping from a national traffic magazine to Aalborg's city engineer:

"There is only one way to solve Aalborg's traffic problems."

"How?"

"By making all the streets one-way to the north!"

"Well, so what happens?"

"Then it becomes Nørresundby's problem."[15]

Nørresundby lies just across the fjord north of downtown Aalborg. Just as this joke has its parallel in the Manhattan–New Jersey traffic joke, Nørresundby might be considered Aalborg's New Jersey.

"A GOOD IDEA WITH A BAD OUTCOME"

With the advantage of hindsight, we can summarize several factors which cause the implementation of the Aalborg Project to deviate from its original intentions. (1) Lack of information to the public about the changes that project implementation would entail. (2) Coincidental traffic problems due to the rebuilding of the Aalborg Theater, district heating work, road repairs, etc. (3) Project implementation occurs during the Christmas shopping season and January "sale" period, where traffic is heavier than normal, with more outside traffic entering the city, and during the most important period of the year for retail sales. (4) Some of the first-stage measures are implemented only partially, and the disadvantages of these measures often dominate, while the benefits will first be realized with full implementation. This is the case, for example, with the closing of the western part of Algade, where the disadvantage for drivers is clear, while the benefits for bicyclists, pedestrians, and local merchants of the planned pedestrian mall and bicycle paths are not achieved. Tactically speaking, this procedure is unwise: it generates resistance without any corresponding support for the project. (5) The project's holistic, comprehensive aspects are destroyed by progressive reductions. The individual parts of the project are mutually dependent on each other to obtain their effect. When one part is taken out, the effects of the other measures are reduced, eliminated, or become counterproductive. (6) Many of the visible constructions lack aesthetic quality, partly because they are unfinished or temporary. (7) The police do not support the project, for example, by refusing to enforce the "No Through Traffic" prohibition at the bus terminal. (8) Finally, there is massive resistance to the project from the Aalborg Chamber of Industry and Commerce and from the *Aalborg Stiftstidende*.

After it becomes public knowledge that the provisionally reopened streets will remain permanently open to vehicular traffic, the Aalborg Project receives its second prize, "The Cold Trick" (*Den Kolde Fidus*), from the Aalborg Journalist Association. Unlike the prize for "good and sensitive planning" awarded

Aalborg by the Danish Town Planning Association two years earlier, the Cold Trick Prize is given for "a good idea with a bad outcome" (*"et godt indfald, som fik et dårligt udfald"*). As the prize is normally awarded to an individual, the Aalborg Journalist Association considers giving it to the alderman for the Technical Department, as he has ultimate responsibility for the project. However, the alderman has already received the prize ten years previously—and also for traffic regulations that were voided following pressure from the Chamber of Industry and Commerce—so it is decided that the prize should be given instead to the leader of the Aalborg Project's Task Force. Taken together, the award from the Danish Town Planning Association and the Cold Trick Prize reflect the way the Aalborg Project has evolved from a design that professional planning and policy circles view as innovative and good to a severely problematic implementation.

THE FIRST CASUALTY OF WAR

Stable power relations are more common than open, antagonistic confrontations. Even though the Aalborg Project contains a number of power relations and situations which could have evolved into confrontation, there are in fact only two real open confrontations in the project's nearly fifteen-year history. The first is the confrontation between the Aalborg Municipality and the North Jutland County regarding the location of the city bus terminal. The second confrontation is that between the Technical Department and the Chamber of Industry and Commerce described in this and the previous chapter. Both confrontations take place during the early part of the project's implementation phase, an experience that is not unusual. It is a general tendency of planning and policy that it is precisely at this point in a plan's or policy's life cycle, where the transformation from idea to reality becomes concrete and has real effects on the economy, environment, and quality of life, that the most significant opposition can be mobilized. The probability for confrontation is thereby greater in this phase.

Implementation of the Aalborg Project can be said to have started on the very day construction began on the city bus terminal. And from here comes the project's first confrontation, that between Aalborg Municipality and North Jutland County. The next major step in the implementation is the inauguration of the project, after construction is completed. Here emerges the second confrontation, that between the Technical Department and the Chamber of Industry and Commerce.

Michel Foucault points out that knowledge-power and rationality-power relations are found in all contexts. While the data from the Aalborg Project confirms Foucalt's assertion, it also shows that in power relations characterized by openly acknowledged antagonistic confrontation, power-to-power relations dominate so as to virtually exclude knowledge-power and rationality-power relations in the sense that rational argument has little or no influence. In such confrontations, "Truth is the first casualty of war," as the proverb has it. In an open confrontation, actions are dictated by whatever works best to defeat the opponent. And once the confrontation is overt, the raw exercise of power tends to be more effective than appeals to objectivity, facts, knowledge, rationality, or the "better argument," even though rationalization may be used to legitimate the exercise of raw power.

That rationality yields to power in situations of open confrontation can to a certain extent be viewed as an extreme instance of the observation that greater power is often associated with less rationality: rationality yields almost totally in those situations where there are optimum conditions for the exercise of raw power: namely, in the open, antagonistic confrontation.

The interplay between rationality and power operates to stabilize power relations, and in effect constitutes such stable relations. Decisions made via rationality-power relations can be justified by an appeal to reason, and thereby gain greater legitimacy than "decisions" based upon raw power-against-power confrontation. Rationality-power relations therefore are found primarily in the context of stable power relations, and the two are mutually dependent. In the Aalborg Project, surveys, analysis, documentation, and technical argumentation are techniques used to try and create consensus; they are the kinds of attempts that characterize stable power relations. Alternatively, such rational analyses are attempts to avoid confrontation, such avoidance also being a characteristic of stable relations. This does not mean, of course, that decisions in stable power relations are always founded upon rational considerations. The Aalborg Project reveals several examples of the contrary. For example, the "summit meetings" between the Technical Department and the Chamber of Industry and Commerce are frequently arranged as power-to-power meetings in which staff members with relevant professional knowledge are excluded. Another example is the relation between the Technical Department and the Aalborg Bus Company, where the latter has refused to deliver or has suppressed documentation concerning public transportation because it saw more advantages in uninformed, purely political decisions.

"Stable" power relations should not be confused with "balanced" power relations. Stable power relations and what Erving Goffman would call a "working consensus" in no way imply "non-coercive (*zwangslos*) consensus" or "communicative rationality," to use two of Jürgen Habermas's terms. Relations of domination in a stable power relation can certainly entail distortions in the production and use of analytic-rational arguments and documentation. In those situations where rational considerations tend to play a role, however, it is within a framework of stable power relations. In the Aalborg Project, the scope in which rationality can have an effect in the project is, quite simply, conditioned by the existence of stable power relations. In conclusion, the significance of this association between rationality and stability is that rationality and the ideals of modernity and enlightenment only stand a chance of having an effect where the exercise of raw power, *Realpolitik,* and confrontation are suspended and replaced by stable relations of power.

Thirteen

THE DREAM PLAN

> In times when the passions are beginning to take charge of the conduct of human affairs, one should pay less attention to what men of experience and common sense are thinking than to what is preoccupying the imagination of dreamers.
>
> *Alexis de Tocqueville*

As in every real game, the Aalborg Project contains a joker. It goes under the name "The Dream Plan" (*Drømmeplanen*). A counterplan to the Aalborg Project, the "Dream Plan" emerges from an unexpected source, the Social Democratic City Council Group. The Social Democrats play their joker before the Technical Department has fully recovered from the Chamber of Industry and Commerce's frontal attack on the project described in the two previous chapters. Less than a year previously, the Social Democrats had helped to ratify the Aalborg Project by a near-unanimous vote in the Aalborg City Council. Why a counterplan now? What is the agenda behind the "Dream Plan"? From where does it get its name? What does it look like? How is it received in the Technical Department and by the other actors involved in the Aalborg Project? What consequences does it obtain? What does it indicate about Social Democracy? And, finally, what can the Dream Plan tell us about the relationship between rationality and power? These questions will be the focus of this and the following chapter.

"IT WAS IN THE AFTERNOON . . . AFTER WORKING HOURS"

Via the documentary and interview research it has not been possible to determine with certainty where the name "Dream Plan" actually comes from. The main force behind the plan, Aalborg's Social Democratic deputy mayor, says in an interview that the name came from the chairperson of the Social Democratic City Council Group. When interviewed, however, the chairperson insists,

> We were not the ones who baptized it the "Dream Plan." It was the press who began using this expression. And I have to say that it irritated me somewhat.

Aalborg's city engineer, however, believes that the term "Dream Plan" is related to the high costs connected with the plan, with its "restructuring . . . tearing down . . . and other things which cost a lot of money. It was therefore called the Dream Plan. I do not know where [the name] comes from, but it is the money, because one thinks, 'They cannot find this money.'" It appears that the name is used for the first time by one of the participants at a press conference the Social Democratic City Council Group held to launch the plan.[1] The name is then picked up by the press and widely publicized the day after the press conference, and, to the dismay of the Social Democrats, remains the name by which the plan is known.

The Social Democrats describe the reasons for their counterplan as follows:

> The protests seem . . . unwilling to "die" in this affair [the Aalborg Project]. This is because the changes have operated so that most people are confused about finding their way around town, and about building up new habits in the pattern of movement. Nearly everyone views the traffic changes as a witch hunt against drivers and as an attempt to harass business and to confuse out-of-town customers trying to find their way, etc. At the same time, it is questionable whether bicyclists, pedestrians, and [those using] public transportation have seen their situation improve. Another objection focuses on the reduced possibilities to get from one neighborhood to another, which is a direct result of the division into zones.[2]

As a solution to these problems, the Social Democrats call for the "establishment of logical and easily discernible ring-road systems to service the downtown area . . . simultaneous with downtown being 'made peaceful' [*fredeliggørelsen af bymidten*], via the introduction of speed-reducing barriers on the smaller streets."[3] This proposal is elaborated in four pages of text and seven pages of sketch maps. Compared to the Technical Department's several hundred pages of planning reports and to the Chamber's counterplan, the Social Democratic plan can best be termed a rough draft. Yet it is a draft whose implementation would radically alter Aalborg's physical appearance. For instance, construction of the proposed ring-road system would involve massive destruction of property, the building of new streets, and the extension and widening of existing ones. Moreover, the proposal calls for the construction of two new large parking garages in the city center and the building of bicycle paths on Vesterbro Street. Finally, the Social Democratic plan will reopen several of the streets now closed to car traffic in the Aalborg Project. In sum, the proposal imposes far fewer restrictions on automobile traffic in the city center than does the Aalborg Project, and it is far more costly.

The Social Democrats' counterplan comes as a genuine surprise to everyone outside the Social Democratic party, and to considerable numbers of party members as well. The head of the Technical Department's Task Force recalls:

> It was in the afternoon. I think that it was after working hours, and for the following two days I would be away taking a course or something. [The city engineer] telephoned and said that he had something very important which he thought I ought to have right away. It was the Social Democratic City Council Group's proposal which I received. And I was simply dumbfounded! I didn't know anything about it being in the pipeline, I had *absolutely* no idea that something like this would come up . . . It contained massive road construction . . . many of the big old projects proposed again, but in altered form. It was entirely confusing what this would result in.

Others on the staff reacted in a more humorous fashion, at least at first. Aalborg's chief planner for public transportation explains:

> It is not normal that you fall down on the floor screaming with laughter. But it was something like that, you know. Because there were principles [in the Social Democratic proposal] which in our opinion were entirely out of date and had been so for many years. And so at first you laugh about it. Afterwards you pull your hair out and become angry because now you have to use several months of work to assess this plan.

Finally, another staff member tells of her reaction:

> Most of what [the Social Democrats] had done was so foolish that you couldn't work with it . . . But we were quite shocked about the plan. I think, and I still believe, that it was absolutely substandard. I can't understand that anybody would sign their name to it . . . When you know that there have been professional planners working on it, and you get this kind of plan which is devoid of argument and incoherent and everything, then you ask yourself, "What the hell does this mean? Are they making fun of us?"

The Social Democrats, by contrast, think of the plan as a professional piece of work. A local architect's office has been the consultant on the plan. The Social Democratic deputy mayor, a member of the City Council Technical Committee, states in an interview, "What we are proposing is professional. Not something with pencil lines, and rough sketches . . . We got a real planner to do it."

In the first days after receiving the Social Democratic plan, the Technical Department staff tend to take it with a grain of salt. The plan is viewed as an anachronism and as technically shoddy. This view is shared by the chairman of the Technical Committee from the center-left Radical Liberal party (*Radikale Venstre*), who finds the Social Democratic counterplan not only out of date but also incompatible with Social Democratic policy:

> I am a rather peaceful person, I believe, but I reacted sharply in the Technical Committee. I think it was strange to take the kind of viewpoint [the Social Democrats had]. Nor do I think [the plan] accorded with what I call the progressive forces within the Social Democratic Party. I think it was a Conservative-Social Democratic plan which lay to the right of the ideas held by the Conservative [Technical Department alderman].

The member of the Technical Committee representing the Socialist People's party thinks much the same way. She explains:

> It has certainly been strange to see how ideas—I nearly said Conservative ideas —emerge within the Social Democratic Party. Whereas [the alderman for the Technical Department] totally rejects something [i.e., the Social Democratic plan] which in reality ought to be his own policy.

THE AALBORG SCANDAL

The Social Democrats, however, are not playing any jokes on either the Technical Department or anyone else. The counterplan is intended as a serious move in Aalborg politics. A closer examination indicates that the Social Democrats' plan has a hidden agenda. It is part of an attempt by the Social Democratic City Council Group to recover its footing and improve its public image following the disaster of the "Aalborg scandal" the previous year.[4] The bribery case against the Social Democratic mayor, a Social Democratic alderman, and others seriously weakened the party and its City Council Group. The mayor was forced to resign and went to prison. As a result, in the first elections after the scandal, votes for the Social Democrats declined by 25% and the party lost six seats in the City Council. The Social Democrats were in shock. They had become a minority. For the first time in more than a half-century they now had to find new methods of policy making and of presenting themselves to the public. The chairman of the Social Democratic City Council Group, who helped launch their counterplan, explains the situation:

> It was right after the City Council elections, and there may well have been some one or other who needed to make themselves and their ideas more visible. The

City Council Group certainly had an enormous need to come out and show that indeed there [still] was a Social Democratic Group, and that we still had some ideas and some plans . . . There had emerged a kind of spiritual freedom within the group [after the mayor had resigned and left]. We were flying high, realizing the fact that there was now more than one person in the group [besides the former mayor] who could do something. People again got the urge to really take up the tasks of local politics.

And one of the things they "take up" is the Social Democratic counterplan to the Aalborg Project.

The week after the Technical Department received the plan, the Social Democrats hold a press conference, and the plan is launched with great fanfare in *Aalborg Stiftstidende.* The Social Democratic spokespersons, including Aalborg's deputy mayor and the party's City Council Group chairman, emphasize that "a unanimous City Council Group stands behind it, and that the 'hinterland' [*baglandet,* i.e., the voters' associations and the party organization] is in agreement."[5] This means that with just five more members of the thirty-one-member City Council willing to support the Social Democratic plan, the Aalborg Project will irrevocably fall. The Social Democrats estimate that the plan will cost 100 million kroner to implement. We will return to the question of cost later.

Three days following the first public mention of their plan, the Social Democratic party obtains support from an unexpected camp: the Chamber of Industry and Commerce. The Chamber is, per tradition and on principle, more often in opposition to Social Democratic policy than in support of it. In an interview, however, the chairman of the Chamber's City Center Committee explains their attitude to the Social Democratic plan with these words: "We of course, exploit [the Social Democratic plan] grossly." The Chamber is again practicing *Realpolitik,* where traditions and principles are subordinate to the goal of achieving results. And again the Chamber strikes with the masterful sense of timing which is the mark of true political adroitness.

In an interview with the *Aalborg Stiftstidende,* the chairman of the Chamber declares that the Social Democratic plan is "a very sensible plan . . . [which] has paid attention to virtually all the points of objection which the Chamber has presented time and again ever since the [Aalborg Project's] start."[6] Parts of the Social Democratic plan, however, are too radical and too partisan toward automobile drivers, even for the Chamber of Industry and Commerce. The Chamber's chairman thus declares, "It seems, for instance, a bit too radical to demolish [the buildings on] the entire side of Dannebrogsgade."[7]

If the Technical Department first thought that there would be an easy way of getting around what they see as an inferior plan, it now becomes clear that this is not the case. Two of the politically and economically strongest groups in Aalborg are now opponents of the Aalborg Project. The projects' future is, therefore, as ominous as ever. Only two weeks remain until the next "orientation meeting" of the City Council regarding the project, and during the coming two months the project will be subject to the definitive vote for ratification in the Council.

Panic spreads. Even though the Technical Department staff find it difficult to take the Social Democratic plan seriously in a *professional* sense, they are now forced to take it seriously in a *political* one. One Technical Department staff member puts it this way:

> It was the entire Social Democratic City Council Group of eleven people who proposed [the plan]. This is eleven out of thirty-one: Only five are needed [to form a majority of sixteen], right? Then *this* becomes *the plan!*

Three days after the Chamber of Industry and Commerce declared its support for the Social Democratic counterplan, the Socialist People's party delegate in the Technical Committee criticizes the plan publicly. A week later it is the turn of the chairman of the Technical Committee, from the Radical Liberal party. In an op-ed piece in *Aalborg Stiftstidende* he writes:

> At the moment it does not sound very logical when [the Social Democratic deputy-mayor] declares to the *Stiftstidende* that an important objective of the plan is to make the center of town peaceful. The published part of the plan seems to indicate, rather, that the result will be exactly the opposite.[8]

The next day, the alderman for the Technical Department adds his name to the list of critics. In an interview with *Aalborg Stiftstidende* published under a four-column headline: "The Social Democratic Party in Aalborg Has Stabbed Me in the Back," the alderman criticizes the Social Democratic City Council Group and its plan in the sharpest of terms:

> I am astounded at the actions of the Social Democratic City Council Group and feel that they have given both myself and my civil servants in the Municipal Administration's Second Department [i.e., the Technical Department] a stab in the back . . . [The] group suddenly calls a press conference and presents a proposal which on several points deviates from the already implemented arrangements, and . . . is in disagreement with those measures which the Social Democrats themselves have approved . . . [The] procedure makes me anxious about future forms of cooperation in the new City Council . . . [The plan] actually costs closer to 300 million kroner [rather than the 100 million kroner estimated by the

Social Democrats]. Furthermore, there is nothing new in the plan. Most of it is archaic and has long ago been abandoned.[9]

Apparently the Technical Department alderman is, once again, heading toward open confrontation about the Aalborg Project, this time with the Social Democratic party as his opponent. Faced with the new turn of events, the Chamber of Industry and Commerce senses the dawn of better things and prepares for the orientation meeting of the City Council, to be held the following week. The Chamber has already decided to hold a general assembly prior to the City Council meeting.

Two weeks previously, the Chamber's Retailer Committee had met in order to prepare for the assembly and had decided that it was now "presumably the last chance to attain influence on the decisions in connection with [the Aalborg Project], making it extremely important that as many members as possible attend [the general assembly] and present their points of view."[10] The chairman of the Retailer Committee also pointed out that "the meeting . . . is not an orientation meeting but a protest meeting."[11] Aside from the Chamber's own members, the politicians from the City Council Technical Committee were also invited, as were the Aalborg Police Department and the local press. The alderman for the Technical Department along with his section heads and staff also were expected to participate by presenting the Aalborg Project's current status and by answering queries.

A week prior to the Chamber's assembly, the Technical Department and Chamber leaders hold one of their closed summit meetings. Minutes of the meeting have the words "INTERNAL MINUTES" printed in special type on the front page, and the participants are limited to the Technical Department alderman, his section heads, and the leaders of the Chamber of Industry and Commerce. As in previous summit meetings, the Aalborg Project's secretary, who also heads the Task Force, is not invited. Only a single point is on the agenda: planning the Chamber's assembly. The course of events is agreed upon. The alderman, the section heads, and the staff will be at the Chamber's disposal to participate in the meeting, and the head of the Task Force will be available to assist the Chamber in the practical preparation and organization of the meeting, together with the Chamber's own section head.[12]

In this extremely pressured situation, where the Aalborg Project is under attack from both the Chamber and the Social Democratic party, and where the Chamber has declared its support for the Social Democrats' counterplan, it is precisely at this juncture that cooperation between the Technical Department and the Chamber is resuscitated. The open confrontation between the two parties is replaced by the more familiar stable relation of cooperation. In this connection, the chairman of the Chamber of Industry and Commerce relates in an interview that he was teased by the alderman when they met, with remarks to the effect that "it looks like you've become a Social Democrat." Nevertheless, the alderman's previous admonition to the Chamber—that "they are not the ones with whom I will discuss future traffic regulations. It will be the users, the citizens"[13]—shows itself to be an empty threat. The alderman brings the confrontation to a halt by simply giving up in the face of the opponent and reestablishing the stable cooperation, with all the coordination and ex ante adaptation of action this entails.

The stable power relation that is first transformed into an antagonistic confrontation and then returns to a stable relation confirms Michel Foucault's findings that power relations are dynamic and reciprocal, in the sense that stable power relations can turn into antagonistic confrontations at any time, and vice versa. As we have seen, however, evidence from the Aalborg Project suggests that Foucault's conclusions must be modified by the finding that the relationship between stable power relations and antagonistic confrontations is asymmetrical: stable power relations are more common than antagonistic confrontations, much as peace—however conflict ridden—is more typical than outright war in most societies; even war usually has long stable periods with inactivity. This observation gains support from further developments in the Aalborg Project, as we shall see later. Actors in power relations tend to actively avoid open, antagonistic confrontations, and when these do appear, they tend to devolve rapidly into stable relations again. The result is that the technical, economic, and organizational conditions which shape planning, administration, and policy making, both in conception and execution, are to a greater degree defined by stable power relations than by antagonistic confrontations.

Confrontations are usually more visible than stable power relations and therefore become conspicuous foci for both power research, press coverage, and public debate. When seen in the total context of relations of power, however, confrontations are less important in comparison to the dynamics of stable power relations. Research, press coverage, or public debate, which center attention exclusively on the confrontational aspects of power, tend to give us an incomplete and distorted picture of power relations.

At the general assembly of the Chamber of Industry and Commerce, the Technical Department informs at some length about the Aalborg Project's status and about the results of an assessment of the first stage which has been carried out by the Technical Department. The Chamber repeats its now well-known criticism of the project and uses the meeting to express its continued opposition to the project's implementation. *Aalborg Stiftstidende* reports from the meeting that the members of the Chamber of Industry and Commerce presented their well-known criticisms in the strongest form. The merchants opposed virtually all of the implemented traffic regulations in the center, and they accused [the Technical Department alderman] and his staff of wanting to create a ghost town where street closings and a confusing traffic system drive away the out-of-town customers.[14]

FROM DREAM TO NIGHTMARE

In the Danish Cyclist Federation there is again serious anxiety about the turn of events in the Aalborg Project. The federation does what it can to exert influence in the public debate and to directly influence the Technical Department. For example, on several occasions during the winter, the Federation requests that the Technical Department maintain its stand on the original Aalborg Project and reactivate the parts that have been dropped. In early spring the Federation arranges a public demonstration on Vesterbro for the construction of bike paths.

The Cyclist Federation also protests the Social Democratic plan. The chairman of the federation's Aalborg chapter is a member of the Social Democratic party. He tries to protest the plan within the party but without success. He explains:

> *Chairman of the Danish Cyclist Federation:* [The Social Democratic counterplan] appears as a *fait accompli,* so I throw a tantrum, "What the hell is this!" And the other, more quiet members in the working group [a group within the Social Democratic party which reviews Technical Department activities] also believe that this is damned strange, for we had not discussed this. [On the contrary,] we would soon be discussing the downtown plan [the Technical Department's project]. And the [Social Democratic] City Council Group had also approved it . . . So I was really very secure until all of a sudden this "Dream Plan" is sprung on me . . . We called it a nightmare . . . I then say to [Aalborg's Social Democratic deputy-mayor, the driving force behind the Social Democratic plan], "[C]an it really be that you people support what the Chamber of Industry and Commerce is supporting . . . ?"
>
> *Interviewer:* Does anything happen, then?
>
> *Chairman:* Not a bit!

According to the Cyclist Federation's chairman, the Social Democratic plan comes as a surprise not only to those outside the party but also to those within it. And the earlier declaration from the main protagonists behind the plan that "the hinterland is in agreement" shows itself to be wrong.

The Danish Cyclist Federation and its Social Democratic chairman work intensively to support the Technical Department and to keep alive the original Aalborg Project. Nevertheless, it is striking to observe the difference between the Federation and the Chamber of Industry and Commerce with reference to participation and influence as concerns the project. We can illustrate this difference by comparing the activities of the two organizations in the weeks prior to the already mentioned City Council orientation meeting. The different treatment accorded the Cyclist Federation and the Chamber by the Technical Department is another example of the unique position held by the Chamber in local city politics and planning. The example is also characteristic of how the Technical Department's leadership accords little significance to the town's grass roots organizations, even when these organizations support the department's projects. The department seems not to want allies.

As early as eight weeks before the City Council orientation meeting, the Danish Cyclist Federation's chairman writes to the alderman for the Technical Department requesting that the Federation participate on an equal footing with other organizations in the meeting. In addition, the same letter requests "an orientation meeting with, for example, [the head of the Task Force] a few days in advance, so that we can come to the meeting reasonably well-prepared."[15] A month later, the Technical Department alderman responds that the Danish Cyclist Federation may participate in the City Council meeting, but that they will not receive any advance orientation from the staff inasmuch as the purpose of the City Council meeting is precisely that of orientation. "The [Technical] Department is therefore not disposed to give advance orientation to those interest organizations invited to participate in the City Council meeting," writes the alderman. "If your organization persists in its desire for an advance meeting, the Danish Cyclist Federation should not expect to be invited to participate in the City Council orientation meeting."[16]

The curt treatment given the Cyclist Federation should be contrasted with the indulgence demonstrated by the alderman and by three Technical Department officials nine days after this letter is sent, when they meet with Chamber leaders, as described earlier. Here the alderman, as mentioned above, permitted himself, his managers, and his staff to participate in the general assembly of the Chamber a week before the City Council meeting. This meeting was arranged precisely in order to orient the Chamber in advance, inasmuch as the Chamber wished to exert influence on Aalborg City Council and on public opinion prior to the City Council meeting. Moreover, the head of the Task Force, the very staff member whom the Danish Cyclist Federation had wished to meet— a request rejected by the alderman—is placed at the disposal of the Chamber by the alderman to assist them in preparing their meeting.

The Cyclist Federation learns about this from the press and from Deep Throat, who reports to the Cyclist Federation from his vantage point within the Technical Department. The Federation sends a second letter to the Technical Department alderman inviting the department to a meeting about the Aalborg Project in the Federation's Traffic Committee. In its letter the Federation also expresses its dissatisfaction with the discriminatory treatment it has suffered compared to the Chamber of Industry and Commerce:

> The [Federation's] Traffic Committee sends this invitation despite the ultimatum contained in the Department's orientation [letter], inasmuch as it may be read in the *Stiftstidende* . . . that the Chamber of Industry and Commerce can hold a meeting with the [Technical Department] on the same issue.[17]

When he receives the letter, the alderman scribbles on it "*not* me" and continues to his staff, "but perhaps someone else if any of you want to." Apparently no one has such a desire. According to the chairman of the Cyclist Federation, no one from the Technical Department showed up for the meeting. The chairman recounts:

> [The letter] is a provocation. We had certainly discovered by that time that the Chamber had been having contacts with the department, right? That is, they had really been on the inside with their arguments. So when we hear that the department is invited over to the Chamber of Industry and Commerce . . . we think, "Damn, we can also invite the staff planners and the alderman to our meeting." But then I think that [Deep Throat] called up and said, "You people can't do this. You must be kidding!"

The Kayerød Neighborhood Association, an early supporter of the Aalborg Project, has been passive during the attacks of recent months. Now the association rises to the occasion. In the week prior to the City Council orientation meeting, the association writes to Aalborg's mayor to call attention to the fact that they have "obvious interests in the traffic conditions in the center of town" and that they therefore request an invitation to the City Council meeting.[18] The Aalborg Project's Task Force had previously recommended to the Executive Committee and to the Technical Department alderman that the Kayerød Neighborhood Association be invited to the City Council meeting, but the alderman rejects the request. In an interview he explains, "As for the residents' associations, we just do not resonate politically." The mayor therefore sends Kayerød a "No" the day before the City Council meeting. Only the Chamber of Industry and Commerce, the Police Department, the Danish Cyclist Federation, and some public transport officials are invited to the meeting.

CALM BEFORE THE STORM

At the start of the City Council meeting, Aalborg's city engineer begins his talk ominously: "Could this be a funeral party we are preparing today? If yes, well then I don't think the main character—the traffic plan—has had fair treatment in its short lifetime."[19] The city engineer's speech is clearly affected by the Chamber's continued opposition to the Aalborg Project and by the Social Democratic counterplan. The day after the City Council meeting, *Aalborg Stiftstidende* writes that the counterplan "was there like a ghost in the background."[20] The city engineer continues:

> [The traffic plan] has been attacked by the nonautomotive road users [*svage trafikanter*], by the motorists [*hårde trafikanter*], by the merchants, by the handicapped, by the press, etc. Attacks from many sides do not have to mean that the attackers are completely right. The pedestrian streets were initially subject to the same massive attacks. And especially from the merchants, too . . .[21]

Here it may be noted that the introduction to the city engineer's speech originally read differently. In its first draft, the speech began as follows:

> [The alderman for the Technical Department] says that we, his staff, may not politicize, but he has never said that we may not be subjective. I will be subjective and express my own personal opinion. [The alderman] and the members of the Technical Committee know that I normally am content with listening to their opinions, so on this occasion I would like to be forgiven.[22]

These introductory sentences are crossed out and replaced with the words, "Let me first be subjective." Over the crossed out lines are the alderman's initials, but as far as I can assess they are not in the alderman's handwriting. Given the Technical Department's daily work routines it is most likely that the city engineer has discussed his speech with the alderman, who has then proposed changes in the introduction.

The first introduction and the actual speech clearly diverge from the city engineer's usual manner. The city engineer is not known for providing his personal opinions about Aalborg's city politics and planning, something he himself mentions in the speech. On the contrary, he is usually very cautious and keeps his opinions to himself and his staff. Furthermore, during the first three to four years of the Aalborg Project, the city engineer has been one of the most conservative members of the Executive Committee as concerns effecting changes in the existing conditions in downtown Aalborg. The city engineer was actively involved in the first reductions of the project, for example, the project's division into stages and the reduction in the bus terminal. Thus, there seems to be a real change in his attitude at this point. He explains his new role in terms of three factors. First, that the documentation produced within the project has helped convince him of its positive aspects. Second, that there will be no problem for automobile traffic even though nonautomotive and public transportation attain increased priority. Third, that in the course of his work with the project the city engineer has generally changed his position toward environmental issues. In my interview with him, he elaborates:

> *Interviewer:* I believe I can detect a change in your attitude . . .
>
> *Aalborg's City Engineer:* You are absolutely right. Maybe it stands out. It is the documentation, but there are other things besides documentation.
>
> *Interviewer:* What are the other things?
>
> *City engineer:* Well! It is a greater desire to pay attention to a better environment—this sounds terrible, I don't like to say things like this. But it also has something to do with this. I have been a supporter, like most traffic planners, of parking places here and parking places there, so that people could park their cars close to the shops. And perhaps I have increasingly recognized that it is not at all certain that [this] is desirable.

Both the city engineer's public appearance before the City Council and the change of attitude the speech reflects indicate that *everyone* in the Technical Department is now willing to fight for the survival of the Aalborg Project, even its most conservative proponents. They refuse to look on passively as attempts are made to kill off the project.

After the city engineer's speech, the Aalborg City Council receives the same orientation about the project's status as the Chamber of Industry and Commerce had received the week before. The Chamber and other interest organizations repeat their former positions without adding anything new. And the alderman for the Technical Department attempts to calm both the Chamber and the Social Democratic party by concluding, now four-and-a-half years into the project, "that there ought to be agreement on the content and extent of the first stage before parts of the later stages are implemented."[23] The other aldermen and the remaining City Council members are silent at the meeting. The silence may be interpreted as the calm before the proverbial storm. The effect of the Social Democratic counterplan is indisputable: the fronts have been consolidated, but it is not clear what the result will be.

Fourteen

KNOWLEDGE KILLS ACTION

Dreams have as much influence as actions.
Stéphane Mallarmé

The Aalborg Project is now approaching its moment of truth: presentation to the City Council for final ratification. After four years of repeated set-backs and reductions, the Technical Department decides to go on the offensive and try to reverse the project's decline. Hence, the department again proposes that the bus terminal at Nytorv be closed to automobile traffic with the intention of salvaging key elements such as the traffic zone solution and a public transportation system that runs on time. Østeraagade is again proposed for permanent closure at Slotspladsen Square. And finally, the proposal again requests that city buses be permanently removed from Danmarksgade so as to allow for the planned reduction of motorized traffic on this street.

The Technical Department, however, has a problem: the project's political status is unclear due to the Social Democratic counterplan.

THE MOMENT OF TRUTH

This situation does not improve when the chairman of the Chamber of Industry and Commerce, four days prior to the City Council meeting, sends a five-page letter to each of the Council's thirty-one members. In great detail, the chairman again explains the Chamber's views, and he asks the council members to alter the project according to the Chamber's wishes:

> In conclusion, on behalf of the Aalborg Chamber of Industry and Commerce, I
> wish to implore the members of the City Council to change the "Traffic Plan"

in accordance with our wishes, which we are convinced will also be to the advantage of the residents and out-of-town guests, tourists, and customers. Aalborg is certainly a regional center, but in traffic terms not so large that it should not be able to avoid having restrictions and prohibitions for cars.[1]

The key request in the Chamber's letter is that the City Council not approve the Technical Department's project. Among other things, the letter asks that the presently closed Østeraagade at Slotspladsen—the last effective street closure for automobile traffic in the implemented project—be reopened. It is interesting to note here that although the Chamber of Industry and Commerce is reiterating its previous criticism of the Aalborg Project, the Chamber has changed its view regarding the bus terminal at Nytorv. Where the Chamber had strongly opposed this scheme and would rather have seen the terminal moved to Aalborg's harbor, the Chamber's chairman now—after the terminal has been in operation for seven months—expresses his satisfaction:

> The reconstruction of Nytorv as bus terminal with optimal transfer possibilities for bus passengers, new bicycle paths, taxis, and possibility for deliveries from Østeraagade to Slotsgade, is generally a success. The modern shelters for waiting bus passengers, the lighting, and the cobblestones and tile all fit in very nicely with both the older and new buildings around Nytorv.[2]

The Chamber's turnabout is reminiscent of the introduction of pedestrian malls in Aalborg and Denmark. First the merchants were strongly opposed to them. But after the malls were introduced, the merchants became their most ardent supporters. Nevertheless, the merchants usually opposed further expansion of pedestrian mall networks until they were implemented anyway, after which they supported them, etc. Another, more banal but perhaps supplementary explanation for the Chamber's revised attitude toward the bus terminal at Nytorv could be that the Chamber acquired a new chairman immediately after the terminal was put into operation, and this new chairman, author of the letter cited above, owns a large shop adjacent to the bus terminal. According to the chairman himself, his shop is doing well because of the many bus passengers and pedestrians now in the area.[3] By comparison, the previous chairman of the Chamber owned a manufacturing company on Nytorv, and with the establishment of the bus terminal encountered problems with deliveries to and from his company.[4]

The Social Democratic counterplan also mentions the reopening of Østeraagade to motorized traffic, and this now becomes a test case for whether or not the Aalborg Project's traffic regulations will be allowed to survive. The Technical Department, in its written comments to the Municipal Administration and to the City Council in preparation for the June meeting, explicitly emphasizes that as far as concrete individual measures are concerned, and with the exception of the closing of Østeraagade, there is no essential difference between the first stage of the Technical Department project now up for ratification—the ninth version of the project over four years—and the Social Democratic plan.[5] The Social Democrats contest the representation of the two projects as essentially similar, and the Technical Department alderman can therefore not count on Social Democratic support at the City Council meeting. Moreover, it appears that the Liberals (*Venstre*) have also begun to reconsider their position toward the Aalborg Project. Hence, it is possible the project will be definitively voted down at the City Council meeting.

The situation remains unclear until the actual City Council meeting. It leads to political maneuvering, which the next day is summarized in an article in *Aalborg Stiftstidende* with the front-page headline: "Rupture on the Right."[6] The alderman explains his attempt to salvage the project:

> It was damn unlucky for a Conservative [like myself] to come to a City Council meeting with a proposal which the Social Democrats would vote down because they agreed with the Chamber of Industry and Commerce. Politically speaking, this just doesn't fit, does it? . . . Perhaps I had been able to figure on Liberal party support in the City Council, but I wasn't completely sure. In any case [the Liberal alderman for the Fifth Department] was not much of a supporter of these measures. And he had repeatedly said so. Now I am not sure that [the Liberals] would have failed me at the decisive moment, but [the Liberal alderman] had repeatedly shown what I would call a lukewarm attitude toward the project, perhaps even a negative attitude. And then it is revealed—this much information I got before the City Council meeting, you know—that the Social Democrats were still very wavering about where they would position themselves.
>
> Then there was a pause in the City Council meeting. I got together with some people from the Technical Committee and some Social Democrats and said, "Listen here, this can all end badly. It can end with the plan being voted down. I understand that you people can't control your own group." "No," [they answered]. "And if I can't trust the Liberals one hundred percent, then all this can collapse completely, and then we can get some decisions that will be practically impossible to reverse again. Wouldn't it be more clever if we postponed the whole mess? . . . It was therefore a *purely* political maneuver . . . and the Liberals were very angry about it, I won't hide that. On an earlier occasion, [the Liberal alderman] had asked me whether I would not help in postponing the project. At that time I said that I could not. It's my project that I'm going with to the City

Council. So I can't stand up and postpone it. Then it is postponed together with the Social Democrats. I can certainly see that it was perhaps not especially appropriate. But I am convinced that it was the *only* possibility to get the project through at a later time.

Two measures, however, are approved at the City Council meeting: (1) replacement of the bus lanes on Vesterbro street with bicycle lanes,[7] and (2) elimination of the winding "ribbon drive" on Danmarksgade around Frederikstorv Square. The rest of the Aalborg Project is postponed.

The project has now been operating for nearly five years, and at no time has it been on a weaker footing. *Aalborg Stiftstidende* follows up the City Council meeting with an editorial entitled "Traffic-Plan Tie-Up" ("*Trafikplan-knude*," the word *knude* can mean both "tie-up" or "knot," implying that the plan itself is in trouble). The editorial, in its customary agreement with the views expressed by the Chamber of Industry and Commerce, attacks the last remaining important measure among the street closures for automobile traffic: the closing of Østeraagade toward Slotspladsen Square. This is an unusually specific topic for an editorial:

> [The Aalborg Project] has become a soap opera [*serieforestilling*] in the Aalborg City Council . . . It must now be clear to everyone that the utopian dream for those people bloated with fantasy, that everyone will use bus, bicycle, or their own legs to get from all of North Jutland to the region's largest business center, cannot be achieved. And precisely the closing of Østeraagade at Slotspladsen, about which the City Council members could not agree, seems to be one of the programmatic issues which seriously clashes with the desire to allow the downtown's car-driving guests to obtain reasonably convenient access and exit.[8]

Supporters of the Aalborg Project are clearly concerned about the outcome of the City Council meeting and about the turn of events the issue has now taken. Opposition to the project now includes not only the Chamber of Industry and Commerce but also the Social Democratic party, the Aalborg Police Department, and the press.

In an article in *Aalborg Stiftstidende*, the City Council member from the Socialist People's party, who is also a member of the council's Technical Committee, appeals to all supporters of the Aalborg Project to mobilize against the Social Democrats' Dream Plan. At the same time, the Socialist member of the City Council uses the occasion to praise the Conservative alderman's struggle to save the project, an uncommon expression of nonpartisan political support for the alderman:

The Socialist People's party believes that the city center plan contains qualities which make a good point of departure for a town which is better to move about in, a town which is better to live in, and yes, generally a town which is alive, also after the shops have closed, . . . and I think that it is worth all praise and respect that a Conservative alderman to this degree takes up the struggle against his own people in order to implement the principles of the city center plan's traffic policy . . . [B]ut if it evolves into a power struggle between the Social Democrats and the Conservatives, it can very easily end with the Chamber of Industry and Commerce and hard-core drivers of cars emerging victorious from the battle. Therefore, the Socialist People's party believes that the next four to five months should be used by all supporters of the traffic plan to begin to exert massive pressure on the Social Democratic party in order to get them to see that their line on traffic policy should not be composed of cars-only streets [*motorgader*] and new right-of-ways [*gadegennembrud*] for roads. This era is long past. The Cyclist Federation, the downtown residents' associations, those who vote Social Democratic, and especially the Social Democratic party members must now seriously spare no efforts in order to prevent the Social Democratic City Council Group from setting developments in the center of town twenty years backwards.[9]

The Socialist City Council member's analysis of the situation highlights the real problem: in a direct power struggle between the Social Democratic City Council Group and the Conservative alderman, the alderman can easily risk losing, especially when the Social Democrats' viewpoints overlap with those of the Chamber of Industry and Commerce. The Technical Department thus desperately needs help. The "massive pressure" on the Social Democratic City Council Group never materializes, however. The only genuine power factor *for* the Aalborg Project and *against* the attacks on the project is the Technical Department itself, headed by its Conservative alderman. In contrast to the Chamber of Industry and Commerce, the Technical Department has done nothing to procure and cultivate allies. They are isolated and weak. In this critical situation one can again try to defend the project in rational terms. One can attempt to use rationality as power when one has no other power. It is this strategy which the Technical Department now employs.

ELIMINATING POLITICS WITH TECHNICS

The Technical Department alderman is quite aware of the problems and the danger of ending up in a direct confrontation with the Social Democrats. He has not forgotten what happened in the open confrontation with the Chamber of Industry and Commerce the year before. And his insecurity at the last City Council meeting speaks its clear language. The alderman gets nowhere by scolding the Social Democrats for "stabbing me in the back" and for producing "archaic" plans, something he has done before.[10] On the contrary, the alderman now realizes that this strategy has brought him to the brink of placing his project in open confrontation yet again, and that it weakens both the project's position and his own.

The history of the Aalborg Project shows that the project is best served by avoiding confrontations, and that the Technical Department therefore has a special interest in keeping power relations stable. In attempts to avoid confrontations, we have already seen the "stroking strategy," in which the Technical Department avoids or plays down criticism of its opponents even when it is directly attacked. The stroking strategy also includes not publishing information that places the counterpart in a bad light, even when this information strengthens the department's position in a publicly known disagreement with the opponent. The Technical Department has employed this latter mode of action earlier and will do so again toward the Social Democratic party in connection with their "Dream Plan." We have also seen the "strategy of technical rationality," in which questions are depoliticized and made less controversial by formulating them, rationally or rationalized, in technical, objective terms rather then in terms of political interests. Finally, we have seen the "strategy of surrender" which is used where no other strategy can prevent confrontation. Here the department avoids an emerging confrontation by simply yielding to its opponent. In relation to the Social Democratic party, the Technical Department now chooses to rely on the strategy of technical rationality in an attempt to avoid having to capitulate, as they formerly had in relation to the Chamber of Industry and Commerce. The Social Democratic City Council Group must be convinced that the Technical Department's proposal is *technically* better than the Social Democrats' counterplan. In the words of the Technical Department alderman: "I have not postponed the traffic plan in order for it to be debated [further], but in order to convince the Social Democrats that it is rational."[11]

We have already seen how technical expertise can be used to rationalize policy. Conversely, we have seen also how politics can be used to eliminate "difficult" technical questions. Now, for the first time, we see an attempt to eliminate politics with the aid of technics. Such depoliticization is itself a political strategy, of course. As the first step in this new strategy, the alderman informs the Social Democratic City Council Group that the Technical Department wishes to subject the group's counterplan to a serious, professional city planning assessment (*byplanfaglig vurdering*).[12] The alderman's approach should be seen in light of the fact that the Social Democratic plan consists of only three pages of text and seven pages of sketch maps, and is therefore unclear on many points of content, and especially on projected consequences. In explaining the technical assessment to the Social Democratic City Council Group, the alderman describes it as something the Technical Department wishes to do for its own information and to help the group obtain a better description of its plan. The alderman explains:

> It was clear to me that if [the Social Democratic City Council Group's] ideas were to be influenced, then they should be influenced in a rational and not political manner. We had to begin the argument on a technical level which could show that what they had done was good or bad . . . Therefore I chose to tell them, "I can certainly meet with you people and explain something to you, but then we will suddenly have two political systems, Conservative vs. Social Democratic, which have the potential to clash with each other. Wouldn't it be much wiser if we asked the city engineer and the chief of city planning and some of their people"—I can't remember whether the city architect was also included—"to enter directly into a discussion [with the Social Democrats] and put all our information and studies at your disposal regarding the potentials of your designs? How will it affect the town altogether—in terms of planning, in terms of land use, and how will it affect the traffic?" They said, "Yes, thank you."

In this way the Technical Department obtains a much needed half-year reprieve for its project in a situation where it is in danger of destruction.

In commencing the technical assessment of the Social Democrats' plan, the alderman asks Aalborg's new Social Democratic mayor if the Technical Department can "approach either one member of the Social Democratic Group or one of the professional planning consultants who have assisted the group so that the Technical Department might obtain further information on some points [in the counterplan] in order for its assessment to be undertaken on the correct basis."[13] It is worth noting that the alderman explicitly requests permission to contact "one of the professional planning consultants who have assisted the group."[14] This again underscores the alderman's strategy of moving the Aalborg Project from the political to the technical and professional domain.

Aalborg's mayor accedes to the alderman's request for contact between the Technical Department and the Social Democratic City Council Group, and in July the alderman and his executive staff meet with a Social Democratic representative. At the meeting, the Technical Department spokespeople reiterate that they "would prefer" to make contact with one of the consultants behind the Social Democratic plan.[15] Here too the Technical Department doggedly pursues its strategy of extracting the plan entirely out of its political framework and instead subjecting it to a professional-to-professional discussion and assessment. The Technical Department staff members see the Social Democratic plan as so technically incompetent that it cannot stand detailed professional evaluation. And they believe that they will have more success by first convincing fellow professionals about this than politicians.

The Social Democratic representative who participates in the July meeting, however, finds himself unable to decide upon the Technical Department's request. He must first consult with his Social Democratic colleagues in the City Council. Four days after the meeting, he phones the Technical Department and informs them that the group is not disposed toward allowing the Technical Department to make direct contact with the consultants behind their plan.[16] Rather, the Social Democrats themselves prefer to meet with the Technical Department. Hence, the professional-to-professional meetings the Technical Department had proposed become meetings between politicians and professionals.

In August two representatives from the Social Democratic City Council Group meet with Aalborg's city engineer, the chief of city planning, the city architect, and a staff member from the Technical Department.[17] The two Social Democrats, besides being City Council members, are also members of the Council's Technical Committee. The meeting is arranged as a "clarification" (*opklarende*) meeting, where the Technical Department asks questions about the Social Democratic plan, and the two Social Democrats attempt to answer the questions. The Technical Department staff agrees to delay until later the actual discussion of problems and its criticism of the plan. It is agreed that the Technical Department will write up the minutes of the meeting and that the two Social Democrats will then receive the minutes for commentary and approval.

In all, five to six meetings and telephone conferences are held over three months. While innumerable aspects of the Social Democratic plan were discussed and evaluated at these meetings, two examples can serve to illustrate the kind of processes which actually took place. The two examples deal with the problems of reopening Østeraagade at Slotspladsen Square and an expansion of Kjellerupsgade. The Social Democratic plan proposes that Østeraagade toward Slotspladsen be reopened to traffic. This part of the Technical Department's project (unlike the once closed and then reopened Nytorv and Algade) has in fact remained implemented. The Technical Department therefore asks the Social Democrats whether they think the street should be reopened in both directions, and how they think traffic could function in the Østeraagade-Slotspladsen intersection.

In response to these questions, and much to their surprise—and relief—

the Technical Department staff learn that Østeraagade is not to be reopened to car traffic at all but only to buses. The following remarks, given in my interview with a participating staff member, illustrate the atmosphere of the meetings:

> *Technical Department staff member:* We thought the [Social Democratic plan] entailed that Østeraagade should be reopened just like that. But [at the August meeting] they explained to us that the reopening was only for public transportation. Okay, everyone kept his mask on, but it was a *great* relief and actually also a surprise. [One of our bosses] was the only one who could not keep a straight face.
>
> *Interviewer:* How did [this boss] react?
>
> *Staff member:* He said something to the effect that he was relieved. And it was perhaps also he who got mixed up in discussions about some of the other points . . . where he kind of jumped ahead to the analysis and tried to show already at this point that [the Social Democratic plan] was a bunch of junk on some points. But we had agreed beforehand that this was only a clarification meeting, and after that we had to hold a few more meetings in order to negotiate.

In the case of Kjellerupsgade, which was not mentioned in the Technical Department project, the Social Democrats' plan calls for the street to be expanded. Moreover, the Social Democratic plan includes the construction of a parking garage in Kjellerupsgade with space for 500 cars.

At the meeting, the Technical Department calls the Social Democrats' attention to the fact that the expansion of Kjellerupsgade presumably entails the destruction of parts of Nordkraft, a large district heating power plant located in the center of Aalborg. The Social Democrats are asked how they intend to avoid problems in relation to the power plant. Moreover, the Technical Department also reminds the Social Democrats that Nordkraft plans to build a new administration building on the same parcel of land on which the Social Democrats have placed the proposed parking garage, and they ask whether the Social Democrats have considered another site for the administration building.[18] The Social Democrats ask for time to ponder these questions. Again they must return to the City Council Group for answers. A good three weeks later, one of the Social Democrats phones the Technical Department and informs them that the group has decided to withdraw its plan for the expansion of Kjellerupsgade.[19] Again the Technical Department can breathe easier.

The Social Democratic City Council Group instead accepts a model for diverting traffic from Kjellerupsgade to Karolinelundsvej, if capacity problems should make it necessary in the future. Moreover, the Social Democrats inform the Technical Department that they will accept another site for the proposed parking garage. The area of Sauers Plads is proposed as a possible site, but this is the same area the Kayerød Neighborhood Association has for several years sought to have classified as a recreational zone. Another conflict is created. The Technical Department then examines the Social Democrats' revised proposals and find that it will cost 40 million kroner to build the proposed parking garage and that the 500 parking places the garage will contain are unnecessary.[20] Subsequently, the Social Democrats also retract their demand for the parking garage.

The total costs for those parts of the Social Democratic plan which concern downtown Aalborg are calculated by the Technical Department to be about 120 million kroner (1982 prices), or about double the Technical Department's own plan.[21] The Social Democratic proposal also contains measures to be implemented outside downtown Aalborg, and these are calculated to cost an additional 297 million kroner. During the negotiations between the Social Democratic City Council Group and the Technical Department, however, it is decided to leave these measures out of consideration and instead place them in the domain of general municipal planning. In a period of economizing, the Technical Department does not fail to use the budgetary argument, the most powerful argument of all, in its "technical" destruction of the Social Democratic plan. Hence,

> construction of the proposed ring roads will in economic terms presumably mean a redistribution of the sums within an unchanged budgetary framework to the Office of the City Engineer and thereby entail poorer financial possibilities to improve conditions for other types of transport (than those driving private cars): pedestrians, passengers in public transportation, bicyclists, and moped drivers . . . Implementation of the Social Democratic proposal will thus entail an increased budgetary framework for the Office of the City Engineer, if the level of service within the other sectors under the Office of the City Engineer is not to decline.[22]

This procedure evolves into a pattern of contact between the Technical Department and representatives of the Social Democratic City Council Group. The Technical Department's strategy of conducting a technical assessment of the Social Democratic plan appears to work: point by point, the staff bring up the problems in the Social Democratic plan, and the Social Democrats withdraw their proposals on each point, until the plan is practically abandoned.

In Chapter 4 we examined Nietzsche's statement: "Knowledge kills action; action requires the veils of illusion." We saw how the Aalborg Bus Company obtained the action it wanted—the bus terminal on Nytorv—by creating "illusions" about the terminal, that is, a manipulated evaluation of the location and size of the terminal. Now we see how the Technical Department succeeds in "killing" action it does not want—implementation of the Social Democratic Dream Plan—by producing knowledge about the effects of the plan. The success of their strategy surprises the staff members in the Technical Department, who did not expect things to be so easy. One staffer recounts:

> What happened was that we held the clarification meeting [mentioned above]. Then at the next meeting, we went through some of the consequences and some of the proposals and changes we *really* wanted to propose . . . And then we gradually evolved the routine that some of the viewpoints we had brought up at the meetings, they reported back to us that these were okay, and on top of that they retracted their own viewpoints. At first I was surprised because we had not asked that they retract anything. But they discussed it within the Social Democratic City Council Group, where they then said "O.K., so we retract this and that." So for several points we made forecasts about some of the consequences—what would it cost and how large was the actual need . . . and then gradually several of the major items were retracted.

"I DON'T LIKE POLITICS, I REALLY DON'T"

What do the Social Democrats themselves think of this procedure? How do they view what happened?

I have interviewed two of the three Social Democrats who were responsible for negotiations with the Technical Department about their plan. One of them, the Social Democratic City Council Group chairperson, presents her version of the meetings:

> *Social Democrat Group chairperson:* The alderman [for the Technical Department] thought that there were some elements in [our] plan, which he didn't like. But there he is positive—and he really is—in the sense that he says, "Then we have to discuss it." And so we are called into a few meetings with the planners where they want to get more information of what we really meant, so that they could work further along with it . . .
>
> *Interviewer:* What role did this come to play for your plan?
>
> *Group chairperson:* It is clear that we had to give in on some points and say, "O.K., if the professionals say that it gives this difficulty and that difficulty, then of course we must consider whether it is sensible." Here we naturally have to see the big picture, that when we go into this kind of work, we do not have the apparatus to go in and do the basics . . . We *never* presented this plan from the start —that's the way I experienced it—as being definitive. So it was an issue for discussion about whether there were some elements in it which were sensible.

The above presentation is what one might call a "nice" story about what happened with the Social Democratic plan. The presentation is characterized by a certain degree of rationalization, as are other passages in my interviews with Social Democrats on this point. Archival research indicates that during the months of contacts with the Technical Department, the Social Democratic party, from having launched its plan with much fanfare as a professionally solid proposal for a new planning scheme for Aalborg, changes its attitude so that they accord less and less significance to their plan, until it is virtually dropped.

Just as the Social Democratic "Dream Plan's" emergence must be understood in the context of the "Aalborg scandal" and the subsequent change of personnel within the Social Democratic City Council Group, including the mayor's forced resignation, the plan's demise must also be seen in the context of a resignation. This time it is the retirement of Aalborg's Social Democratic deputy mayor, who ostensibly retires "because I don't like politics, I really don't, it is too lowly, elbowing your way through and all that—people have to try it before they can ever believe how dirty it is!"[23] The deputy mayor, also a member of the City Council Technical Committee, initially goes on sick leave, but later on retires permanently, citing reasons of health. The deputy mayor has been the driving force behind the Social Democratic plan. In his work in the party, in the Technical Committee, and in the Aalborg City Council, he has concerned himself with issues of town and traffic planning, something unusual for a Social Democratic politician in Aalborg. The Social Democrats have tended to be more involved in the social service sector, education, sports, and culture. When the deputy mayor retires, there is no one else in the Social Democratic party who can seriously support the plan. The chairperson of the party's City Council Group describes what it is like to take over responsibility for promoting the plan after its main sponsor leaves the scene.

> It is certainly true that when you assume [responsibility for] a child, you can't do it with the same spirit as the person who was the real godfather. I, especially, was at a loss. Sure, I was chairperson [of the Social Democratic City Council Group] . . . but I have some totally different areas which I am involved in. So in all these talks [about the plan] I was in fact there just to mediate, so that I at least knew what had been discussed and I transmitted some feedback to the group. Because some of the discussions the planners had, I didn't understand a bit of it, you know. . . But it is *absolutely* certain, I think, that things would have turned out differently if [the deputy mayor] had been able to continue in the City Council. We know that when we ourselves have started something, we ourselves have gotten an idea, and when you get support for it, then you push it straight through.

Moreover, it occurs that the individuals assigned to the Social Democratic plan to replace the deputy mayor are new and inexperienced in City Council politics. City and traffic planning, as mentioned, are low-priority areas in the Social Democratic party, and they become domains where novice Social Democratic City Council members are allowed to get their political feet wet. The individual who takes the deputy mayor's seat on the City Council and on the Technical Committee also took part in the meetings with the Technical Department. He explains:

> *Interviewer:* Did you and [the other contact person in the Social Democratic party] support the plan as much as the deputy mayor did?
>
> *Social Democratic member of Technical Committee:* No, I don't think so. Because he was the one who had done all the work with it. And both of us came in as new members. We weren't well acquainted with the plan either, and we did not have the possibility to become so. For myself, at least, I did not have the possibility.
>
> *Interviewer:* Would it have made any difference if it was the deputy mayor [in his capacity as Social Democratic councilman] who had been sitting across from the Municipality [represented by the Technical Department] during these negotiations?
>
> *Social Democratic member:* Yes, I think so. If I had done something and it was still me who was sitting there and arguing for it, then I think that I would have been more uncompromising on my points. I definitely think so . . . you'll argue your viewpoints more when they are something you yourself have come up with. No question about this.

Finally, the demise of the Social Democratic plan is also due to the fact that it does not have backing from the party ranks beyond the City Council Group. The group originally thought it had this support, or had at least tried to give such an impression to the press and to the public. More and more people, however, including those from within the party, come to view the Social Democrats' proposal as an anachronism, both professionally and politically. The chairman of the Danish Cyclist Federation's Aalborg chapter, also a Social Democrat and a member of a Social Democrat working group for matters regarding the Technical Department, explains:[24]

> Either [NN] or [PP] [Social Democratic members on the City Council Technical Committee] had told the [*Aalborg Stiftstidende*] that there is indeed support [for the plan] in the local party organizations [*baglandet*]. . . But it is a fact that there was no agreement among members of the working group. We had a long discussion about it, and [the deputy mayor] thought that he had been stabbed in

the back, by me of all people. He thinks that he has my acceptance, right? He has not asked about it, in my opinion, but he still goes out in the public and says that he has it.

The deputy mayor tells his side of the story:

> *Aalborg's Deputy Mayor (Social Democrat):* We made a system which would be so goddamn democratic with all these working groups for the various munici-pal departments. But these were also places where we could not air our ideas. New politicians would become members of the groups and then you never knew when they would declare the news [to the press]. Then perhaps, the news might come at the wrong time. Therefore we had to suddenly say, "Now we have made this plan". . . . Just as soon as we publicize it, so [the Social Democrat chair-man of the Danish Cyclist Federation] and the Socialist People's party as well—[the Cyclist Federation chairman] is somewhat more disposed toward the Socialist People's party—they come out against the plan. They will not support "motor streets" [*motorgader,* i.e., high capacity streets for motorized traffic]. In this way you suddenly get a label pinned on you, "motor street," right? They are crazy! And then problems arise out in the western part of town in trying to get the system to work.
>
> *Interviewer:* Yes, at Dannebrogsgade, the houses on one side have to be torn down.
>
> *Deputy Mayor:* Yes, and you simply have to do this . . . How the hell would you otherwise get the heavy traffic to drive around [downtown]? . . . It must be horrible to live on such a street with all the big heavy trucks . . .
>
> *Interviewer:* Was the [Social Democratic] support in good shape?
>
> *Deputy Mayor:* [The chairman of the Cyclist Federation] was frightened when the Socialists spoke out against [the plan] . . . And then [the Social Demo-cratic Group chairperson] happened to say that it was a Dream Plan.[25] Already at this point it sounds suspect. It will cost twenty million [kroner] in a time of cutbacks and everything else.[26] So you can well see that it is already lost. One could discuss whether this was the intention with some of them, too.

There is much evidence to show that the deputy mayor is correct when he hints that the intentions among other prominent Social Democrats were that the Dream Plan should be dropped. But the Social Democrats are not wont to talk so much about this point in the Dream Plan's history. A city official close to the course of events sees both the Dream Plan's deroute and the deputy mayor's exit as direct consequences of the Social Democratic power struggle, following the Aalborg scandal, and of the filling of the vacuum left by the res-ignation of the former mayor. The official explains:

It was because of the Dream Plan that the deputy mayor retired (was thrown out!) from the City Council. He had tried to use the Social Democratic power vacuum for his own benefit but lost! (Parenthesis in original)[27]

THE PHANTOM REPORT

In the autumn, the Technical Department completes a report about the Social Democratic plan.[28] In a document of thirty-eight pages, four times that of the original Social Democratic plan, the technical and financial problems connected with the Social Democratic proposals are described. As usual, the Technical Department is thorough. Now it also shows political flair. The Technical Department alderman ensures that the Social Democratic party is quietly approached with the intention of clarifying whether the party would like the report published. "Decision regarding the memorandum's formal status awaits the result of the approach," read the minutes from a Technical Department Executive Committee meeting.[29]

The result is that the Technical Department's devastating critique of the Social Democrats' Dream Plan is neither printed nor published. Its front page is marked with the words "INTERNAL USE! Not transmitted and must not be transmitted out of the house." After which it is filed deep in the city engineer's archives.

At the same time, the Technical Department alderman sends a letter to Aalborg's Social Democratic mayor, in which he provides the official termination of the Dream Plan affair:

> On the basis of the agreement reached between the [Technical] Department and the Social Democratic City Council Group, it is considered unnecessary to carry out further assessments of the proposal from the Social Democratic City Council Group in regard to downtown Aalborg. For its part, the [Technical] Department will therefore undertake no further evaluations concerning downtown Aalborg unless a specific request is made to do so.[30]

Indeed, no further requests are made. The matter is closed.

A member of the Aalborg Project's Task Force tells of the decision about not publishing the assessment report and not following up the matter any further.

> It was decided to stop the report, simply because [publishing it] had no purpose. There was nothing left of the Social Democrats' proposal, and the intention behind making an assessment of a proposal must be to analyze it and then to get a decision about it . . . So politically speaking, I would perhaps say that there was

no purpose in publishing the report. And, well yes, O.K., the alderman's judgment was simply that there was no reason to kick somebody when he was already down. If we published the report . . . it would appear to the public as a total retreat for the Social Democrats. He couldn't see that there was any reason to do this. Presumably, it was also something political-tactical. He wanted very much to see implemented what he advocated in the first stage of the city center plan. So there was no reason to create a division with the Social Democrats.

Besides the Technical Department's decision not to publish the assessment of the Dream Plan, two additional factors cause the Social Democrats not to completely lose face. First, it is decided to make the closing of Østeraagade toward Slotspladsen Square temporary instead of permanent, such that there remains a theoretical possibility to return to the Social Democratic proposal to reopen Østeraagade just for buses. Second, the Technical Department considers a Social Democratic proposal to construct bus stops for city buses in front of the regional bus depot and railway station so as to ensure better conditions for transfer between regional and city buses and trains.

CONSEQUENCES OF THE DREAM PLAN

Two weeks after the Social Democrats and the Technical Department agreed to table the Social Democratic plan for good, the *Aalborg Stiftstidende* writes that the Social Democrats' plan "is expected to make for the winter's biggest battle in the City Council."[31] Thereafter one hears no more about the Dream Plan. For once, *Aalborg Stiftstidende* is curiously out of touch with current developments in the Aalborg Project. Perhaps it is because this is a case where the Chamber of Industry and Commerce is not involved. In cases with Chamber involvement, the paper has had intimate knowledge of all developments in the project, again underscoring the close links between the paper and the Chamber.

The Dream Plan may have been a political chimera, but it was not without political significance. Despite the fact that the plan is an anachronism in relation to existing tendencies in society and in the areas of environmental, traffic, and urban policy and planning; despite the fact that the plan is professionally substandard; despite the fact that one might ask, as did several of those interviewed, whether the Technical Department's project does not serve the interests of Social Democratic voters better than the Social Democrats' own plan; despite the fact that the Dream Plan enters the political process in an untimely and unsophisticated manner; and despite the fact that the plan does not obtain the influence originally intended, it was nevertheless far from clear when the

Social Democratic plan first appeared that it would, like a "dream" or chimera, fade away. After all is said and done, the plan was a real risk for the Technical Department and had real consequences for the outcome of the Aalborg Project.

With only five additional votes in the City Council, added to the Social Democrats' eleven, there would have been a majority for the Dream Plan, regardless of its lack of professional standard, and regardless of how much the plan were to conflict with existing tendencies in social developments. With the support of the Chamber of Industry and Commerce and with the Liberal party's insecurity about the Technical Department's project, this majority might well have materialized if the plan had come to a definitive vote in the City Council chambers. This is why the Technical Department took the plan so seriously, even though, as the interviews indicate, they also ridiculed it.

Seen from the perspective of the Technical Department, the strategy of winning time by initiating a professional assessment of the plan certainly paid off. The Technical Department successfully points out major weaknesses in the plan. Moreover, they experience a stroke of luck when the political force behind the plan—the Social Democratic deputy mayor—retires during the assessment period and is replaced by political ingenues without special knowledge or interest in the plan. Hence, the Technical Department encounters less opposition, and the assessment achieves greater effect. The political demise of the deputy mayor becomes the sustenance of the Aalborg Project.

One way in which the Social Democratic plan gains real significance is that it becomes yet another event that creates political frictions in the Aalborg Project. In encountering such events year in and year out, the Technical Department becomes ever more cautious regarding how far it dares to go in implementing the project. The chairman of the City Center Committee under the Aalborg Chamber of Industry and Commerce comments in an interview:

> The [Social Democratic plan] puts a brake on the alderman, and he has to fight a hell of a lot and use a ridiculous amount of time to get [his project] moved ahead. This is the effect which it has . . . When as a leader you have responsibility for a domain and the other politicians can also see that there is someone who constantly touches on something, then you become more cautious. This is the effect I think it has. Also because the arguments in [the Social Democratic plan] were really our own [i.e., the Chamber's]. This certainly strengthens our position without it attaining any generally big influence. But these are just a lot of small things which, when taken together, suddenly make things go a bit more in the direction we had wanted.

This view is supported by the fact that the eleventh version of the Aalborg Project, presented after the Social Democratic plan has fallen, is somewhat more conservative than the previous version. The Technical Department's de-sire to again close the bus terminal at Nytorv to automobile traffic is aban-doned once more. Østeraagade's closing does not become permanent but remains temporary. Danmarksgade does not become devoid of buses. The in-tegrated bus stop for city and regional buses on Vingaardsgade is again post-poned. The Technical Department's offensive, and the hoped-for comeback for the department's project, collapses. Instead there occurs yet another round of small reductions in the project. The Chamber of Industry and Commerce thus becomes the real winner in the case of the Social Democratic Dream Plan. This helps defuse further resistance from the Chamber against the Aalborg Project, increasing the likelihood of ratification by the City Council.

The lessons of the Dream Plan confirm the maxim stated earlier that the less the power, the more an actor has to depend on rationality. Both in terms of *Realpolitik* and in formal politics, the Technical Department is virtually power-less when confronted with the Social Democratic counterplan. The depart-ment must rely on reason and luck to win out over the Social Democrats, and in large part it succeeds. The events surrounding the Dream Plan are further evidence for the mutually constitutive character of rationality and stable power relations. After almost getting himself into an antagonistic confrontation with the Social Democrats over their counterplan, the Conservative alderman backpedals and deliberately stabilizes the situation. He wins by reducing the element of politics and increasing the element of rational analysis. Manipulat-ing the relation between the political and the rational is politics too, needless to say.

Fifteen

MINUTIAE MATTER

> All the problems of politics, of social organization, and of education
> have been falsified through and through . . . because one learned to
> despise "little" things.
>
> *Friedrich Nietzsche*

With the demise of the Social Democratic Dream Plan, the Aalborg Project's path to ratification by the Aalborg City Council is again cleared. Or more correctly: the path is cleared for the eleventh version of the project. Before this version is presented to the City Council for approval, however, two events occur which contribute to the project gradually reaching that lowest common denominator the dominant political actors seem to be able to agree upon. First, yet another major element of the project, the integrated bus stop for city and regional buses on Vingaardsgade, is abandoned, having been opposed by the Chamber of Industry and Commerce. Second, another retail shopping survey is carried out, which again disproves the claims made by the Chamber regarding declining sales in the city center. We shall examine these two events in this and the following chapter.

❧ THE FRAGILITY OF POLICY IMPLEMENTATION ❧

Project designers originally viewed the integrated bus stop for city and regional buses on Vingaardsgade as a crucial element in the total Aalborg Project. The bus stop was intended to ensure the coordination of local and regional public transportation in the city center. It is abandoned, as a result of a combination of structural and organizational factors and specific events, including the following: (1) a delay in obtaining environmental certification for the bus stop, (2) a projected decline in automobile traffic in the city center that did not occur, (3) an organizational restructuring involving a less important role for public transportation in Aalborg Municipality's administrative structure, (4) the forced resignation of Aalborg's mayor, (5) the Social Democratic "Dream Plan," (6) opposition to the bus stop by the Police Department and the Chamber of Industry and Commerce, and (7) structural changes in the national and international economies.

The "demise of the bus stop" thus comprises its own drama which illustrates the complexities of implementation decisions as well as their fragility, reciprocal dependence, the influence of timing and happenstance, and dependence on both actor-centered and structural conditions. Let us examine this complex set of factors.

As explained in Chapter 10, the integrated bus stop was first postponed, and thus did not make the first stage, due to the delay by North Jutland County in processing an application for environmental certification of the bus stop. North Jutland County claimed that it had a conflict of interest in the matter, but this came out only after the application had languished in county offices for six months. The case was thereafter sent to the Danish Environmental Protection Agency, where it was approved on the stipulation that various environmental improvement measures be implemented for reducing air and noise pollution caused by bus operations in Aalborg.

It now transpires, however, that the Environmental Protection Agency's decision is appealed to the Danish Environmental Appeals Board, one of the appellants being none other than the North Jutland (County) Transit Authority. The Transit Authority is uncertain regarding the "economic and administrative consequences [of] the Environmental Protection Agency's stipulations" and fears that the conditions attached to the approval certificate may harm the company's finances and its autonomy.[1] The Transit Authority fears, for example, that it may be required to have its buses modified so that they pollute less. Hence, they appeal to prevent extra costs and control. The appeal is successful, and the Environmental Appeals Board certifies the integrated bus stop "without special stipulations," that is, without requirements for special environmental improvement measures connected to the establishment of the bus stop.[2]

The decision of the Environmental Appeals Board is viewed with some surprise by both the Environmental Protection Agency in Copenhagen and by the staff of Aalborg's Technical Department. They do not believe that the concept "certification without special stipulations" exists, and they consider that the board's decision does not accord with existing environmental legislation. As an Environmental Protection Agency staff member puts it in an interview:

> The Environmental Appeals Board made the case completely ridiculous. A certification without conditions! You just *can't* do that. It doesn't exist. It's nonsense.[3]

Similar views come from Technical Department staff members, one of whom comments:

> The environmental approval we have received from the Environmental Appeals Board certainly isn't legal. Actually, you can't obtain an environmental approval without stipulations . . . I had several discussions with a staff member in the Environmental Protection Agency . . . He said that they would consider whether they should appeal [the Appeals Board's decision], or what the heck they should do. Because he didn't think that they can issue an environmental certificate without stipulations. If it was without stipulations, what is it they have certified, then? If you have approved it without stipulations, then the noise level can rise from 55 to 75 [decibels], right? And on this point he believed simply that in relation to the law, it could not be done. He said to me that for the moment they would discuss it internally [within the Environmental Protection Agency], and if they concluded that they would do something about it, then we would of course hear about it. As we have not heard anything, I guess they haven't done anything about it.

The Environmental Appeals Board's certification stands. It is issued one month into the trial period for the first stage of the Aalborg Project, and it is therefore given too late for the city and regional bus stop to be included in this stage as first planned. It is given early enough, however, for the bus stop to be included in a planned subsequent expansion of the first stage.

In the course of the Aalborg Project's trial period, the planned decline in automobile traffic on Vingaardsgade does not materialize. Traffic declines by only 14% instead of the planned 30–40%. The decline is not big enough to allow available space for the daily traffic of 1,150 city and regional buses the bus stop would serve.[4] The insufficient decline is hardly surprising. It is a direct consequence of the failure to establish the zone boundary for cars in the city center, which in turn allows drivers to enter and pass through the center via Vingaardsgade instead of using the ring roads. It becomes a kind of domino effect where the falling down of one brick in the project (the zone boundary) leads to the collapse of other pieces. If the integrated bus stop is established in this situation, one can expect conflict between buses and cars on Vingaardsgade and further controversies about the project. The question is whether the Technical Department is ready for such controversies.

The city engineer, for one, is not. Despite his change of attitude mentioned in Chapter 13, he still retains his old sense for avoiding unpleasantries. He is the first in the city administration to have second thoughts about the establishment of the bus stop. He thus informs both the chief planner for public transportation and the head of regional transportation for the North Jutland Transit Authority that he "is not 100% certain that [he] at the present time dare recommend the establishment of the integrated bus stop on Vingaardsgade."[5] For his part, Aalborg's chief planner for public transportation disagrees with the city engineer and is not prepared to abandon the bus stop. He informs the Technical Department of this.[6] However, the chief planner and his whole office and the Aalborg Bus Company no longer have the same strong political support or the same central organizational position they once had. Times changed rather abruptly for public transportation when Aalborg's influential Social Democratic mayor was forced to resign in connection with the "Aalborg scandal" (see Chap. 13). Until then, public transportation had been placed directly under the mayor, in Aalborg Municipality's central administration, and had been strongly supported by the mayor, also known by the nickname "Bus-Marius" because of his fondness for public transportation. Now public transportation has been moved to the more peripheral Fifth Department, containing the city's public utility companies. The Fifth Department is headed by an alderman from the Liberal party (*Venstre*) whom the chief planner for public transportation considers a "supermotorist" (*supermotorist*):[7]

> [This alderman's] basic attitude is that no restrictions should be placed on private cars. They should be able to drive wherever they want. This is the principal orientation for him.

The alderman for the Fifth Department is the same alderman who, during the controversy over the Social Democratic Dream Plan, wavered in his support of the Aalborg Project. Both public transportation and the Aalborg Project have much lower priority for him than for the former Social Democratic mayor and for the Conservative alderman for the Technical Department. In sum, then, both the organizational position of public transportation and its political support are considerably weakened. Public transportation in Aalborg no longer defines reality; it now simply reacts to it.

The political struggle over the Social Democratic Dream Plan discourages the Technical Department from again raising the issue of the Vingaardsgade integrated bus stop, for it is opposed by both the Social Democrats and the Chamber of Industry and Commerce. Now the Technical Department's lack of enthusiasm in pursuing the integrated bus stop is reinforced by the fact that the Aalborg Police Department also comes out against it. A police spokesman explains:

> We didn't really believe that Vingaardsgade in its present form was appropriate [as an integrated bus stop] . . . [We] would end up with more large buses down-

town, buses which in fact did not need to be there. So we insisted that the regional bus depot should be retained as the regional bus center.

This police official overestimates the role of the Police Department, however, when in the same interview he asserts, "It was certainly we who were behind the fact that [the integrated bus stop] did not materialize." The Police Department's opposition is but one of many factors which contribute to the bus stop ultimately being abandoned.

During the first four years of the Aalborg Project, public transportation had been a growth industry, and not just in Aalborg but throughout Denmark. Two-digit growth rates in expenditure and patronage were common during this period, as were three- and four-digit percentage increases in subsidies (see Chap. 2). The leading causes were two international oil crises, an economic recession with falling real income and stagnant sales of private cars, heavily increased taxes on gasoline, and new laws to strengthen public transportation. Now this growth period has drawn to a close. The economy has adjusted to the new situation, and a new conservative government is less willing to support public transportation. Subsidies are cut and utilization rates begin to decline.

These structural and socioeconomic changes also affect Aalborg. They erode the economic, political, and ideological will to continue investing in public transportation, including the investment in the integrated bus stop, already on shaky ground for the reasons cited above.

A NEW PROJECT PHILOSOPHY?

In a letter to the Public Utilities Department, Aalborg's city engineer and the Technical Department alderman summarize the problem of the integrated bus stop as they now see it:

> It was a prerequisite for the establishment of the integrated bus stop that the volume of automobile traffic be reduced by 30–40%; otherwise we would acquire operational problems . . . The recently gathered observations have shown that the volume of traffic on Vingaardsgade following the implementation of the first stage is of the same order as earlier. We therefore regret that it will not be possible to establish the integrated bus stop. It will be difficult—and perhaps not desirable either—to have the City Council approve the necessary additional restrictions so that the volume of traffic on Vingaardsgade can be reduced to the requisite level.[8]

The last paragraph explicitly reflects a changed attitude, not only as regards the integrated bus stop but about the entire Aalborg Project: the Technical Department had been arguing that a reduction of automobile traffic in down-town Aalborg was necessary in order to improve the environment and to improve the traffic conditions for pedestrians, bicyclists, and public transportation. The "additional restrictions" cited above are therefore not new; nor are they "additional." On the contrary, they are part of the original project. These restrictions, however, have been abandoned because of opposition to the project.

Abandoning the integrated bus stop and the change in attitude which it expresses thus mark a new situation for the Aalborg Project. It denotes a decisive turning point: the original rationality behind the project no longer has support in the Technical Department. The initial rationality has been turned completely on its head, such that the goal is now to avoid the very reduction in automobile traffic which was a purpose of the integrated bus stop in the first place. The Technical Department has apparently given up and has made the logic of the Chamber of Industry and Commerce, the Police Department, and the *Aalborg Stiftstidende* its own logic. The Aalborg Project now seems to be without effective institutional support.

Instead of the integrated bus stop on Vingaardsgade, the Technical Department proposes that transfer possibilities between city and regional buses be improved by having the westbound bus traffic in the city center use the city bus stop on Algade while eastbound buses use the existing bus stop in Vingaardsgade. This proposal is opposed, however, by both the Aalborg Planning Office for Public Transportation and by the North Jutland Transit Authority, presumably because "automobile traffic, especially through Algade, causes much too great a delay in the regional bus traffic."[9]

The story ends with the existing situation being maintained. No integrated bus stop for city and regional buses is established on Vingaardsgade, nor are the above-mentioned alternative transfer possibilities instituted. Instead, a change of the plaza in front of the Aalborg Bus Depot is planned, so that city buses passing the depot may stop at the plaza and thereby come into closer contact with the regional and suburban bus network and the railway station.[10] As mentioned in Chapter 14, this change is the outcome of negotiations between the Technical Department and the Social Democratic party as regards the party's Dream Plan, and they now become a new element in the eleventh version of the Aalborg Project.

"THE BASIC CONCERNS OF LIFE ITSELF"

After the decision is made, the Technical Department alderman seems satisfied that the integrated bus stop will not materialize. He explains in an interview:

Today I think that everyone says, "Well, the solution [the bus stop] will never come. It wouldn't be the right [solution] either." Those staff members who at that time were enthusiastic about the Vingaardsgade solution say this, too. I think that it has simply been accepted that the conditions for public transportation today . . . are adequate, and that one does not need to burden Vingaardsgade with the integrated bus stop . . . And I think that everyone will come and say, "Well, O.K., so we spared ourselves the debate we would have gotten if the [buses] were to be driving in both directions along Vingaardsgade and motorists had to drive in one [direction], from Vesterbro. And it is absolutely certain that even though all the transportation planners maintained that it would all work out, for myself—and for lots of people I talked with, including the police—there was a very strong fear that it would not come to function well.

While it is correct that staff and politicians no longer believe that the integrated bus stop will ever be realized, the alderman may be mistaken in assuming that his staff believe that this is the correct decision. The city engineer, who had had reservations about the timing of the bus stop, now recounts:

City engineer: I think that what is called the integrated bus stop on Vingaards-gade has been dropped. I think that it has been dropped forever. And I think that this is absolutely wrong . . . because I believe that the transfer possibility there is important. I also think that the fact that the passengers can get off at that location has a certain importance for business here in the town.

Interviewer: Isn't it just as good to obtain transfer possibilities at [the regional bus depot] as it is now planned?

City engineer: In my assessment, not at all. No. I think it has a certain immediate influence that one can get off in the center of town.

The head of the Planning Office for Public Transportation agrees with the city engineer but goes further in his assessment of the abandoning of the integrated bus stop:

The chief planner for public transportation: Here in the Municipality, the decision by the Environmental Appeals Board was interpreted to mean that there was no [legal] case regarding the environment. [The case] should never have been opened. This indicates that the legislation really does not cover these kinds of cases. It is a pity to find out afterwards that there was no case. Because in my judgment if we had [just gone ahead and] constructed the integrated bus stop in Vin-gaardsgade simultaneous with the implementation of the plan, then we would have been forced to retain the Algade closure and retain more of the important parts of the plan than we did.

Interviewer: So allowing some of the other measures to fall away would have been ruled out in that case?

Chief planner: Yes.

In this interpretation, which in my analysis is a realistic scenario, construction of the integrated city and regional bus stop—and the investment of municipal funds and prestige it would have entailed—would have forced the city to take serious measures to reduce automobile traffic on Vingaardsgade; otherwise the bus stop and the flow of cars in the street would have been unable to function. This, in turn, would have meant that the planned street closures on Nytorv and Danmarksgade, and with it the two-zone solution, could not have been abandoned as they were. Also, it would have made possible the closure of Algade to motor traffic and its conversion into a pedestrian and bicycle street. In this manner, construction of the integrated bus stop as part of the first stage might have helped the Aalborg Project achieve its declared goals. Instead, the actual course of events was a vicious circle: Nytorv and Danmarksgade were not closed to through-car traffic; the required reduction of traffic volume on Vingaardsgade did not occur; the bus stop predicated on this reduction—was not built; so Algade could not be closed; and the pedestrian and bicycle street not established even after permission to build the bus stop had been granted by the Environmental Appeals Board. It was too late. The dominos had fallen, one after the other.

Nietzsche teaches us not to "despise 'little' things," because they are "the basic concerns of life itself," here the life of the Aalborg Project.[11] With the reservations that apply to all retrospective explanations, we may conclude that the six months it took North Jutland County to declare itself in conflict of interest, followed by its refusal to decide about the integrated bus stop, may be the "'little' thing," the minor detail, with the great effect, that is, the first brick of the domino effect. Postponement of the integrated bus stop which followed from the county's delay made possible the vicious circle. Opposition, especially from the Aalborg Chamber of Industry and Commerce, the police, and the press, toward restrictions on automobile traffic thereafter set the dominos in motion. Perhaps the county's delay was meant as an act of revenge against the municipality for Aalborg's mayor having refused to grant the county supervisor's request to locate the city bus terminal at the bus depot and railway station. If so, the revenge of the county has been fully successful.

ACTION REQUIRES ILLUSION

The decision of the Environmental Appeals Board to approve the integrated bus stop at Vingaardsgade has consequences for the city bus terminal at Nytorv.

It will be recalled that the Nytorv terminal was approved by the Environmental Protection Agency on the condition that Aalborg Municipality implement several antipollution measures for bus operations (see Chap. 9). At the same time, the Environmental Protection Agency asked the North Jutland County Administration to assess the terminal's environmental impact after a year in order to determine whether additional environmental protection measures should be undertaken. After the approval of the integrated bus stop by the Appeals Board "without special stipulations," however, the North Jutland County Council concludes that there is a lack of congruence between the Environmental Appeals Board decision for the Vingaardsgade bus stop and the Environmental Protection Agency's recommendations regarding the Nytorv bus terminal. The County Council therefore concludes that there is no basis for assessing pollution at the city bus terminal.[12] Quality control of the project thereby collapses.

In the meantime, automobile traffic on Nytorv has become substantially greater than expected, partly because of the refusal of the Aalborg Police Department to enforce the "No Through Traffic" regulations at the bus terminal (see Chap. 12). Even without this additional traffic, projections for the bus terminal's environmental impact show that it approaches or exceeds various national and international pollution limits. This was the basis for the Environmental Protection Agency's reservations about the terminal and why it sought to exert controls on it via stipulations. And this was why the North Jutland Office for Public Health objected to the plans for the terminal. Quite simply, the terminal is regarded a health hazard. With the additional traffic through the terminal, the pollution is greater than originally estimated by the Environmental Protection Agency and by the Office for Public Health. The largest and single most important subproject in the Aalborg Project has thus been certified on a foundation which subsequently shows itself to have been false. From an environmental protection perspective, it is especially unfortunate that the quality control desired by the Environmental Protection Agency fails to materialize.

Again we are reminded of Nietzsche's dictum, "Knowledge kills action; action requires the veils of illusion."[13] Perhaps if knowledge about the actual consequences of the bus terminal at Nytorv had been accurate, the project would not have been certified in its present form. In this sense, one can view the terminal as a project which may have been implemented only because its consequences were not correctly predicted. This element of unpredictability is linked not to mere chance but to power, especially the power exercised by the Chamber of Industry and Commerce, the two corporations Dansk Supermarked and Salling, the Police Department, and the *Aalborg Stiftstidende*.

Sixteen

MYTHS DIE HARD

I suggested long ago that convictions might be more dangerous enemies of truth than lies. This time I should like to pose the decisive question: Is there any difference whatever between a lie and a conviction?

I call a lie: wanting *not* to see something one does see, wanting not to see something *as* one sees it . . . [D]esiring not to see as one sees, is virtually the primary condition for all who are in any sense *party:* the party man necessarily becomes a liar.

Friedrich Nietzsche

The Chamber of Industry and Commerce's main argument against the Aalborg Project is that it will lead to a decline in sales for the shops in downtown Aalborg. The "falling revenues" argument is repeated at formal and informal meetings with the Technical Department, in the press, in the Chamber's counterplan, at both orientation and voting sessions of the Aalborg City Council, and in letters from the Chamber to individual City Council members. The argument has had very real and drastic consequences: it has destroyed the original form of the Aalborg Project and has produced a hybrid in which negative effects are rampant.

A second argument against the Aalborg Project used by the Chamber was that the project would turn away the most important customer group, those in private cars. This argument, let us call it "the driver is most important," was undermined, however, by a shopping survey showing that each of the three main customer groups—motorists, nonautomotive shoppers, and those using public transportation—accounted for about one-third of the sales in the city center (see Chap. 10).[1] Even though the "driver is most important" argument is thus technically invalidated by the survey, the argument lives on as rhetoric within the Chamber of Industry and Commerce, a rhetoric with a definite objective. The argument still has *political* importance.

KILLING THE FALLING RETAIL SALES ARGUMENT

Immediately after the implementation of the Aalborg Project's first stage, while the Chamber of Industry and Commerce is employing the "falling 183

revenues" argument, the Technical Department decides to execute a second retail survey to test this argument as well.[2] Like its predecessor, this second survey is sparked primarily by the Chamber's opposition to the project. As justification for the survey, the Technical Department cites the following:

> Especially on the part of several businesspeople, it has been remarked that the traffic changes would produce a drop in retail sales in downtown Aalborg. As part of an analysis of the effect of the traffic plan's first stage, it has therefore been decided to conduct a survey . . .[3]

Retail sales in the quarter immediately following implementation of the first stage are compared to sales over the previous two years. The choice of survey periods—before and after implementation—is important. The period immediately following implementation is the point in the project's history where the Chamber of Industry and Commerce most intensively—and with the most far-reaching consequences for the project—asserts that sales in downtown Aalborg are declining (see Chaps. 11 and 12).[4] This point in time also turns out to be the absolute low point of a decade-long recession in the Danish economy. The year of implementation of the Aalborg Project, and the year previously, are the only years during this decade where personal consumption is declining in Denmark.[5] It is useful here to examine the Aalborg Project at both the actor and structural levels. The main actor, the Chamber of Industry and Commerce, claims a drop in sales "which exceeds the decline generated by the existing economic situation [the general recession]."[6] At the structural level, the Danish and international recession would also lead one to expect declining sales in downtown Aalborg, other things being equal. Thus, without the Technical Department being aware of it, the choice of survey period proves critical for the assessment of trends in sales: if the Chamber's assertion of declining sales due to the Aalborg Project cannot be supported for the period chosen, then it cannot be expected to hold generally.

This second survey, like its predecessor, shows the Chamber of Industry and Commerce to be incorrect: retail sales in downtown Aalborg rose 1.6% (fixed prices) during the survey period. This compares to a 2.1% national decline during the same period, yielding a relative increase for Aalborg of 3.7%. If one uses current instead of fixed prices, that is, if one does not adjust for inflation, downtown Aalborg experiences an increase in sales of 19.5% during the survey period. Aalborg's merchants, therefore, are not affected by Denmark's general economic downturn. On the contrary, they are experiencing an upswing. The "falling revenues" argument is fallacious.

If one divides sales into the categories "groceries" (*dagligvarer*) and "specialty goods" (*udvalgsvarer*), it appears that sales of specialty goods have risen by

3.2% in downtown Aalborg versus a national decline of 6.9% (fixed prices). This corresponds to a relative increase in sales of specialty goods in Aalborg of 10.1%. In current prices the increase in specialty goods sales reaches 20%. It is especially interesting that sales of specialty goods show greater increases than other goods, inasmuch as the Chamber of Industry and Commerce has repeatedly claimed that the Aalborg Project would be especially hard on precisely these types of goods, which are purchased by a larger proportion of customers driving their own cars.

If the specialty goods sector is further subdivided into "textiles" (*tekstilvarer*) and "genuine specialty goods" (*egentlige udvalgsvarer*), one finds some justification for the Chamber's assertions of a decline in sales. Hence, the total 3.2% increase in specialty goods sales consists of an increase in the sale of textile goods of 7.1% coupled with a 3.2% decline in earnings from genuine specialty goods (fixed prices). For Denmark as a whole, however, sales of genuine specialty goods declined by a much steeper 11.2% (fixed prices), yielding a relative increase for downtown Aalborg of 8%. Measured in current prices, downtown Aalborg experienced a 20.3% increase in sales of genuine specialty goods.

A division of the downtown area into districts further indicates that the eastern zone, with its concentration of shops around the Nytorv bus terminal and the bus street running under the Civic Center, has experienced a slight increase in the share of total sales, from 59.2% to 60.3%.

In relation to the Aalborg Project, the increase in earnings experienced by Aalborg's downtown shops can be interpreted in at least two ways. First, it may be seen to confirm the conclusion that the "have-your-cake-and-eat-it-too" strategy of the Chamber of Industry and Commerce has succeeded: the Chamber seems to have succeeded in transforming the actually implemented project so that the customer base derived from nonautomotive and public transportation increases, while simultaneously maintaining those customers who drive their own cars.

Second, it can be concluded that implementation of the initially conceived project, in which improvements for nonautomotive and public transportation were offset by restrictions on automobile traffic, would most likely have had either no effect or a positive effect on sales. The statistics quoted above indicate that any loss of customers driving cars caused by the original project could have been offset, or more than offset, by increases in sales from customers using bikes or public transportation.

There is no evidence to support the claim made by the Chamber of Industry and Commerce that the original project would have had catastrophic consequences for retail sales. This conclusion accords with the experiences of other towns where similar projects have been implemented.[7]

"THE CITY *HAS* BECOME BETTER"

The fact that Aalborg's merchants claim declining sales, while the real figures show just the opposite, is probably linked to the national economic recession already mentioned. Both private consumption and investments were falling in real terms. Economic instability led to political instability: Denmark's Social Democratic minority government collapsed and was replaced by a center-right coalition just when the Aalborg Project was being implemented. The national and local press, radio, and television brought daily reports, analyses, and doomsday assessments about the sorry state of Denmark's economy. For example, there was much rhetoric of the Danish economy's road toward "the abyss" (*afgrunden*) during this period.[8]

With hands-on knowledge from their own cash registers, one might have expected Aalborg's merchants to realize that the national decline in private consumption did not apply to Aalborg, that they, in fact, found themselves on an "island of progress." Yet this was apparently not the case. The local merchants paid more attention to the media than to their own sales figures. Or they were simply invoking the general economic downturn against the Aalborg Project.

Had the ratification and implementation for the Aalborg Project not overlapped with the most depressed years of Denmark's decade-long recession, the Aalborg Chamber of Industry and Commerce might have been less negative toward the project, or their arguments would have carried less weight. The project then may have been implemented more in accord with its original intentions. Here again we see how a social and structural conjuncture of the economy is transformed by a main actor into a factor of significance for the Aalborg Project. And again we see how coincidence, or bad luck, can be as significant in determining outcome as other factors.

The Technical Department concludes its retail survey in now characteristically cautious style:

> On the basis of this survey there exist no grounds to conclude anything regarding the extent to which the traffic regulations during the first stage have influenced the above-mentioned changes in retail trade in downtown Aalborg. Retail trade in downtown Aalborg has done well . . . especially in comparison with trends in the country as a whole. Downtown Aalborg therefore continues to be a main regional center for retail trade, especially as regards branches such as textiles and other specialty goods; this is a result of, dependent on, or despite the first stage traffic regulations.[9]

The Chamber of Industry and Commerce, the press, and the public receive the potentially very provocative results of this newest retail trade survey with near-complete silence. The survey's significance is consciously underplayed and underpublicized by the Technical Department, and this second survey does not attain the same immediate political attention as the previous study. Nevertheless, the survey is important for understanding the changing attitude of the Chamber of Industry and Commerce toward the Aalborg Project.

The Technical Department chooses not to publish and not to publicize the results of the survey. The survey is not even printed up as a genuine report, as was the previous study. Instead, the results are written up as a short memorandum which circulates internally within the Technical Department, and the memo is sent to the Chamber of Industry and Commerce. It is also sent to the press, but apparently not until two-and-a-half months later and only after the City Council has finally ratified the Aalborg Project.[10]

The Technical Department is relying once again on its "stroking strategy," this time stroking the Chamber of Industry and Commerce and the press. It is the same strategy that was used with the Social Democratic party, when it was decided not to publish the department's devastating assessment of the Social Democrats' Dream Plan (see Chap. 14). After five years of stormy existence, in which the Aalborg Project's very survival has been at stake several times, the Technical Department does not wish to embarrass anyone or create more trouble. The continually revised project is starting to gain some acceptance.

Evidence as to how the retail trade survey is received and viewed by the Chamber of Industry and Commerce exists in interviews and in the Chamber Archives. According to the Chamber's Retailer Committee,

> An increased market share in our trade area together with significant tourist trade from our neighboring countries of Norway, Sweden, and West Germany have meant that retail sales in downtown Aalborg had a greater growth [during the survey period] compared with the national average. This is demonstrated in a newly published report by the municipality on the effects of the first stage [of the Aalborg Project], which had just begun to take effect at this time on a trial basis. The [Chamber's Retailer] Committee and the Technical Department can both look with satisfaction at the positive trends, especially for sales of specialty goods in the downtown area, and now that the first stage has been ratified by the City Council, taking into consideration some of the changes which we proposed . . . we hope that we can also contribute positively to future changes in the traffic and city plan.[11]

The Retailer Committee's presentation of the Technical Department's survey memorandum is not only equivocal but also incorrect. The Technical Department's survey says nothing about the city center's "market share in our trade area" nor about the extent of "tourist trade from our neighboring countries." It is not true that the survey "demonstrates" that an "increased market share" and "significant tourist trade" "have meant" greater growth in retail trade in downtown Aalborg. Also, no other studies exist which document these claims. The Chamber of Industry and Commerce again attempts to define a reality from preconceived notions, which are now ascribed to the Technical Department, as if this reality derived from factual documentation produced by the department.

Moreover, in relation to the actual course of events, it is manipulation to say that "both [can] look with satisfaction" and that the Chamber hopes that it "can also contribute positively to future changes in the traffic and city plan." The impression conferred upon the reader is that the Aalborg Project has been executed as a cooperative endeavor between the Chamber of Industry and Commerce and the Technical Department, which is correct for certain phases of the project but certainly not for the period and for those changes mentioned in the Chamber's report. Here the situation was characterized by open, antagonistic power struggle between the two parties.

Why does the Chamber of Industry and Commerce make creative additions to the Technical Department's survey and falsify its presentation of it? And why are conflicts manipulated and covered over with doubletalk and overconfident inanities? The Chamber is trying not to lose face and therefore feels it necessary to find causes for the increase in sales earnings which have not been formulated in terms of the Aalborg Project. That the claimed explanations are rationalizations created out of thin air apparently means little. On the other hand, the Chamber cannot continue its confrontational strategy toward the Aalborg Project. After all, it has gradually obtained changes in nearly all the project's main elements. And with the survey, if not before, it is becoming clear to the Chamber that the project has not had the negative consequences they said it would have. How should a 10% increase in sales of specialty goods, in the context of a national decline, be possible if the project was supposed to have all the negative consequences previously claimed? Hence the Chamber's effort to take the edges off previous conflicts. The Chamber of Industry and Commerce continues to present to the outside a harmonious image of consensus. This is perhaps especially important in connection with the Chamber's general assembly, where the report quoted will be presented, and where the invited guests will traditionally include Aalborg's mayor, the alderman for the Technical Department, the city engineer, and the chief of city planning.

This interpretation of the Chamber's motives is supported by my interviews with the chairmen of the Chamber and its City Center Committee. The latter explains:

Interviewer: How does it happen that you people [from the Chamber] go to the municipality and say that your sales are dropping because of the project, while sales are in fact increasing? . . .

Chairman of the Chamber's City Center Committee: The city *has* become better. It *has* become better to get around in. We had various things changed, and the fact that so much is being invested in the downtown area also makes it attractive to come there, and this means an improvement in the flow of customers. Absolutely. But the change occurs after we get [Algade and Nytorv Square] opened up [to car traffic], together with all this attention focused on the opening of the bus terminal. This certainly has an influence, too.

Interviewer: Do you think that sales increase because you succeed in getting Algade and Nytorv reopened?

City Center Committee chairman: . . . The investment [in the Aalborg Project] seen as a whole has perhaps been more important than the opening of the streets, but [the opening of Algade and Nytorv] at least contributed to the Christmas sales also being salvaged. An argument which I also need to use, of course.

OVERINTERPRETATION AS WEAPON

Why does the chairman of the City Center committee feel the "need to" argue that the reopening of Algade and Nytorv have helped increase retail sales? Because the Chamber of Industry and Commerce, and especially the chairman of its City Center Committee, have personally invested so much time, energy, prestige, and power in pressuring the Technical Department, the City Council politicians, the press, and the public that they would lose face if they did not emphasize their role.

In a response to this interpretation, and to my claim that the Chamber of Industry and Commerce manipulated and falsified the Technical Department survey, the chairman of the Chamber's Retailer Committee commented:

> I am entirely in agreement with your assessment. There was a conscious over-interpretation on my part, especially with reference to market shares and tourism. I wanted to create a positive atmosphere, first because if during the recession we did not appear successful in all areas, then we—Aalborg and the retailers, for whom I was chairman—would be no better than the others, i.e., the rest of North Jutland and especially ["City South," a large shopping center just south of Aalborg and the city's major competitor for customers]. Second, tourism was not accepted as an economic factor and as having developmental potential at that time. The retail sector, the politicians, and industry viewed tourism as an inferior mom-and-kids occupation [*kone-børn erhverv*]. The Aal-

borg Shipyard had not yet been closed, but in the overinterpretation I wanted to call attention to the fact that it was precisely we here in North Jutland who had to exploit tourism. Finally, as newly elected chairman of the Retailer Committee and member of the board of the Chamber of Industry and Commerce, I promised myself and others to create a "city association" [*cityforening,* a merchants' association]. To do this I needed to strengthen the self-esteem and heighten awareness of Aalborg City's [i.e., downtown's] function for all of North Jutland. Otherwise we would lose to "City South." This is why I made the overinterpretation, and I believed that the future would prove me right.[12]

The logic, here and elsewhere in the Aalborg Project, seems to be that if you want the future to prove you right—or want a future that is right for you—then it is perfectly acceptable to "overinterpret" the present.

The chairman of the Chamber, who is not a retailer himself but runs a manufacturing company, provides the following assessment of the retail survey:

Chairman of the Chamber of Industry and Commerce: It has perhaps been a somewhat weak point among us that the statements we have made with reference to sales declining or rising are based on statements from various merchants. I will not say that they are incorrect, but one can perhaps get the idea that they are somewhat colored by the situation.

Interviewer: Do you mean an underestimate?

Chairman: Perhaps an underestimate, yes. When one then has the view [that restricting auto traffic will harm sales], then you perhaps evaluate it in a more distorted way. I will certainly admit to that. And it is also true, and it is something which I am often upset about in all this debate—especially when one talks with retailers—that it is all very passionate, very emotional.

Interviewer: Does one not have to be objective when running a store or a business?

Chairman: Yes, but it isn't that. It is the changes you are afraid of. You are afraid of *the changes.* You are afraid that they will affect your company. Afterwards it turns out that they just don't. But in the period where you don't know, you are uncertain.

Interviewer: One might still think that people who run businesses are used to looking into the future and evaluating what might come along, and take account of it when they invest, hire personnel, etc. Can't this be transferred to other things than business? City planning problems, for example?

Chairman: Yes, that's right. Yes. We have a mother organization called the Provincial Chamber of Commerce [*Provinshandelskammeret*], and I would certainly say we ought to have some more help from there, someone from the organization who comes and says, "Trends are heading in this and that direction, and now you shouldn't be so afraid of this." I mean, one might be able to get some support from a mother organization with *professionals*. And we haven't gotten any [support]. I have to admit this. In this we have stood completely alone. And remember, none of us are city planners.

The chairman of the Chamber of Industry and Commerce touches on two factors relevant to our understanding of the Chamber's role in Aalborg politics: the retailers' conservatism, and their apparent ignorance about actual developments. Modern political history has given us innumerable examples whereby ideological conservatism, sheer ignorance, and an excessive concentration of power can form an unfortunate, if not a tragic, constellation. This, too, is the situation in the case of the Aalborg Project.

THE AALBORG PROJECT, VERSION 11.0

Following the collapse of the Social Democratic Dream Plan, the demise of the integrated bus stop on Vingaardsgade, and the retail survey's demonstration that the Aalborg Project has not led to declining sales, enough barriers to implementation are again cleared so that the Technical Department dares to send the project to a vote in the City Council. After five years of repeated revisions, the *eleventh version* of the project is finally approved by a large majority, again including the Social Democratic council members. The Liberals, whose support had been uncertain, also cast their vote in favor of the project.

The project's first stage—there is no more mention of any second and third stage—thus acquires the following features: (1) the bus terminal at Nytorv remains as already constructed; (2) the integrated bus stop at Vingaardsgade is abandoned as an element in the first stage, the downtown city and regional bus networks remain unchanged, and transfer possibilities between the city and regional buses at the bus depot will be improved; (3) bicycle lanes on Vesterbro will be replaced by genuine asphalted bicycle paths with raised curbs; (4) the east–west bike path on Østerbro-Borgergade-Kastetvej will be constructed as planned; (5) a reduced speed zone [*stillevej*] will be constructed on Danmarksgade; (6) the western part of Algade will remain open to automobile traffic, the pedestrian and bicycle street is dropped; (7) the western part of Nytorv, including the bus terminal, will remain open to automobile traffic; (8) the closing of Østeraagade's opening toward Slotspladsen Square is retained as a temporary barrier but is given an "aesthetically more satisfactory form."[13]

A representative from the Social Democrats publicly explains his party's change of mind: "We in the Social Democratic Party have had to acknowledge that our otherwise so excellent traffic plan is surpassed by this one. The alderman's proposal is better."[14] The alderman for the Technical Department cautiously adds: "This is only the first stage, but when it will be followed up, about that I dare not promise anything."[15] With this version of the Aalborg Project, a consensus project seems finally to have been achieved.

RATIONALITY NEEDS STABILITY

The Technical Department's "stroking strategy" is central to the consensus that has now been reached regarding the Aalborg Project. Let us therefore examine this strategy. The "stroking" has been used in several instances: for instance, when Aalborg's chief of city planning declined to publish his article criticizing the Chamber of Industry and Commerce, when the Technical Department declined to publish its critique of the Social Democrats' Dream Plan, and when the department declined to publish the results of the study disproving the Chamber's claim of falling retail sales.

On first sight one might see the stroking strategy as a sign of weakness in the Technical Department. In the struggle over the Aalborg Project, the Technical Department apparently dares not pressure its opponents, even when the facts would seem to support the Technical Department's position. One might conclude that passivity by the Technical Department is one explanation why the implemented version of the Aalborg Project is just a faint reflection of the original project eleven versions earlier.

A more detailed examination of the relations between rationality and power in the project, however, shows that whenever struggle over the project evolved into confrontation, it was the Technical Department and its project that lost. Let us see why, but let us first point out that given this fact it is understandable that the Technical Department has consciously sought to avoid conflicts and escalation into confrontations, and that they see an advantage in acting conciliatory even toward those opponents whose goal it is to undermine the Technical Department's position.

Apparently the Technical Department took a bit of time to learn that conflict is a losing strategy. During the project's early years, the department was less concerned about conflict and the consequences of escalation. The turning point came when the Technical Department lost the direct confrontation with the Chamber of Industry and Commerce regarding the reduction of automobile traffic in the city center. After that point, the Technical Department alderman began cooperating with the Chamber even after having publicly declared that he would no longer do so. Forcing people to change their minds is partly what power is about.

The Technical Department learned from bitter experience that it can better achieve its goal via stable power relations than by open antagonistic confrontations. The level of information is typically higher in a stable relation than in a confrontation, and actions decided by consensual agreement are more likely to be implemented than those measures on which there is open disagreement. Finally, open confrontations use up more resources, are often experienced as unpleasant, and tend to delay, if not kill off, other activities.

It should be added, however, that the implicated parties will be very differently positioned with respect to benefiting from stability and confrontation. The Chamber of Industry and Commerce, being a privately operated interest organization, has much more freedom than the Technical Department to exploit confrontations; for example, overt politicization, pulling strings, making undocumented assertions, manipulation of facts, outright lying, using the press, personal letters to key persons, drawing on outside parties to use their muscle—these are all part of the arsenal of private interest organizations. They are accountable only to their members, not to the public interest as such.

In a formal sense, the Technical Department is, or should be, the institutionalization of the public interest, including the rules of democratic behavior and rational argument, technically and legally. The scope for the Technical Department to make use of confrontational behavior is therefore much more limited. Whenever confrontation between the two parties had built up, the prime mover was invariably the Chamber of Industry and Commerce. And during the one instance of open confrontation between the two, it was the Chamber which took the step that triggered confrontation and won by doing so. Compared to a powerful private interest organization like the Chamber, the Technical Department's "arsenal" is limited so that it must achieve its results within the framework of stable power relations. As mentioned earlier, professional arguments carry weight particularly in those situations characterized by negotiation and consensus seeking. It is in such situations that professional argument can contribute to the creation of a common framework of understanding. The Technical Department, being the institutional embodiment of professional argument, therefore has an interest in seeing problems and decisions defined and maintained within the framework of stable power relations; hence, the reliance on the conciliatory "stroking strategy."

This difference between the Chamber and the Technical Department in their ability to benefit from stability and confrontation exemplifies a generally unequal relation between rationality and power—and between formal politics and *Realpolitik*. In such unequal situations, formal rational argument tends to have the weaker position, and this weakness cannot be overcome by utilizing the methods of *Realpolitik* and confrontation. This does not mean that one must passively accept this inequality or the status quo. Rather, it means that if one wishes to expand and straighten the field of stable power relations and of rationality, then one must rely on strategies that can limit the use of confrontational behavior.

Stable power relations leave space for the power of rationality, that is, the force of the better argument making an impact. Antagonistic confrontations, on the other hand, are dominated by the rationality of power. If we seek to maintain rational discourse, it is therefore crucial that power relations be controlled. Without such control power relations evolve into antagonistic confrontations and open power struggles. It is this project of control which is central to both modernity and to modern rationality itself, a project of control currently exemplified by Jürgen Habermas's work on "communicative rationality" and "discourse ethics."[16] One may speculate that maintaining the power of rationality in society can only occur where confrontation and pure power play are restricted. If this is the case, rationality can be viewed as a relatively fragile entity—and as we have seen in Chapter 8, also as a historically young entity. To the extent that the power of rationality is to be ensured in society—at local, national, or international levels—it must be secured by developing strategies and tactics capable of limiting the raw exercise of power.

Seventeen

EXIT THE INNOVATORS

> [K]ingdoms which depend on the virtue of one man do not last long,
> because they lose their virtue when his life is spent.
>
> *Niccolò Machiavelli*

For the first time in four years, the situation around the Aalborg Project is calm. Having survived the stages of genesis, design, political discussion, approval, trial implementation, conflict, power struggle, stalemates, and repeated modifications, the project again moves toward implementation. The work again settles down to detailed planning, drafting, and execution of the individual subprojects within the total project.

"WE LEARN, TOO, YOU KNOW"

Over the next two years the most important subprojects will consist of the following: (1) construction of bicycle paths on the southern part of Vesterbro (the north-south route), (2) drafting proposals for the east-west bicycle paths on Borgergade and Ved Stranden streets, (3) conversion and beautification of Gåsepigetorvet Square at Vesterbro, (4) improving the roadblock at the end of Østeraagade at Slotspladsen Square, (5) conversion of Danmarksgade to a reduced-speed zone (*stillevej*) with narrow lanes and speed bumps, (6) planning for the rebuilding of the railroad station plaza (John F. Kennedy Square).

On Vesterbro, bicycle paths are constructed along the Vingaardsgade–Østre Allé section. Several analyses of traffic accidents have pointed to Vesterbro as an especially hazardous street, and it is accorded first priority in the policies designed to reduce accidents.[1] It is worth noting that the changes on Vesterbro were originally planned as part of the Aalborg Project's second stage. In this sense, the second stage has now begun, even though the first stage is not yet completed, and even though no one actually speaks of the Vesterbro bike path project as part of a second stage, or of any second stage at all for that matter. Having been "burned" once, a member of the project's Task Force explains, "We do not operate with the concept of 'second stage' anymore."[2]

That the alterations on Vesterbro proceed relatively quickly reflects the fact that the Technical Department, the Chamber of Industry and Commerce, the Vesterbro Street Association, the Danish Cyclist Federation, and a majority in Aalborg City Council are now supporting these changes, despite scattered protests.[3] As we have seen on several occasions, those aspects of the project not opposed by the business community proceed rapidly. And in this case the merchants are active supporters, since Vesterbro has gradually become so heavy with traffic that it is considered to be adversely affecting sales on the street. The chairman of the City Center Committee under the Chamber of Industry and Commerce explains:

> We realize that if Vesterbro is not altered, then Vesterbro will die. There is no one in the City Center Committee of the Chamber of Industry and Commerce who does not realize this.

Similar remarks come from the chairman of the Chamber:

> Vesterbro is not at all the shopping street it used to be because people race right through it. It is possible that narrowing the street [due to the building of bicycle paths and environmental measures] can mean that we get a more sensible shopping environment up there. In any case, the people involved in it sure hope so.

In the meantime, the Technical Department decides that the remaining section of the north-south bicycle route through downtown Aalborg, that is, the stretch of road from Vingaardsgade to the Limfjord Bridge, will be built immediately after the completion of the first section of the route, thus achieving one of the main goals of the total project. Nevertheless, this does not happen. The north-south bicycle route remains unfinished on the most narrow stretch of the road where most accidents involving cyclists take place. The political will to help bicyclists by reducing the capacity for cars does not materialize until nearly a decade and a half later.

The status of the project's second main element for nondrivers, the east-west bike route, resembles that of Vesterbro. Toward the east, the route is laid out by building paths on Nytorv and Østerbro; toward the west, paths are built on the western part of Borgergade and Kastetvej. These two sections, however, are not connected to each other as planned. Missing are 200 heavily traveled meters at Borgergade-Grotumsgade-Ved Stranden, what comes to be known in Danish as the "*missing link.*" According to the version of the Aalborg Project approved by the City Council, Borgergade will become a one-way street on this stretch of road. Because of the broad opposition to the project as a whole and particularly to restrictions on cars, however, the Technical Department conveniently "forgets" about the one-way construction. This causes problems with obtaining the necessary physical space for the bicycle paths. The Technical Department works out a draft proposal with bicycle paths and two-way car traffic and expects that the paths will be built in the near future. However, a decade will pass before construction begins.

As for the square on Vesterbro, *Gåsepigetorvet,* it is redesigned and reconstructed as part of environmental improvements and aesthetic changes on Vesterbro. There had originally been no plans to reconstruct Gåsepigetorvet before building the bicycle paths on Vesterbro. The order of priorities has changed, however, and it is the general view among Technical Department personnel that this change in priorities is linked to the City Council elections taking place during this stage of the Aalborg Project. A planning staff member comments on the Gåsepigetorv project:

> Gåsepigetorvet is one of those things which are moved toward the top [of the agenda], and because the [Technical] Department had to save money, the bike paths on Vesterbro were postponed . . . The money is then used to construct Gåsepigetorvet instead of additional meters of bike paths. And this is connected to the fact that there is an election [to the City Council]. Such a square looks nice . . . It is awfully regrettable, I think, but you know, it's all political. [Constructing a square] produces a few more votes than some bike paths. The alderman himself admitted this when I asked why.

The reconstruction of Gåsepigetorvet Square is finished just prior to the City Council elections.

As for the improvement of the barrier where Østeraagade terminates at Slotspladsen Square, the City Council's approved version of the Aalborg Project states that the barrier should be maintained only temporarily but should be given an "aesthetically speaking more satisfactory form."[4] In other words, the unsightly temporary concrete and plank barrier closing the street to cars, used for the past two years, should be made to look nicer. On closer examination, however, it appears that something more than aesthetics lies behind this decision.

In the original project, the Technical Department had proposed that the closing of Østeraagade toward Slotspladsen be made permanent. That it instead remained temporary and approved as such by the City Council is due to the face-saving concession made by the Technical Department to the Social Democratic party in connection with the negotiations on the party's Dream Plan (see Chap. 14). The Technical Department staff, however, does not want to see a reopening of Østeraagade toward Slotspladsen because it is the last remaining street closing of those originally planned for downtown Aalborg, and because a reopening, they believe, would generate more automobile traffic in the city center and especially through the bus terminal at Nytorv and Østeraagade. The Technical Department therefore utilizes a "sunk-cost" strategy: they make sure that so many additional costs are tied to the temporary street closing that it would be too expensive and look bad to reopen it. The associated waste of resources would give a bad image to the municipality.

The "aesthetically speaking more satisfactory form" measure is the first step in the "sunk-cost" strategy. More than a half million kroner are now used to beautify this temporary closing.[5] The second step consists of installing traffic lights at the Ved Stranden intersection close to Østeraagade. This traffic signal cannot be used and must therefore be taken down again if the closing of Østeraagade is not maintained. A Task Force member explains this use of aesthetics and technics as politics:

Task Force member: I was the one who made the change [in the Project] so that the [closing of Østeraagade toward Slotspladsen] would obtain an aesthetically speaking better form. And this is what it has gotten now . . . It is temporary, but it looks very permanent to most people. So there are not many who think of what is down there as being a temporary closing . . .

Interviewer: How much money did you receive to carry out this aesthetic improvement?

Task Force member: Oh God! That's a sensitive point. No money was allocated, of course, because it came on top of something else. I think that 100,000 kroner was allocated, and this was not enough at all. I can't remember it anymore. [The actual cost was 562,000 kroner].[6] But the design work alone was fantastically expensive because it was discussed down to every detail.

Interviewer: Was it a strategic maneuver on your part to make [the street closing] as permanent as possible?

Task Force member: Yes, you might call it that . . .

Interviewer: Do you think that Østeraagade will ever be reopened?

Task Force member: I don't really think so, and I can tell a story which says something about this. Each year we make a list of priorities for building traffic signals [and] the analysis showed that the intersection we call "Three Times Ved Stranden" [the T-intersection Ved Stranden-Ved Stranden] . . . ought to be regulated by a traffic light. And so I proposed this in the Technical Committee . . . But in order to propose it, we wanted to be reasonably sure that the temporary closing would last for at least a certain number of years. For if it was reopened again in two years, then the money [spent on the traffic lights] would be largely wasted. And there were many people in the Technical Committee who got hot under the collar that it was proposed in this way. How could the Technical Department staff return the ball like this? But we maintained that we would not install a traffic signal [without the certainty that Østeraagade was not reopened in the near future] . . . So this thing with it being temporary, it can last for a long time, of course.

The Chamber of Industry and Commerce was originally opposed to the closing of Østeraagade at Slotspladsen. The closing had long been one of the elements in the project which was highest on the Chamber's "wish list" of measures they wanted changed. For example, the closing was one of three street closings they sought to reopen, when two years previously, together with the firms of Salling and Dansk Supermarked, they put pressure on the Technical Department to change the implemented first stage of the Aalborg Project. The two other closed streets—Nytorv west and Algade west—were reopened, but Østeraagade remained closed (see Chap. 11). The Chamber now seems to have come to terms with the closing of Østeraagade and does not seek any change. The chairman of the Chamber's City Center Committee comments:

> We would have liked to have avoided the closing of the exit [from Østeraagade to Slotspladsen], but today I must say that it functions reasonably well, and it has certainly reduced the traffic so much that we can perhaps avoid a total closure of Østeraagade. And this is better. We learn, too, you know, and the solution which has been found functions reasonably well. We also agree that unnecessary traffic should not drive through [downtown]. And then we have gotten the parking spaces [at the end of Østeraagade] and we have gotten a few trees and things like that.

It is worth noting that the "aesthetically speaking more satisfactory" street closure also includes parking spaces camouflaged with trees and bushes, that is, "green" parking spaces. For keeping Østeraagade closed, the parking spaces are an ingenious—and hardly coincidental—move on the part of the Technical Department. The business community loves parking spaces, and with this move the Technical Department has tried to insure against Østeraagade being reopened. Apparently, the Technical Department is now practicing the form of tactical implementation formerly lacking in the Aalborg Project. In any case, the "aesthetically more satisfactory" closing of Østeraagade appears to be permanent.

Compared to the first four subprojects, work proceeds more slowly with the reduced-speed zone on Danmarksgade and the conversion of the railroad station plaza. The reduced-speed zone on Danmarksgade is drafted without the originally planned closing to automobile traffic, but the actual implementation of the project is postponed for several years, possibly because a majority of the shop owners on the street are against the project, and because the Technical Department and the Fifth Department (public transportation) cannot agree on the physical form of the bumps, locks, and other speed-reducing devices.[7] In connection with district heating repairs on the street, a speed-reducing zone is implemented on part of the street five years later.[8]

The rebuilding of John F. Kennedy Square, as mentioned earlier, was not part of the original Aalborg Project but emerged later as part of the negotiations between the Technical Department and the Social Democratic City Council Group. The alderman for the Technical Department, however, has reservations about this new element in the project, and it is therefore not promoted in the political-administrative system. Aalborg's city engineer explains:

> [O]ur alderman is somewhat reserved. I will not say that he is against it, but he is reserved in the sense that it's not absolutely necessary, traffic-wise that [the rebuilding of John F. Kennedy Square] take place. In spite of everything the traffic still moves. And then he goes over there and says that the population does not desire a rebuilding of the square. Therefore we must not proceed too quickly.

Hence, the work with John F. Kennedy Square does not yet produce any actual changes in Aalborg's townscape, despite comprehensive planning work and an exhibition showing how the changes could be implemented in practice. Not until a decade later is this project revived and finally implemented.

THE BUSSINESS COMMUNITY COMES AROUND

At the same time as the Technical Department is concentrating on individual subprojects in the Aalborg Project, Aalborg's business community now shows itself, for the first time, to begin to accept the project's basic idea: that improvements in the environment and in traffic safety can become an asset for downtown Aalborg, despite limitations on drivers' freedom of movement.

We have already discussed the changes on Vesterbro and on Gåsepigetorvet, where a merchants group, the Vesterbro Street Association (*Vesterbro Gadeforening*) expresses the following wishes the year before Vesterbro and Gåsepigetorvet are remodeled:

> The Vesterbro Street Association supports the establishment of bicycle paths on both sides of Vesterbro street . . . We also seek the establishment of a pedestrian crossing on Vesterbro . . . We want to see trees planted along the road or something like that in order to make the street more attractive to move in and thereby

emphasize Vesterbro as a shopping street [rather than just a thoroughfare] . . . We would like to see a bus stop established on Vesterbro at Bispensgade . . . Gåsepigetorvet should be beautified. In this connection we can also underline the replacement of the existing hot-dog stand with one which is more attractive . . . [Vesterbro Street Association] proposes that there be an open-air produce market once a week at the site of the old bus station [at Vesterbro and Stengade].[9]

The list of requests could have been taken directly from the Technical Department's set of "Proposals for the Restructuring of Vesterbro" published four years previously.[10] With the emphasis on environment and nondriving road users, the list expresses the same priorities as those which lay behind the original Aalborg Project.

Similarly, six months after the Vesterbro merchants, the shopkeepers of the Boulevarden Street Association present their desire to convert Boulevarden into a "real" boulevard with trees, as the street originally appeared, before a previous generation of city and traffic planners demolished them:

> The Boulevarden Street Association appeals to [the Technical Department alderman] to seriously consider the plans to recreate a "real" boulevard with trees, also because Boulevarden is Aalborg's face to outsiders who come to the town by train. We believe that Boulevarden ought to be recreated like it was before, when the street had trees along the roadside—trees brutally felled in connection with the installation of pipes and cables in the street . . . The name "Boulevard" itself inspires us to make it green and charming, and we would also like to propose that benches be placed on the sidewalks and parking places between the trees . . . We of the Boulevard Street Association will work so that the plans to make Boulevarden more beautiful do not become postponed far into an uncertain future— we believe that the Boulevard ought to have its new image simultaneously with the completion of the projects at each end of the Boulevard . . .[11]

The "projects at each end of the Boulevard" are the conversion of John F. Kennedy Square mentioned above as well as the conversion of Østeraagade as part of the bus terminal at Nytorv-Østeraagade. These projects, as mentioned, were not implemented until many years later, whereas trees were planted on a part of the boulevard before that.

As a third and more surprising example of the business community's increasing interest in environmental improvements, the pedestrian mall and bicycle street in the western part of Algade—once part of the original Aalborg Project but abandoned due to massive pressure from the Chamber of Industry and Commerce—is now proposed to be reintroduced by the businessmen on

Algade and by the Vesterbro Street Association; and the proposal is now supported by none other than the Chamber of Industry and Commerce. At the
same time, the shopkeepers propose that there be established yet another
pedestrian mall on Jens Bangs Gade.[12]

Whereas the Technical Department has grown accustomed to hearing the
businessmen complain of being overlooked by planners, administrators, and
politicians and their numerous pedestrian projects, bicycle paths, and other
measures for nondriving road users, the retailers now argue quite the reverse.
In a letter to the Technical Department, a group of Algade merchants implores
the alderman, "Let Aalborg center be for the businessmen [not cars]. Build another pedestrian mall—ALGADE" (emphasis in original).[13]

As justification for a new pedestrian mall, the shopkeepers provide the following argument:

> Aalborg center is being pulled eastwards (toward the Civic Center), where there
> are many pedestrian malls. Algade . . . is beginning to lose its character of being
> part of the center . . . With the steadily increasing traffic, it is nearly unbearable
> to be a shopper and retailer on Algade. The shops are filled with carbon monox-
> ide many times a day because of the continuous line of traffic from Gravensgade
> to Vesterbro. More than 150 buses drive through Algade per day. We therefore
> propose that this part of Algade be converted into a pedestrian mall. We have
> conducted a petition which shows 100% support.[14]

Algade has long been so burdened with traffic that it affects the possibilities
for—and quality of—other activities in the street than just traffic movements.
The heavy traffic is gradually turning the street and surrounding buildings into
a slum. It has taken the shopkeepers much longer to realize this than the Technical Department. It was these factors that led the department, more than five
years earlier, to propose that the street be converted into a pedestrian mall and
bicycle street, and led to closing the street to automobile traffic, until pressure
from the business community forced its reopening.

Now that the shopkeepers want the project implemented, the Technical
Department is more restrained. The alderman, after years of fighting with the
merchants, is tired and not very enthusiastic about bringing the formerly abandoned proposal back onto the agenda of Aalborg politics. He replies to the Algade merchants:

> [Y]our idea of converting Algade between Vesterbro and Gravensgade into a
> pedestrian mall will be evaluated as part of the comprehensive planning of
> downtown Aalborg. Your group will be informed when something more spe-
> cific happens. I regret that I cannot inform you when that will be. To make mat-

ters clear, I can inform you that Algade was [previously] closed to through car traffic (buses excepted). At that time I decided to reopen Algade to automobile traffic as a result of protests from, among others, the Aalborg Chamber of Industry and Commerce . . . As mentioned, I am disposed to evaluate your proposal, but to set the record straight I must call your attention to the fact that at the moment, no funds have been allocated to the budget for building the pedestrian mall on Algade.[15]

Seven years after the Aalborg Project's start, the roles of initiator and opponent have apparently been reversed. Now it is the business community that presses for specific changes, while the Technical Department cautiously sticks to the subprojects over which it has reached—after many years of conflict, struggle, and delay—a lowest-common-denominator consensus. The Technical Department has learned its lesson, and it is called *caution*. As part of this caution, all talk of the project's "second stage" is avoided. "Second stage" simply disappears from the Technical Department's vocabulary.[16] The concept is no longer seen as politically expedient. The department has had enough problems with the "first stage" and sees no reason to repeat it. A Technical Department staff member summarizes the situation more succinctly:

> There will never be a second stage. Never! I think the plan would suffer if we tried to set up a second stage.

A DEAD PROJECT?

As mentioned in the introduction to this chapter, a calm has settled over the Aalborg Project, and the Technical Department now has reservations about any new initiatives and about reviving old ones, as we have seen. This calm and reservation, however, is not due solely to the Technical Department's experience that caution is necessary in the project. It is just as important to look to the immediate future if we seek to understand what happens with the project, as several important forthcoming events now appear to influence the project.

First, Aalborg's city engineer of many years retires, and a new leader must be found for the project's Executive Committee. Second, the previously mentioned City Council elections influence the project. And third, the politically responsible leader of the project, the alderman for the Technical Department during the last sixteen years, plans to retire in connection with the elections.

A middle manager, not previously related to the Aalborg Project, is promoted to acting city engineer and thus becomes the new leader of the project's Executive Committee.[17] This is the first personnel change in the core group behind the project since its start more than six years previously.[18] The city en-

gineer's retirement will reveal itself to be the first of a near total replacement of
the individuals in this group, from top to bottom. A new generation is taking
over, and an era in Aalborg's planning history comes to a close.

For the present, the acting city engineer, after some months of monitoring the activities of the Aalborg Project's Executive Committee and Task
Force, proposes that the two organs be dissolved.[19] He asks that the remaining
major subprojects in the overall project be implemented via ad hoc project
groups. A more comprehensive organization will be reestablished only if necessary for the planning of the project's second stage. The veterans of the Aalborg Project are far from satisfied with this proposal. Aalborg's chief of city
planning and the members of the project's Task Force insist that a forum need
to be maintained for "the exchange of information with the objective of giving the individual offices the possibility to come up with potential points of
view before decisions are made in individual cases."[20] For his part, the chief
planner for public transportation proposes that while the Task Force can be dissolved, the Executive Committee, of which he is a member, should be retained.

The acting city engineer, however, sticks to his proposal, and the minutes
of what is apparently the final gathering of the project's Executive Committee
read as follows: "[The acting city engineer] concluded that agreement could
not be reached [regarding the dissolution of the project's Executive Committee and Task Force] and stated that he would recommend to [the alderman for
the Technical Department] that the Executive Committee and Task Force be
dissolved."[21] The minutes end with the following notation (in capital letters):
"IN THAT IT IS PRESUMED THAT THE EXECUTIVE COMMIT-
TEE AND TASK FORCE ARE DISSOLVED, THANKS ARE GIVEN
FOR THE GOOD COOPERATION IN THE PAST YEARS."[22] As a self-
contradictory detail, indicative of the problems in abolishing the Executive
Committee and Task Force, the same minutes reveal the following previously
cited passage regarding an idea from the shopowners on Algade street in connection with converting part of it into a pedestrian mall: "[The] idea of converting Algade between Vesterbro and Gravensgade into a pedestrian mall will
be evaluated as part of the comprehensive planning of downtown Aalborg."[23]
It is precisely this "comprehensive planning," however, which is proposed
abolished elsewhere in the same minutes with the proposal to close down the
Aalborg Project.

After the discussion with the Executive Committee, the acting city engineer sends his proposal for dissolving the Executive Committee and Task Force
to the Technical Department alderman.[24] Following this, the two groups no
longer hold meetings, the comprehensive planning within the Aalborg Project

ceases, the activity levels of the various subprojects decline further, and the Technical Department alderman does *not* make any decision on the acting city engineer's recommendation. The project's status is unclear.

The forthcoming City Council elections also put a damper on project activities. Local government tends to function at a slower pace during an election period. Prior to the elections, politicians are preoccupied with campaigning and other activities directly linked to the election; moreover, they wish to avoid controversial issues. On this latter point, it seems to be the case that politicians, voters, and the press typically regard action as more controversial than inaction. In the period following an election, a low level of activity may be due to reorganization of governmental institutions; that is, due to changes in the City Council's political composition and in the alderman positions. This is certainly the case for the Aalborg Project around the time of the elections to the Aalborg City Council.

Finally, within the Technical Department itself, inactivity can be linked to the decision of the alderman not to stand for reelection. The alderman has held his post since the establishment of Aalborg Municipality and the Technical Department, and he would certainly have won it again had he decided to run Instead, he decided to run for the City Council only. In choosing this option, however, the end of his tenure as leader of the Technical Department does not give him the same interest and involvement in the Aalborg Project that he previously had.

Taken together, these factors result in the once active Aalborg Project now lying dormant for almost two years. The project is viewed by many—politicians, administrators, planners, and the general public—not as completed but as dead.[25]

Eighteen

A SINGLE DRAMA . . . WITH AN ENDLESS PLAY
OF DOMINATIONS

Repetition is reality, and it is the seriousness of life.

Søren Kirkegaard

Following the City Council elections, the Technical Department and the Aalborg Project, to the degree that the project still exists, obtain a new commander-in-chief. The new alderman, like his predecessor, comes from the Conservative People's party. At the same time, the leadership of the Fifth Department, which runs public transportation and public utilities, also changes, with the former Liberal alderman now being replaced by a councilwoman from the Socialist People's party.[1] The new Fifth Department alderwoman is known as a strong proponent of public transportation and supporter of the original Aalborg Project, which she has defended publicly on several occasions. Less well-known are the views of the new Technical Department alderman toward environmental planning, public transportation, traffic and city planning, and toward this specific project.

BACK TO SQUARE ONE

Together with the Planning Office for Public Transportation, the new Socialist alderwoman for the Fifth Department takes the initiative to extract the Aalborg Project from its unclear status as a potentially terminated project and bring it back onto the agenda of politics and planning. In a letter to the new Conservative alderman for the Technical Department, she writes:

> [T]he first stage of the traffic plan for downtown Aalborg has been in operation for five years. During this period the plan has been changed, and certain parts of

it has never been implemented or have later been removed . . . [W]e find that it is time that more fundamental considerations be begun as to how traffic should be managed, not just in the Nytorv area, but in the entire city center. In our opinion, downtown Aalborg does not function well compared with the intentions which lay in the ratified traffic plan . . . We believe that a basic prerequisite for the traffic plan—namely, the reduction of automobile traffic on several streets—has not been achieved, and that we therefore now ought to discuss whether we should pursue this objective—which is our view—or whether another traffic plan should be elaborated based on other objectives, with all the consequences this might entail.[2]

In more untraditional fashion, the Fifth Department also attempts to mobilize public opinion on the Technical Department and the City Council in order to revive the Aalborg Project. They do this by discussing the problems of the project in a "debate newspaper" (*debatavis*) published as part of the ten-year anniversary of the municipality's having acquired the Aalborg Bus Company. A lead article in the debate newspaper makes the following remarks about the Aalborg Project:

Aalborg City Council approved the establishment of a "traffic zone solution" in the city center. The main principle was that the downtown area would be divided into four zones separated from each other by roadblocks which were not to be crossed by normal automobile traffic. Bicycles and buses, however, would be able to move unhindered through the city center's road network . . . Only a small part of the traffic zone solution has been implemented, however, and the many positive consequences of the plan—in the form of better environment, improved conditions for pedestrians, bicyclists, and bus traffic, for example—have been correspondingly absent.[3]

Regarding the area around Nytorv, the debate paper writes:

Quite opposite the intentions, the number of traffic accidents on Nytorv has risen considerably, and downtown automobile traffic is as heavy as ever. Neither the environmental nor the safety improvements which were the goals have been achieved. At Nytorv, in the 2 years prior to its conversion [into the bus terminal] there occurred 4 traffic accidents resulting in personal injury. During the first 2 years following the rebuilding there have been 10 traffic accidents with personal injury.[4]

In an even more untraditional bent, the debate newspaper, which is a government document, goes on to identify "the merchants" as having caused the project's nonimplementation, and it expands on what "most people" would prefer to see in downtown Aalborg:

The reason why the plan has not been implemented must be found partly in a strong opposition on the part of the merchants . . . [The Aalborg Project] was formulated with environmental improvements as an objective, which continues to be valid. Most people want better conditions for the nondriving road users: pedestrians, bicyclists, and the bus passengers. When will the plan begin to work?[5]

The initiative from the Fifth Department is successful in the sense that the project again returns to Aalborg's political agenda. The project's Executive Committee is reunited, nearly two years after the acting city engineer—now officially constituted—proposed the elimination of both the Executive Committee and the Task Force. In fact, several of the staff members involved in the project had assumed that the two groups had been dissolved.[6] Resurrected, they now meet again because "several factors regarding traffic and urban renewal demand a discussion and clarification."[7] A staff member from the Technical Department explains in an interview:

The reason why [the Aalborg Project] was revived was that there were several projects [being planned] in the city center, and you cannot consider all these projects in isolation . . . Therefore it was formally the same Task Force . . . and it was within this that . . . follow-up [on the Aalborg Project] was worked out.

The objective is to revive the project in its original, comprehensive form rather than as the fragmented, decimated project it was when the Task Force and Executive Committee ceased functioning.[8] The Executive Committee and Task Force are each given the same functional composition they had prior to their temporary dissolution.[9] The leader of the Task Force, who is again secretary to the Executive Committee, is the same person who has held this post since the Aalborg Project's inception nearly ten years ago.

The planners are back to "square one" as illustrated by the following passage from a report on the situation in downtown Aalborg at this stage in the project: "Better traffic conditions, especially for [noncar and public transportation] users, and reduced negative environmental impacts can only be achieved via a reduction of automobile traffic in the city center's inner street network."[10] These words could just as well have been written nearly a decade earlier, at the start of the Aalborg Project.

THE OLD TRIUMVIRATE IS REUNITED

As mentioned, planning is again approached in a more comprehensive fashion, as was the case when the Aalborg Project started. However, as was also the case before, it quickly happens that the project's problem child and status symbol *par excellence,* the bus terminal at Nytorv, comes to dominate the work. *Aalborg Stiftstidende,* its main office still on Nytorv Square, reintroduces the Aalborg Project by focusing on Nytorv under the following four-column headline: "Demands Nytorv Closed to All Motorists."[11] In the article, the Socialist alderwoman for the Fifth Department criticizes the lack of follow-up on the Aalborg Project:

> [T]he city center plan does not work. It is a good plan, especially if it were re-
> spected. This is not happening at Nytorv, for example, where through traffic in
> private cars is creating major problems for the city buses.[12]

The Fifth Department alderwoman refers here to the "No Through Traffic" ban on cars driving through the bus terminal, a prohibition that the police have not enforced for five years, and which is largely ignored by drivers (see Chap. 12). In the original project, the Nytorv bus terminal was conceived as being free of private cars. Currently, the daily traffic in the bus terminal is 4,000 cars, 50% of which drive through illegally.[13] The *Aalborg Stiftstidende* had earlier interviewed an Aalborg Police Department spokesman about the "No Through Traffic" regulations.

> *Police spokesman:* It is certainly correct that we have not taken the task [of en-
> forcing the "No Through Traffic" prohibition] very seriously . . .
> *Aalborg Stiftstidende:* Has anyone been cited . . . ?
> *Police spokesman:* Not to my knowledge. It should be remembered that the
> Police Department still has the task of making priorities. And the ban on
> through traffic can only be enforced effectively if there is a continuous police
> presence at Nytorv. Twenty-four hours a day. We do not have the resources for
> this . . . I [will] propose to the politicians that the ban [on cars] be lifted.[14]

Once again we see opposing sides consolidating their positions: the proponents of the ban are now being led not by the Conservative Technical Department alderman as before but by the Socialist Fifth Department alderwoman;
the opponents are the Aalborg Police Department who wish to see the ban on
through traffic lifted, and presumably also the silent majority of drivers who
violate the ban with impunity. The police also wish to reopen Østeraagade
toward Slotspladsen.[15] If the "No Through Traffic" prohibition on Nytorv is
formally lifted, rather than just being ignored as it has been for so many years,
so collapses the last remnant of the project's traffic zone solution, that is, the division of downtown Aalborg into four separate traffic zones, once considered
the backbone of the entire project.

The Chamber of Industry and Commerce soon joins sides with the police. The chairman of the Chamber's Retailer Committee, quoted in *Aalborg Stiftstidende,* labels the alderwoman's call to enforce the ban on through car traffic "exaggerated and unacceptable."[16] At the same time, the chairman echoes the police in proposing that Østeraagade be reopened toward Slots-pladsen Square: "In fact, I think that the problems at Nytorv cannot be solved without the Toldboden intersection [i.e., Østeraagade toward Slotspladsen] being reopened," he now declares.[17]

Finally, the editors of *Aalborg Stiftstidende* close ranks with the police and the Chamber. The old triumvirate is reunited:

> Sometimes one gets the impression that there are people in the municipal ad-ministration who have too much time on their hands. In recent years we have seen several traffic barriers introduced into the streets of Aalborg and other towns. They want to determine how the citizens should drive through the town in their cars . . . The newest innovation is that traffic on Nytorv in Aalborg is to be revamped again . . . [The Fifth Department alderwoman] claims that private cars delay city bus services.[18]

As usual, *Aalborg Stiftstidende* is concrete and detailed in its advice to the mu-nicipality's politicians and planners. And as before it conjures up the specter of "traffic death," though in an entirely different connotation than generally un-derstood:

> There are signs which forbid through traffic on Nytorv. The signs have been there for four years [actually it is five], and they are not respected. As far as we know, the police have never cited any driver for violating the prohibition. If such violations are so openly accepted, one can naturally not expect that the signs have the intended effect, and one cannot judge the result of the conversion carried out four years ago. So take the signs down . . . The traffic situation today does not justify closing downtown Aalborg to private cars, and no one can be interested in choking the city center by imposing traffic death [*trafikdød*] on it.[19]

As mentioned, the opponents constitute the familiar constellation of the Aal-borg Chamber of Industry and Commerce, Aalborg Police Department, and *Aalborg Stiftstidende.* On the side of the proponents, however, a decisive change has occurred. Up to now, the Technical Department and the Fifth Depart-ment's Planning Office for Public Transportation, despite their differences, have been in agreement as to the project, and have been its two most ardent supporters. It now transpires that the Fifth Department and the Planning Office for Public Transportation come to stand alone, for the alderman for the Technical Department is unwilling to endorse the closing of the bus terminal to through automobile traffic. Instead he would like to see Nytorv made one-way so as to reduce the volume of cars passing through the terminal.

The planners in the Aalborg Project Task Force, following an agreement between the Fifth Department alderwoman and the Technical Department alderman, conduct a feasibility study of two alternatives for the bus terminal in cooperation with a local consulting company.[20] The two alternatives are (1) *"No Entry"on Nytorv:* Nytorv is to be closed to normal auto traffic; (2) *One-way traffic at Nytorv:* Nytorv would be made one-way from east to west, combined with a prohibition on left turn at Østeraagade and at the exit from Braskensgade (Salling's parking lot).[21]

The implementation of the proposed measures is expected to result in a significant reduction of automobile traffic on Nytorv, Østeraagade, Boulevarden, and Algade, ranging from 85% on Nytorv for Alternative 1 down to 20% on Østeraagade north of Nytorv for Alternative 2. Car traffic on Nytorv would be reduced by 50 –70% for the latter alternative. According to both proposals it is expected that the city buses would obtain a smoother and more rapid flow in the downtown area, especially in Alternative 1. Finally, it is expected that the total number of traffic accidents would decline on an order of magnitude corresponding to the reduction in automobile traffic.[22]

Summing up the two proposals, the planners who elaborated them maintain that "the first is in total agreement with the [Aalborg Project], while the second is a modified edition of the first proposal."[23]

"ONE STEP AT A TIME"

In deciding which of the two proposals to implement, the new Conservative alderman for the Technical Department shows that he will continue his department's tradition for close cooperation with the Chamber of Industry and Commerce. First, the Chamber's board and those members having businesses in the Nytorv area, twelve persons in all, are invited to a meeting with the Aalborg Project's Task Force on "traffic conditions in downtown Aalborg."[24] Second, the alderman and the Aalborg Project's Executive Committee meet with seventeen representatives of the Chamber, two from the Aalborg Police Department and three from the Fifth Department (public transportation), also to discuss "traffic conditions."[25] This is the usual pretreatment, in terms of *Realpolitik,* of the issue with the Chamber of Industry and Commerce before matters proceed to *formal* political treatment in democratically elected committees, in the Municipal Administration (*Magistraten*) and in the City Council. This procedure has functioned through the entire life of the Aalborg Project and is now continued.

The Socialist alderwoman from the Fifth Department, who prior to assuming the alderwoman post had on several occasions criticized the cozy relationship between the Chamber of Industry and Commerce and the Technical

Department, now takes part in this cooperation. Moreover, she surpasses her Conservative colleague in the Technical Department by calling an independent meeting with the Chamber three months before the Chamber's meetings with the Technical Department. The only participants in this meeting are the leadership of the Fifth Department and the leadership of the Chamber.[26]

In its meetings with the Technical and Fifth Departments, the Chamber of Industry and Commerce expresses its continued opposition to closing the bus terminal to automobile traffic. Minutes of the Task Force meeting with the Chamber indicate

> great opposition from the merchants to a closing of Nytorv. After much debate, support from the merchants was achieved for making Nytorv one-way.[27]

Two weeks later, at the Executive Committee's meeting with the Chamber, the alderman for the Technical Department maintains that "nothing has been decided yet."[28] The purpose of the meeting is said to be simply to give the Chamber of Industry and Commerce and the Aalborg Police Department the opportunity to comment upon the proposals before a decision is made.

The Chamber now states that it will accept a one-way street solution on Nytorv in the bus terminal, but that traffic be directed one-way eastward instead of the westward solution desired by the Technical Department. The Chamber believes that rerouting traffic one-way toward the west would make it more difficult for drivers to gain access to Dansk Supermarked's two department stores on Nytorv—Salling and Føtex—and to a major parking garage there. At the same time, the Chamber reiterates its desire to see Østeraagade toward Slotspladsen reopened.[29]

The Police Department's basic attitude is that traffic conditions in the bus terminal function satisfactorily as they are. The only measure proposed by the police is the lifting of the legal ban on through traffic, such that the formal regulations are brought into line with actual practice; illegal through traffic is to be made legal. If another change is to be implemented, the Police Department, like the Chamber, desires a one-way solution instead of a closure; like the Chamber, the police believe that a one-way solution must be in an eastwardly direction. The police tactically link the westward one-way arrangement with a reopening of Østeraagade toward Slotspladsen, that is, should the Technical Department choose the westward arrangement, the police will work for a reopening of Østeraagade, which the Technical Department certainly does not want to see happen. The Police Department also emphasizes that the closing of Algade "can wait."[30]

The Fifth Department alderwoman, as head of public transportation, supports the closing of both Nytorv and Algade and keeping Østeraagade toward Slotspladsen Square closed.[31]

Finally, the Technical Department alderman once again emphasizes that he has not taken a final position on the proposals. Instead, he states that further planning in downtown Aalborg should be based on the following principles: (1) "[O]ne step at a time," (2) "The key person is the customer [for downtown businesses]," and (3) "As few restrictions [on automobile traffic] as possible should be implemented."[32]

The day after the joint meeting, the Technical Department alderman discusses these principles in an interview in *Aalborg Stiftstidende*. The alderman's remarks are in sharp contrast to the position of the Socialist Fifth Department alderwoman, and this contrast generates the paper's headline: "Prospects for Political Battle on Downtown Traffic." The alderman declares:

> My position is that business customers should have the best conditions to find a parking place in the inner city. We should not have traffic restrictions which scare customers coming from the outlying areas away from downtown. On the contrary, the task must be to lure customers in . . . I am strongly opposed to closing Nytorv in order to give the city buses a time advantage . . . Public transportation must have reasonable conditions, but such a demand is reminiscent of minute and second hysteria [*minut- og sekundhysteri*]. The yellow buses are not holy cows, only able to tolerate pedestrians and bicyclists in their proximity.[33]

Any prior doubts about where the new Conservative Technical Department alderman stands in relation to the Aalborg Project and toward public transportation have now been dispelled. A year into his tenure, the alderman demonstrates that he is a friend of auto traffic and of commerce. With his philosophy of "one step at a time," a slogan he later terms his "court slogan" (*haf udtryk*),[34] his priority to business customers before other groups, his resistance toward restricting automobile traffic, and, finally, with his talk of "minute and second hysteria" in public transportation, the new alderman demonstrates that he supports what we might term "the planning of marginal changes." These incremental changes stand in diametric opposition to the more grandiose planning perspective of both the original and the revived Aalborg Project, which emphasize innovation and comprehensive "overnight" solutions, in addition to giving greater priority to environmental improvement, pedestrians, bicyclists, and public transportation while downgrading automobile traffic. Later on, the new Technical Department alderman openly acknowledges, "I do not share the [Aalborg] Project's objective."[35]

The alderman's planning ideology accords well with the view propagated by the Chamber of Industry and Commerce, the *Aalborg Stiftstidende,* and the Aalborg Police Department, ever since the "life or death meeting" at the White House Hotel eight years earlier.[36] This view was previously forced upon the Aalborg Project as an outcome of intense power struggles between the Technical Department and the Chamber, with devastating consequences for the project. Now, with the alderman's "one-step-at-a-time" philosophy, that which was a *condition* in the unequal power relationship between the Technical Department and the Chamber is elevated into a *planning principle*. It is thereby internalized into the project and city government in Aalborg.

It comes as no surprise, then, that the Technical Department alderman, faced with the more radical measure of closing the bus terminal to automobile traffic, opts instead for the one-way solution. On the advice of his staff, however, he chooses a westward one-way solution rather than the eastward solution desired by the Chamber and the Police Department. The Technical Department believes that a westward one-way solution will result in a reduction of automobile traffic on Nytorv by 50–70%, versus the 40% reduction expected from an eastward one-way solution.[37]

When the alderman's one-way recommendation is sent to a vote in the City Council, the Socialist People's party City Council Group revives its counterproposal, originally advocated by the party's alderwoman, and proposes that Nytorv be completely closed to auto traffic. The Socialist proposal is rejected by a 26–5 vote, while the Technical Department's recommendation is approved.[38] Five months later, the decision takes effect: seven years after the City Council first approved the central zone boundary for automobile traffic in the bus terminal at Nytorv, this boundary is now partially established.

Around this time, Aalborg's chief of city planning, a member of the project's Executive Committee for well over ten years and one of the key figures behind the Aalborg Project, goes into retirement. At the same time, the head of the project's Task Force also leaves. This individual, also part of the project for over a decade, and who besides heading the Task Force had been secretary for the project's Executive Committee, chooses to leave the Technical Department and Aalborg altogether, seeing no future for "his" project in this town. As the city architect and city landscaper have also retired, the core group behind the Aalborg Project has now effectively disappeared. With the change of aldermen two years previously, the project lost its political platform in the Technical Department, in the Municipal Administration, and in the City Council. With the exit of its core group, the project has now also lost its professional platform.

The partial zone boundary on Nytorv Square and the previously mentioned reduced speed zone on a section of Danmarksgade Street become the only visible results of the attempt to revive the Aalborg Project.[39] Without support from the Technical Department alderman and with the majority of the original innovators behind the project gone, it proves impossible to get the project moving again.

Yet again, the project activities come to a halt.

THE ART OF THE IMPOSSIBLE

So far, public parking in Aalborg has been free. From the very beginning of the Aalborg Project, however, the Technical Department staff had recommended the introduction of fees and stricter time limitations on parking in downtown Aalborg in order to curb all-day commuter parking.[40] In the area of parking, too, Aalborg has maintained its tradition of being in the forefront of new *ideas* in town and traffic planning. As for *implementation* of these ideas, however, several other Danish towns had already implemented similar solutions in their downtown areas. In Aalborg parking fees were under consideration for thirteen years before they were implemented.[41]

The fees come as a surprise to the town, since neither of the two Conservative aldermen who have headed the Technical Department and the Aalborg Project have been proponents of stricter parking measures. On the contrary, the first alderman made it clear from the project's start that during his term as alderman there would be no parking fees in downtown Aalborg, despite the recommendations of his staff. And the second alderman has shown himself to be significantly more partisan toward shopping motorists than the first.

The explanation for the sudden interest in parking fees in downtown Aalborg does not derive from any desire to fulfill the objectives of the Aalborg Project, even though this measure is central to the original project. What is decisive is the general financial crisis in Aalborg's municipal budget. The budget is so hard-pressed that Aalborg's mayor and four aldermen, including the alderman for the Technical Department, will resort to any idea which can generate revenues. Hence the idea, subsequently approved by the City Council, to introduce parking fees for downtown Aalborg.[42] The fees are expected to provide the municipal treasury with net revenues of 3–4 million kroner per year and could be adjusted up or down according to experience and need.[43]

The Chamber of Industry and Commerce, however, quickly emerges as an opponent of the parking solution. "They're Chasing Our Customers Out of Town" is the headline in the *Aalborg Stiftstidende,* which quotes the chairman for the Chamber's Retailer Committee calling the parking fees "an additional tax" and "yet another step in the politicians' attack on private transportation."[44] The chairman adds, "It is the retailers who lose when the City Council comes up with new ideas to put money into the municipal coffers."[45]

The Technical Department alderman soon follows the Chamber, its members being his political constituency. He now makes a 180-degree change of mind and publicly appeals for the introduction of parking fees to be postponed indefinitely, saying:

> The purpose of introducing the fees [is] exclusively to generate income for the municipal treasury, and I find this very unfortunate . . . I believe that we should introduce the fees only on the day where it shows itself to be necessary for traffic and parking-related reasons.[46]

Two days prior to the City Council meeting in which the proposal will be put to a vote, *Aalborg Stiftstidende* can inform its readers that two of the largest department stores in Aalborg, Salling and Føtex, are opposed to the introduction of parking fees. In an article headlined "Salling and Føtex: 'No' to Parking Fees," Salling's manager declares:

> We are opposed to the parking fees in the city's center and do not think that the costs can be offset by the income. If a majority of the City Council support the parking fees, it will be difficult to get customers from out of town to come and shop in downtown Aalborg.[47]

The manager of the Føtex store agrees, adding, "Parking fees are not our favorite dish, and we would like to do without them."[48]

The Technical Department alderman, however, is in the minority in the City Council. By a vote of 18–12, with the Social Democrats and the Socialist People's party in favor, including the now nonaffiliated alderwoman for the Fifth Department,[49] the Technical Department alderman's proposal to postpone the introduction of parking fees is voted down.[50] *Aalborg Stiftstidende* criticizes the City Council's decision in an editorial, again echoing the views of the Chamber of Industry and Commerce. The editorial, entitled "Tax on Commerce," states:

> If anyone asks why it should suddenly cost money to use the parking lots in downtown Aalborg, the answer is that a majority in the Aalborg City Council have found a new object for taxation . . . It made no impression on the City Council majority that [the alderman for the Technical Department] could show the result of a study which . . . demonstrates that Aalborg has not yet reached the kind of emergency situation that could justify so drastic a step as imposing a penalty fee for having business to attend to in the regional urban center . . . Nor did it make any impression on the City Council majority that the Chamber of Industry and Commerce in Aalborg has vehemently protested against the parking fees. Understanding the business community's problems does not weigh on

the majority. Such an understanding is something they only talk about on fes-
tive occasions, but seldom practice . . . The fees do not create a single extra parking place. They irritate the users and indirectly encourage them to go elsewhere.
This cannot be the intention.[51]

The majority of Aalborg's City Council, however, thinks otherwise and ratifies the parking fee measure by a vote of 17–11.[52]

What twelve years of arguments for environmental improvement, traffic
safety, and improving conditions for pedestrians, bicyclists, and public transportation have not been able to accomplish is now achieved by the persuasive
power of economics, that is, by the desire to add an extra 3–4 million kroner
per year to the municipal treasury. Former Danish Prime Minister Jens Otto
Krag said that politics is the art of the possible. And up to now parking fees have
been impossible to introduce into Aalborg. Now economics, that is, an empty
municipal treasury, makes the impossible possible. And the Aalborg Project
moves yet another step toward realization.

TOWARD THE YEAR 2050

The time is approaching when we must leave the Aalborg Project. In the last
few chapters we have allowed the story of the project to become repetitious
and even dull because such is the reality of the project. The project is not implemented as planned, nor does it burn out. It just gradually dissolves into an
impasse. After five years in which only one of the original subprojects is fully
implemented and two others but partially accomplished, the project is pro-
gressing at a pace so slow as to be hardly detectable. The parking policy, moreover, was implemented solely for budgetary reasons and not out of any
concern for the project as such.

In a radio program on the Aalborg Project broadcast by the national Danish radio, the interviewers touched on these factors in the following questions
to the alderman for the Technical Department:

> *Radio interviewer:* What does a political ratification actually mean in your
> opinion? Citizens of Aalborg might well believe when they look back on what

happened [when the Aalborg Project was first ratified by the City Council] that the approved project should now be implemented . . . And I think you have said that it is your decision whether [implementation] is a hundred percent, or fifty percent, or ten percent?

Alderman for the Technical Department: No, I definitely did not say that . . . We have piles of municipal plans lying around which show what kind of development is desired, but there is nothing at all which states at what point in time they should be implemented.

Interviewer: May I then ask, will [the project] be completely implemented at some given point in time?

Alderman: That I dare not say at all . . .

Interviewer: Won't it be difficult for the voters to keep up when the City Council first ratifies something, and where they perhaps believe that it is a good project and a good City Council, but then later on you sit as alderman and say that it may well be that we have ratified it, but then we can just decide, without changing the ratification, either, that we don't want to implement it?

Alderman: No, it cannot be depicted in such a way, certainly not. What we have done with regard to the ratified project is to gradually evaluate when things should be set in motion.[54]

And, as mentioned, the "gradual evaluations" seem to indicate very long prospects, indeed, for the final implementation of the Aalborg Project.

This is the situation at the time we leave the project. It is not the only possible situation, and this is not to say that we must wait until the middle of the next century before ideas similar to those in Aalborg first become reality in Aalborg, or elsewhere.

There is no grand finale to the story of the Aalborg Project. There is only a Nietzschean "single drama . . . the endlessly repeated play of dominations."[55] And the play of dominations is at this time affected by conservative forces to a greater extent than at any previous moment in the project's history.

The play does not operate in a vacuum, of course. It can be affected. New actors may appear, existing power bases may erode, new power bases may emerge, economic conjunctures may take on new forms, social structures may change, genealogies and case histories may be written, and environmental problems may become so serious that even conservatives find themselves unable to defend the status quo.

This is the stuff of which the future is made.

Nineteen

REALITY CHECK

> Man is the only animal that laughs and weeps; for he is the only animal
> that is struck by the difference between what things are and what they
> might have been.
>
> *William Hazlitt*

For nearly a decade and a half, Aalborg's city government has been trying to implement what politicians, administrators, and planners talk about in urban areas everywhere: reduce car traffic in downtown areas, get people to use other means of transportation, improve air quality, reduce traffic accidents, lower noise levels, improve the quality of public spaces and of urban life generally. These objectives have repeatedly been affirmed by the Aalborg City Council, and the Municipal Administration has used considerable resources to realize them. The city government, however, has never evaluated how well it has succeeded in actually achieving its objectives. Hence, it does not know whether its policies and plans work or not. Nor has it any intention of finding out. Therefore, in this chapter I present my own evaluation.[1]

PLAN AND REALITY

Let us compare the objectives the Aalborg City Council has set for the project with actual developments in Aalborg and in Denmark as a whole. The comparison covers the first decade in the life of the project.

Instead of the planned 30–35% reduction of automobile traffic in downtown Aalborg, the ten-year period actually saw an increase of 8%. While considerably less than the 25–30% national increase in automobile traffic, the increase corresponds to trends in downtown Copenhagen, where no similar policies or plans have been implemented.

An increase in noncar and public transportation in the downtown area of approximately 50% combined with increased automobile traffic has meant more congestion in the downtown area. As a result, the city bus system finds itself unable to keep to its own timetables.

Instead of the planned comprehensive network of bicycle paths in downtown Aalborg, a series of unconnected stretches have been built, scattered around the downtown area; together they comprise but 30% of the planned bike path network.

Before implementation of the Aalborg Project, a bicyclist traveling one kilometer in the city center was fourteen times more likely than a driver to end up in a traffic accident with personal injury. Therefore, the most important single goal of the Aalborg Project was a 40% reduction in personal injuries for bicyclists. This goal has not been achieved. Instead, compared to the period before the project, the number of killed and injured bicyclists in downtown Aalborg has increased a good 40% following the implementation of the Aalborg Project's first stage.[2] In Denmark as a whole, the number of killed and injured bicyclists in urban traffic remained relatively constant during the same period.

A projected 30% overall reduction in the number of traffic deaths and injuries has not been achieved, nor has there even been a trend in the desired direction: instead of a decrease there has been a 5% increase in traffic injuries and fatalities. By contrast, Denmark's overall number of killed and injured in urban traffic has declined by a good 25% during the period. The difference between downtown Aalborg and the entire country is even more drastic, in that total automobile traffic at the national level rose 10–15 times faster during the period than automobile traffic in downtown Aalborg. As for the figures on traffic accidents in Aalborg, no effect can be discerned from either the Aalborg Project nor from the general increase in traffic safety at the national level.

For pedestrians, the goal was an unspecified decline in traffic injuries. A decade of the Aalborg Project produced no significant improvements in the number of killed and injured pedestrians. At the national level, the number of pedestrians killed and injured in urban traffic fell by about 30% during the same period.

Drivers of mopeds are the only traffic group showing a reduction in traffic accidents, the number of killed and injured moped drivers having fallen by 23%.[3] Yet this decline was barely half the national decline of 50%.

The Aalborg Project does not operate with a target for personal injuries involving drivers of automobiles. There occurred no significant difference in the number of killed and injured motorists prior to and after implementation of the project's first stage.[4] At the national level, the number of killed and injured drivers in urban traffic fell by 25%.

Instead of the planned reductions in noise in the inner city streets of 2–5 db(A), measurements show levels to be unchanged, and noise levels in the most heavily traveled streets of downtown Aalborg are 70–76 db(A), substantially exceeding both Danish and international maximum limits.

Instead of the planned reduction of noise on the main artery of Vesterbro, whose measured peak values of 90–99 db(A) are seen as a special problem in the Aalborg Project, there occurred a 10% increase in automobile traffic in this street and hence a slight increase in noise levels.

Given the existing data, the level of air pollution in the most heavily traveled "street canyons" in downtown Aalborg approaches the limits set by the Danish Environmental Protection Agency, the European Union, and WHO for environmentally hazardous and health-threatening materials, that is, nitrogen oxides, carbon monoxide, airborne particles, and soot.

Instead of the planned reduction in air pollution which was supposed to result from reduced traffic in the most heavily traveled "street canyons," existing data suggest that the level of pollution emanating from motor vehicles has remained largely unchanged for nitrogen oxides and carbon monoxide, while there has been an increase in the level of airborne particles and soot, the steep growth in bus traffic being the main source of the increase.

The planned concentration of public transportation on fewer streets in the downtown area and an improvement in the transfer possibilities between city and regional buses has not occurred.

Instead of a projected reduced waiting time for pedestrians to traverse the streets of the downtown area, the result has been unchanged or increased waiting time due to either unchanged or increased traffic.

FROM COHERENCE TO FRAGMENTATION

The consistent lack of goal achievement in the Aalborg Project reflects the trajectory described in the preceding chapters of a project which has moved from comprehensiveness, innovation, and praise to fragmentation, stagnation, and critique. It would be misleading, however, to view the Aalborg Project as a classical implementation failure, that is, as a project that has simply collapsed and whose intended effects are therefore lacking. The Aalborg Project is not just fragmented; it is fragmented in a specific way, with its own specific consequences. Let us briefly examine the project's pattern of fragmentation and its consequences.

It has already been mentioned that the Aalborg Project has come to consist largely of forty-one subprojects, and that the history of the project is largely a tale of how these subprojects move on and off the political agenda, with only a small portion of the subprojects finally implemented. During the first decade of the project—having been originally designed to be implemented as a whole, overnight—only six of the forty-one subprojects were fully implemented, equivalent to an "implementation rate" of 15%. An additional eight subprojects, or 20% of the total, have been only partially implemented, while twenty-seven subprojects, or 65%, have remained on the drawing board. Thus, a decade after the project's start and a full eight years into "project implementation," more than two-thirds of the entire project remains unfinished. Unfinished projects mean unachieved objectives.

Let us explore the pattern of implementation—or more accurately, non-implementation—of the Aalborg Project. A comparison of the status of implementation for the forty-one subprojects with their main objectives shows that implementation is lowest for those subprojects whose goal is to reduce automobile traffic in downtown Aalborg. Only five out of fifteen planned subprojects with restrictions on automobile traffic are entirely or partially implemented, and of these five, three were first implemented eight to nine years after the projects' initial ratification by the City Council. Until that time, only 15% of those subprojects with restrictions on automobile traffic had been achieved in whole or in part, while the implementation rate for those subprojects involving improvements for pedestrians, bicyclists, and public transportation lay at 40–50%.

With roughly a 50% increase in bicycle and public transportation in downtown Aalborg during the first decade of the project, and without the projected 35% decline in automobile traffic, the actual situation stands in sharp contrast to what was envisioned. According to the plan, it was a cardinal prerequisite that improving conditions for pedestrians, bicyclists, and public transportation could only occur via a simultaneous downgrading of automobile traffic—road space in downtown Aalborg was already fully utilized, and a political decision had been made against street extensions, new right-of-ways, and the like. Without the downgrading of automobiles, the pressure on downtown road space would produce harmful effects on environment, traffic safety, and traffic flow. It is this very situation the Aalborg Project was supposed to prevent but has exacerbated instead. This paradoxical situation is due to the project's fragmented and distorted form, in which subprojects that would have restricted automobile traffic were not implemented, combined with the simultaneous implementation of several subprojects that promote pedestrian, bicycle, and bus traffic.

Here lies part of the explanation as to why the general improvement in traffic safety at the national level has not been reflected in downtown Aalborg, despite the enlightened policy and planning traditions of the city and the zeal of the politicians and planners. In similar fashion, one sees no effect of the safety measures—or measures to reduce air and noise pollution—which were in fact implemented as part of the Aalborg Project.

WHO WINS, WHO LOSES . . . WHO GOVERNS?

As shown in the previous chapters, the pattern of fragmentation in the Aalborg Project is due primarily to continued opposition by the Aalborg Chamber of Industry and Commerce, which has fought the project from its inception. In particular, the Chamber has been a vehement opponent of the project's efforts to restrict automobile traffic, with the argument that such restrictions would harm Aalborg's business. This opposition penetrates directly into the project in the above-mentioned implementation rates for the various types of sub-projects.

The main viewpoints of the Chamber of Industry and Commerce concerning the project have overlapped with the views of the Aalborg Police Department and the *Aalborg Stiftstidende*. As the *Stiftstidende* has a near monopoly on the printed press in Aalborg, and as the police held a powerful position in questions of traffic policy, this threefold overlapping of interests endows the Chamber's viewpoints with a special impact.[5] The *Realpolitik* for the Aalborg Project is shaped by these interests in classic Machiavellian style, while the *formal* policy making activities in democratically elected bodies like the City Council, the Municipal Administration (*Magistraten*), and political committees have had and continue to have only minor impact on the project. Unbalanced relations of power have produced an unbalanced project. Power has defined a reality in which the *real* Aalborg Project, that which has become reality, deviates from, and in key objectives directly contradicts the *formal* Aalborg Project, that ratified by the City Council.

The acquiescence of the City Council, and especially the Technical Department, in the face of challenges from the city's business community is an indication that the democratic process has not functioned in connection with the Aalborg Project. The city government's inability to enforce its own decisions and the Police Department's failure to support the approved project have prevented environmental improvements in downtown Aalborg and have allowed a rate of traffic accidents far in excess of the national average and the planners' projections.

The losers in the struggle over the Aalborg Project are those citizens who live, work, walk, ride their bikes, drive their cars, and use public transportation in downtown Aalborg, that is, virtually all of the city's and the region's half-million inhabitants. Every single day residents and commuters in downtown Aalborg are exposed to increased risk of traffic accidents, higher levels of noise and air pollution, and a deteriorating physical and social environment. The taxpayers are also losers, because the considerable funds and human resources used in the Aalborg Project have largely been wasted.

The winners are the business community in downtown Aalborg, who, via their strategy of opposing measures to restrict cars combined with grudging acceptance of improvements for public transportation, pedestrians, and bicyclists, have seen their customer base substantially increased. The commercial success is evidenced by a documented increase in retail sales in downtown Aalborg following the implementation of the Aalborg Project, while sales figures at the national level during the same period declined (see Chap. 16).

The physical lack of balance in the Aalborg Project, with certain subprojects being implemented while others are blocked, is paralleled by a social lack of balance in the project's effects, with certain groups gaining and others losing. There is considerable evidence to indicate that Aalborg's overall situation would have been better had the Aalborg Project not been implemented at all. It can be argued that the project has actually helped worsen the very situation it was supposed to have improved. This conclusion should not be seen as a general argument against environmental, traffic, and urban planning for better cities, in Aalborg or elsewhere. It is simply to say that the kind of politics, administration, and planning that produces the kinds of results we see in the Aalborg Project ought to be avoided.

Twenty

POWER HAS A RATIONALITY THAT RATIONALITY
DOES NOT KNOW

> Democratic contrivances are quarantine measures against that ancient
> plague, the lust for power: as such, they are very necessary and very
> boring.
>
> *Friedrich Nietzsche*

AALBORG AS METAPHOR

The Aalborg Project may be interpreted as a metaphor of modern politics, modern administration and planning, and of modernity itself. The basic idea of the project was comprehensive, coherent, and innovative, and it was based on rational and democratic argument. During implementation, however, when idea met reality, the play of Machiavellian princes, Nietzschean will to power, and Foucauldian rationality-as-rationalization resulted in the fragmentation of the project. It disintegrated into a large number of disjointed subprojects, many of which had unintended, unanticipated, and undemocratic consequences. The grand, unifying, and prize-winning policy and plan degenerated into the string of petty incidents described in the previous chapters. Planners, administrators, and politicians thought that if they believed in their project hard enough, rationality would emerge victorious; they were wrong. The Aalborg Project, designed to substantially restructure and democratically improve the downtown environment, was transformed by power and *Realrationalität* into environmental degradation and social distortion. Institutions that were supposed to represent what they themselves call the "public interest" were revealed to be deeply embedded in the hidden exercise of power and the protection of special interests. This is the story of modernity and democracy in practice, a story repeated all too often for comfort for a democrat. The problems with the Aalborg Project do not derive from Aalborg being especially plagued by corrupt policies or incompetent planning and administration. Most people interested in politics know one or more "Aalborg Stories," and the policy studies literature is replete with examples of failed policies, confused administration, 225 and unbalanced planning. "You don't get to comfort yourself very long with the thought that they aren't too smart in Aalborg," observed one commentator on previously published results from the Aalborg study. "The description of what went wrong and why contains many elements familiar to anyone who works with planning in practice."[1] At a more general level, the Aalborg case confirms Charles Taylor's observation that central tenets of the Enlightenment legacy can be maintained primarily as goals and hope but not as reality.[2]

One such tenet is Francis Bacon's famous "Knowledge is power." Bacon's statement encapsulates one of the most fundamental ideas of modernity and of the Enlightenment: the more rationality, the better. Our study of the Aalborg Project certainly demonstrates the relevance of Bacon's statement. Yet it also shows that power and knowledge cannot be separated from each other in the way Bacon does; and even if one were to speak in Bacon's terms, the Aalborg study shows that the relationship between knowledge and power is commutative: not only is knowledge power, but, more important, power is knowledge. Power determines what counts as knowledge, what kind of interpretation attains authority as the dominant interpretation. Power procures the knowledge which supports its purposes, while it ignores or suppresses that knowledge which does not serve it. Moreover, the *relations* between knowledge and power are decisive if one seeks to understand the kinds of processes affecting the dynamics of politics, administration, and planning. There is a long tradition from Thucydides over Machiavelli and Nietzsche to Foucault for providing such an understanding. The case study of Aalborg was carried out in this tradition, and in our conclusions we will remain within it. Thus, the principal question to be addressed in this final chapter is, "What basic relations of rationality and power have shaped the Aalborg Project and have led to its lack of balance, fragmentation, and lack of goal achievement?"[3]

This question will be elucidated by summarizing ten propositions about rationality and power. The empirical evidence for the propositions has been described earlier in this study. Here we will use the ten propositions to construct a "grounded theory," understood as theory inductively founded upon concrete phenomenology. While the propositions obviously derive from the case of Aalborg, and thus cannot be seen as general theory, they can serve as useful guidelines for researching rationality and power in other settings. The ten propositions may also serve as a phenomenology for testing, refining, and further developing the classical statements about power, knowledge, and rationality found in Bacon, Machiavelli, Kant, Nietzsche, and more recently in Michel Foucault, Jürgen Habermas, Richard Rorty, and others.

The order of presentation of the ten propositions will begin with a focus on the rationality of power and gradually move toward describing the power of rationality.

PROPOSITION 1: POWER DEFINES REALITY

Power concerns itself with defining reality rather than with discovering what reality "really" is. This is the single most important characteristic of the rationality of power, that is, of the strategies and tactics employed by power in relation to rationality. Defining reality by defining rationality is a principal means by which power exerts itself. This is not to imply that power seeks out rationality and knowledge *because* rationality and knowledge are power. Rather, power *defines* what counts as rationality and knowledge and thereby what counts as reality. The evidence of the Aalborg case confirms a basic Nietzschean insight: interpretation is not only commentary, as is often the view in academic settings, "interpretation is itself a means of becoming master of something"—in this case master of the Aalborg Project—and "all subduing and becoming master involves a fresh interpretation."[4] Power does not limit itself, however, to simply defining a given interpretation or view of reality, nor does power entail only the power to render a given reality authoritative. Rather, power defines, and creates, concrete physical, economic, ecological, and social realities.

PROPOSITION 2: RATIONALITY IS CONTEXT-DEPENDENT, THE CONTEXT OF RATIONALITY IS POWER, AND POWER BLURS THE DIVIDING LINE BETWEEN RATIONALITY AND RATIONALIZATION

Philosophy and science often present rationality as independent of context, for example, in universal philosophical, ethical, or scientific imperatives, a current example being the "theory of communicative rationality" and "discourse ethics" of Habermas. If these imperatives are followed, the result is supposed to be rational and generally acceptable actions. Our study of politics, administration, and planning in Aalborg shows rationality to be a discourse of power. Rationality is context-dependent, the context often being power. Rationality is penetrated by power, and it becomes meaningless, or misleading—for politicians, administrators, and researchers alike—to operate with a concept of rationality in which power is absent. This holds true for substantive as well as communicative rationality. Communication is more typically characterized by nonrational rhetoric and maintenance of interests than by freedom from domination and consensus seeking. In rhetoric, the "validity" and effect of communication is established via the mode of communication—for example,

eloquence, hidden control, rationalization, charisma, using dependency relations between participants—rather than through rational arguments concerning the matter at hand. Seen from this perspective, Habermas cuts himself
off from understanding real communication when, in developing his theory
of communicative rationality and discourse ethics, he distinguishes between
"successful" and "distorted" utterances in human conversation; success in
rhetoric that is not based on rational argument is associated precisely with
distortion, a phenomenon demonstrated repeatedly in the Aalborg study.[5]
The assertion of Harold Garfinkel and other ethnomethodologists that the
rationality of a given activity is produced "in action" by participants via that
activity is supported by the Aalborg case. In addition, we have seen that
whenever powerful participants require rationalization and not rationality,
such rationalization is produced. Rationalization is a pervasive feature of the
Aalborg Project and is practiced by all key actors.

PROPOSITION 3: RATIONALIZATION PRESENTED AS RATIONALITY IS A PRINCIPAL STRATEGY IN THE EXERCISE OF POWER

In the same way that political science, following Machiavelli and Ludwig von
Rochau, distinguishes between formal politics and *Realpolitik,* evidence from
the Aalborg study indicates the need for the study of politics, administration,
planning, and modernity, to distinguish between formal rationality and *Realrationalität,* real rationality. The freedom to interpret and use "rationality" and "rationalization" for the purposes of power is a crucial element in enabling power
to define reality and, hence, an essential feature of the rationality of power.

The relationship between rationality and rationalization is often what
Erving Goffman calls a "front-back" relationship. "Up front" rationality dominates, frequently as rationalization presented as rationality. The front is open to
public scrutiny, but it is not the whole story and, typically, not even its most
important part. Backstage, hidden from public view, it is power and rationalization which dominate. A rationalized front does not necessarily imply dis-
honesty. It is not unusual to find individuals, organizations, and whole societies
actually believing their own rationalizations. Nietzsche, in fact, claims this self-
delusion to be part of the will to power. For Nietzsche, rationalization is necessary to survival.

Even though rationalization is a principal strategy in the rationality of
power, and even though several of the most important events in the Aalborg
Project have been profoundly affected by rationalization, the case study indicates that the freedom to rationalize is neither universal, inevitable, nor
unlimited. All political and administrative activity cannot be reduced to ratio-

nalization; different degrees of rationalization exist; and rationalizations can be challenged—both rationally and by means of other rationalizations.

While it is possible to challenge rationalizations, this seldom occurs in the Aalborg Project. The "untouchable" position of rationalizations may be due to the fact that rationalizations are often difficult to identify and penetrate: they are presented as rationality, and, as demonstrated in the case study, often only a thorough deconstruction of an ostensibly rational argument can reveal whether it is a rationalization. In other cases, actors may be prevented from revealing a rationalization because so much power lies behind it that critique and clarification may become futile. A final explanation for actors' unwillingness to reveal rationalizations is that doing so may be dangerous: attempts at deconstruction and critique may lead to confrontations, to the destabilization of the decision-making process, or to negative sanctions on those actors who reveal rationality as rationalization.

PROPOSITION 4: THE GREATER THE POWER, THE LESS THE RATIONALITY

Kant said, "The possession of power unavoidably spoils the free use of reason."[6] On the basis of the Aalborg study, we may expand on Kant by observing that the possession of more power appears to spoil reason even more.

One of the privileges of power, and an integral part of its rationality, is the freedom to define reality. The greater the power, the greater the freedom in this respect, and the less need for power to understand how reality is "really" constructed. The absence of rational arguments and factual documentation in support of certain actions may be more important indicators of power than arguments and documentation produced. Power knows that which Nietzsche calls "the doctrine of Hamlet," that is, the fact that often "[k]nowledge kills action; action requires the veils of illusion."[7] A party's unwillingness to present rational argument or documentation may quite simply indicate its freedom to act and its freedom to define reality.

In a democratic society, rational argument is one of the few forms of power the powerless still possess. This may explain the enormous appeal of the Enlightenment project to those outside power. Machiavelli, however, places little trust in rational persuasion. "We must distinguish," he says in *The Prince,* "between . . . those who to achieve their purpose can force the issue and those who must use persuasion. In the second case, they always come to grief."[8] "Always" may be somewhat exaggerated, and much has changed in terms of Enlightenment and modernity since Machiavelli. Nevertheless, Machiavelli's analysis certainly applies to the Aalborg Project, which in this sense is premodern and predemocratic.

Nietzsche puts an interesting twist on the proposition "the greater the power, the less the rationality" by directly linking power and stupidity: "Coming to power is a costly business," Nietzsche says, "power *makes stupid*" (emphasis in original).[9] Nietzsche adds that "politics devours all seriousness for really intellectual things." In a critique of Charles Darwin, Nietzsche further points out that for human beings the outcome of the struggle for survival will be the opposite of that "desired" by Darwinism because "Darwin forgot the mind," and because "[h]e who possesses strength divests himself of mind."[10] Nietzsche identified the marginalization of mind and intellect by power as a central problem for the German *Reich,* and on this basis he predicted—correctly, we now know—the fall of the *Reich.*[11] Aalborg's mayor also suffered from the marginalization of mind by power, something which ultimately cost him his political life. Will to power is a will to life, but it may well lead to self-destruction.

In sum, what we see in Aalborg is not only, and not primarily, a general "will to knowledge" but also "a far more powerful will: the will to ignorance, to the uncertain, to the untrue! Not as [will to knowledge's] opposite but—as its refinement!"[12] Power, quite simply, often finds ignorance, deception, self-deception, rationalizations, and lies more useful for its purposes than truth and rationality. Yet Nietzsche is wrong when he says, "Who alone has good reason to lie his way out of reality? He who suffers from it. But to suffer from reality is to be a piece of reality that has come to grief."[13] What makes Nietzsche wrong here is the "alone" in the first sentence of the quote. In Aalborg, we have come across other groups that have good reasons to lie and rationalize, groups that do not suffer from reality. These are groups that stand to gain from propagating certain interpretations, rationalizations, and lies about reality and that use politics to create the reality they want. When it comes to politics, even Plato—the ultimate defender of rationality—recommended the "noble lie," that is, the lie which would be told to the citizens of his model state in order to support its moral and political order.[14]

PROPOSITION 5: STABLE POWER RELATIONS ARE MORE TYPICAL OF POLITICS, ADMINISTRATION, AND PLANNING THAN ANTAGONISTIC CONFRONTATIONS

Michel Foucault characterizes power relations as dynamic and reciprocal: stable power relations can at any time evolve into antagonistic confrontations, and vice versa. The data from Aalborg confirm Foucault's conclusion, but we must also modify it by noting that the reciprocal relationship between stable power relations and antagonistic confrontations is asymmetrical: stable power relations are far more typical than antagonistic confrontations, much as peace is more typical than war in modern societies. Antagonistic confrontations are actively avoided. When such confrontations take place, they are quickly transformed into stable power relations. The result is that the issues shaping politics, administration, and planning are defined more by stable power relations than by antagonistic confrontations.

Because confrontations often are more visible than stable power relations, confrontations tend to be frequent topics of research on power and of public debate and press coverage. Concentration on the most visible aspects of power, however, results in an incomplete and biased picture of power relations.

PROPOSITION 6: POWER RELATIONS ARE CONSTANTLY BEING PRODUCED AND REPRODUCED

Even the most stable power relations, those with historical roots going back several centuries, are not immutable in form or content. Power relations are constantly changing. They demand constant maintenance, cultivation, and reproduction. In the Aalborg case, we saw how the business community was much more conscious of this—and substantially more skilled and persevering—than were politicians, administrators, and planners. Through decades and centuries of careful maintenance, cultivation, and reproduction of power relations, business created a semi-institutionalized position for itself with more aptitude to influence governmental rationality than was found with democratically elected bodies of government.

PROPOSITION 7: THE RATIONALITY OF POWER HAS DEEPER HISTORICAL ROOTS THAN THE POWER OF RATIONALITY

From the historical perspective of what Fernand Braudel and the French *Annales* school call the *longue durée,* ideas like democracy, rationality, and neutrality, all central to modern institutions, are young and fragile when compared to traditions of class and privilege. In the Aalborg study, centuries of daily practice have made the latter so firmly entrenched in social institutions that they have become part of modern institutions. Policy, administration, and planning in the Aalborg Project are marked as much by premodern relations of power as by modern rationality, by tribalism as much as by democracy. This is despite the fact that the very raison d'être of modernity has been to eliminate, or attenuate, the influence of tradition, tribe, class, and privilege, and even though modernization has been going on for more than two centuries. One consequence of this state of affairs is what by modern standards is called the "abuse of power" in modern institutions.

Modern institutions and modern ideas such as democracy and rationality remain in large part ideals or hope. Such ideals cannot be implemented once and for all. We again need to remember that to call governments "democratic" is always a misleading piece of propaganda.[15] We may want the democratic element in government to grow greater, but it is still only an element. Efforts at implementing democracy are a constant, never-ending task existing in conflict with traditions of class, tribe, and privilege. The interrelationship between such traditions and modernist initiatives gives rise to new traditions. In this sense, modernity and democracy must be seen as part of power, not the end points of power. Modernity and democracy do not "liberate man in his own being," nor do they free individuals from being governed, as Foucault says. Modernity and democracy undermine religion and tradition and compel man "to face the task of producing himself," and of practicing government that will not obstruct, but will instead advance, "the undefined"—and never-ending—"work of freedom."[16]

PROPOSITION 8: IN OPEN CONFRONTATION, RATIONALITY YIELDS TO POWER

Foucault says that knowledge-power and rationality-power relations exist everywhere. This is confirmed by our study, but modified by the finding that where power relations take the form of open, antagonistic confrontations, power-to-power relations dominate over knowledge-power and rationality-power relations; that is, knowledge and rationality carry little or no weight in these instances. As the proverb has it, "Truth is the first casualty of war."

In an open confrontation, actions are dictated by what works most effectively to defeat the adversary in the specific situation. In such confrontations, use of naked power tends to be more effective than any appeal to objectivity, facts, knowledge, or rationality, even though feigned versions of the latter, that is, rationalizations, may be used to legitimize naked power.

The proposition that rationality yields to power in open confrontations may be seen as an extreme case of proposition no. 4, "the greater the power, the less the rationality": Rationality yields completely, or almost completely, to power in open, antagonistic confrontation because it is here that naked power can be exercised most freely.

PROPOSITION 9: RATIONALITY-POWER RELATIONS ARE MORE CHARACTERISTIC OF STABLE POWER RELATIONS THAN OF CONFRONTATIONS

Interactions between rationality and power tend to stabilize power relations and often even constitute them. This stabilization process can be explained by the fact that decisions taken as part of rationality-power relations may be rationally informed, thereby gaining more legitimacy and a higher degree of consensus than "decisions" based on naked power-to-power confrontations.

Stable power relations, however, are not necessarily *equally balanced* power relations, understood as relations in which the involved parties act on equal terms. In other words, stability does not imply justice, and stable power relations imply neither "non-coercive [*zwanglos*] communication" nor "communicative rationality," to use Habermas's terms. Stable power relations may entail no more than a working consensus with unequal relations of dominance, which may lead to distortions in the production and use of rational or quasi-rational arguments. Where rational considerations play a role, however, they typically do so in the context of stable power relations.

PROPOSITION 10: THE POWER OF RATIONALITY
IS EMBEDDED IN STABLE POWER RELATIONS
RATHER THAN IN CONFRONTATIONS

Confrontations are part of the rationality of power, not the power of rationality. Because rationality yields to power in open, antagonistic confrontations, the power of rationality, that is, the force of reason, is weak or nonexistent here. The force of reason gains maximum effect in stable power relations characterized by negotiations and consensus seeking. Hence, the power of rationality can be maintained only insofar as power relations are kept nonantagonistic and stable.

Special interest groups have substantially more freedom to use and to benefit from the full gamut of instruments in naked power play than do democratically elected governments. Democratic government of the modern Western variety is formally and legally based on rational argument and is constrained to operate within the framework of stable power relations, even when dealing with antagonistic interest groups, unless such groups go on to break the law and trigger police or military intervention. This difference in the mode of operation of governments and interest groups results in an unequal relationship between governmental rationality and private power, and between formal politics and *Realpolitik,* such that governmental rationality and formal politics end up in the weaker position. Inequality between rationality and power can be seen as a general weakness of democracy in the short-run struggle over specific policies and outcomes. It is a weakness, however, that cannot be overcome by resorting to the instruments of naked power, and modern democracy's ability to limit its use of naked power can be seen as its general strength.

The fact that the power of rationality emerges mostly in the absence of confrontation and naked power makes rationality appear as a relatively fragile phenomenon; the power of rationality is weak. If we want the power of reasoned argument to increase in the local, national, or international community, then rationality must be secured. Achieving this increase involves long term strategies and tactics which would constrict the space for the exercise of naked power and *Realpolitik* in social and political affairs. Rationality, knowledge, and truth are closely associated. "The problem of truth," says Foucault, is "the most general of political problems."[17] The task of speaking the truth is "endless," according to Foucault, who adds that "no power can avoid the obligation to respect this task in all its complexity, unless it imposes silence and servitude."[18] Herein lies the power of rationality.

THE CHALLENGE TO DEMOCRACY

In sum, while power produces rationality and rationality produces power, their relationship is asymmetrical. Power has a clear tendency to dominate rationality in the dynamic and overlapping relationship between the two. Paraphrasing Pascal, one could say that power has a rationality that rationality does not know. Rationality, on the other hand, does not have a power that power does not know.

Modernity relies on rationality as the main means for making democracy work. But if the interrelations between rationality and power are even remotely close to the asymmetrical relationship depicted above—which Aalborg and the tradition from Thucydides, Machiavelli, and Nietzsche tell us they are—then rationality is such a weak form of power that democracy built on rationality will be weak, too. The asymmetry between rationality and power described in the ten propositions makes for a fundamental weakness of modernity and modern politics, administration and planning. The normative emphasis on rationality leaves the modern project ignorant of how power works and therefore open to being dominated by power. Relying on rationality therefore risks exacerbating the very problems modernity attempts to solve. Given the problems and risks of our time—environmental, social, demographic; globally and locally—I suggest we consider whether we can afford to continue this fundamental weakness of modernity. The first step in moving beyond the modern weakness is to understand power, and when we understand power we see that we cannot rely solely on democracy based on rationality to solve our problems.

Let us probe this point at a more concrete level. Constitution writing and institutional reform are the main means of action, in theory as well as in practice, in the modernist strategy of developing democracy by relying on rationality against power.[19] Whereas constitution writing and institutional reform may often be essential to democratic development, the idea that such reform alters practice is a hypothesis, not an axiom. The problem with many advocates of institutional reform is that they reverse the axiom and the hypothesis: they take for granted that which should be subjected to empirical and historical test. In Aalborg such testing showed us that even the police—supposedly the guard of the law—refused to follow and enforce the constitutional principles institutionalists rely upon to promote democracy, not to speak of the many other actors in the case who again and again, for personal and group advantage, violated the principles of democratic behavior they were supposed to honor as civil servants, politicians, and citizens in one of the oldest democracies in the world. We saw, in fact, that political actors are expert at judging how far a democratic constitution can be bent and used, or simply ignored, in nondemocratic ways. Such findings demonstrate that the question of how existing constitutions and their associated institutions can be utilized more democratically may frequently be more pressing than the question of how to establish more democratic constitutions and institutions as such. The Aalborg study certainly confirms Robert Putnam's general observation that "[t]wo centuries of constitution-writing around the world warn us . . . that designers of new institutions are often writing on water."[20]

Putnam's study of civic traditions in modern Italy is one of the few other studies of the practices of democracy combining a micro approach with the historical perspective of the *longue durée,* the very long run. Like the Aalborg study, Putnam and his associates find that social context and history profoundly condition the effectiveness of institutions; premodern social practices that go back several centuries drastically limit the possibilities for implementing modern democratic reform. Such conditioning is not only a problem for democracy in Italy and Denmark. In most societies entrenched practices of class and privilege form part of the social and political context and limit the possibilities of democratic change. Putnam notes that the effects of deep historical roots on the possibilities of modern democracy is a "depressing observation" for those who view constitutional and institutional reform as the main strategy for political change.[21] Nevertheless, such is currently the evidence. This does not mean, needless to say, that changing formal institutions cannot change political practice. It does mean, however, that institutional change typically moves much more slowly and circuitously than is often assumed by legal writers and institutional reformists.

But looking at democracy in the time perspective of the *longue durée* is only depressing to those impatient for instant change. For it is also by employing this time perspective that we begin to see what it takes to make democracy work in practice. It is in this perspective we see that people working for more democracy form part of a century-long and remarkably successful practical tradition that focuses on more participation, more transparency, and more civic reciprocity in public decision making. The fact that progress has generally been slow within the tradition by no means makes such progress less significant; quite the opposite. The tradition shows us that forms of participation that are practical, committed, and ready for conflict provide a superior paradigm of democratic virtue than forms of participation that are discursive, detached, and consensus-dependent, that is, rational. We see that in order to enable democratic thinking and the public sphere to make a real contribution to democratic action, one has to tie them back to precisely what they cannot accept in much of modern democratic theory: power, conflict, and partisanship, as has been done with the Aalborg study.[22]

In the *longue durée,* we see that in practice democratic progress is chiefly achieved not by constitutional and institutional reform alone but by facing the mechanisms of power and the practices of class and privilege more directly, often head-on: if you want to participate in politics but find the possibilities for doing so constricting, then you team up with like-minded people and you fight for what you want, utilizing the means that work in your context to undermine those who try to limit participation. If you want to know what is going on in politics but find little transparency, you do the same. If you want more civic reciprocity in political affairs, you work for civic virtues becoming worthy of praise and others becoming undesirable. At times direct power struggle over specific issues works best; on other occasions changing the ground rules for such struggle is necessary, which is where constitutional and institutional reform come in; and sometimes writing genealogies and case histories like the Aalborg study, that is, laying open the relationships between rationality and power, will help achieve the desired results. More often it takes a combination of all three, in addition to the blessings of beneficial circumstance and pure luck. Democracy in practice is that simple and that difficult.

Let us return one final time to Machiavelli's warning about the dangers of the normative attitude: "[A] man who neglects what is actually done for what should be done learns the way to self-destruction."[23] The focus of modernity and modern democracy has always been on "what should be done," on normative rationality. What I suggest is a reorientation toward the first half of Machiavelli's dictum, "what is actually done," toward *verita effettuale.* We need to rethink and recast the projects of modernity and democracy, and of modern politics, administration, and planning, in terms of not only rationality but of rationality and power, *Realrationalität.* Instead of thinking of modernity and democracy as rational means for dissolving power, we need to see them as practical attempts at regulating power and domination. When we do this we obtain a better grasp of what modernity and democracy are in practice and what it takes to change them for the better. This is what I have attempted to do with this book.

Postscript

Not every end is a goal. A melody's end is not its goal.

Friedrich Nietzsche

In March of 1995, Aalborg's reputation for being in the forefront of European urban policy and planning was confirmed when the European Union in Brussels awarded city officials its "European Planning Prize." Triumphing over 300 nominees, Aalborg received the prize for having developed what the jury viewed as an innovative, democratic urban policy and planning with particular emphasis on the involvement of citizens and interest groups.

Since 1991, Aalborg's new approach to planning policy has evolved as an antithesis to the Aalborg Project, which officials and the public had viewed as being incapable of solving the city's problems, preserving its key aesthetic assets, or improving environmental quality. Awareness of these inadequacies came about partly because of the public debate generated by this study when it first appeared in Danish.[1]

The awarding of the European Planning Prize does not end the Aalborg story, however. One Aalborg planner commented: "I do not agree with the jury that this is Europe's best planning document, since it does not contain any planning! . . . Has the process been democratic?"[2] Skepticism of this kind lends credence to the need to conduct another case study concerning how the new approach is operating in Aalborg's present-day planning and policy environment. Such a study would evaluate whether the new approach is leading to more democratic and more positive changes in Aalborg's physical, economic, ecological, and social realities and would evaluate the implications for politics, planning, and democracy in other contexts. Carrying out this kind of research would be a reaffirmation of Foucault's maxim that "we are always in the position of beginning again."[3]

Appendices

Appendix A

MAIN ACTORS IN THE AALBORG PROJECT

Aalborg city government consists of an elected City Council (*Byrådet*) and a Municipal Administration (*Magistraten*). The Municipal Administration is subdivided into five "departments" (*afdelinger*) each having several "offices" (*kontorer*). The five departments, called First, Second, etc., cover, respectively, (1) administration and finance; (2) technical affairs, and planning for city, traffic, and environment; (3) social affairs; (4) cultural and educational affairs; and (5) public utilities. Each department is headed by an elected alderman (*rådmand*). The alderman for the Second (Technical) Department formally heads the Aalborg Project. The mayor, who is also an alderman, heads the First Department (administration and finance). During the design phase of the Aalborg Project, the Aalborg Bus Company was part of the First Department. Later on, during implementation and operation, the bus company was transferred to the Fifth (Public Utilities) Department.

The relations of the city government to other main actors in the Aalborg Project, and to the project itself, are outlined in the figure opposite. While only the Task Force, Executive Committee, and private consultants are active at the start of the project, its activities eventually expand to include all the actors shown.

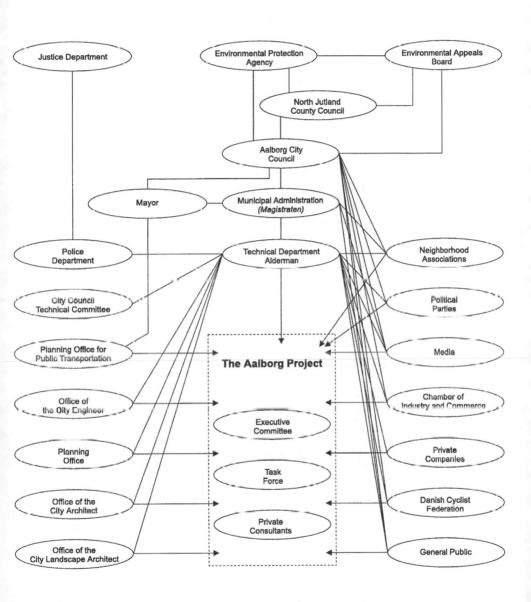

Appendix B

CHRONOLOGY OF THE AALBORG PROJECT

October 1977	The Aalborg Project is initiated
1978	Elaboration of project design and proposal covering urban renewal, land use, traffic, and environment
February 1979	Project design is completed
1979	Public hearings
November 1979	The Aalborg Chamber of Industry and Commerce publishes counterplan to the Aalborg Project
December 1979	The Danish Town Planning Association awards the project the association's prize for "good and sensitive planning"
1980	Project revision
June 1980	Aalborg City Council ratifies the project by a 25–1 vote
1980–81	Detailed planning and drafting of subprojects
March 1981	Implementation begins
October 1981	Inauguration of the first stage of the project
1981–82	Confrontations between the Technical Department and the Chamber of Industry and Commerce
February 1982	The Aalborg Journalist Association awards the project its "Cold Trick" prize, given for "a good idea with a bad outcome"
April 1982	The Social Democratic City Council Group publishes its counterplan to the Aalborg Project, the so-called Dream Plan
January 1983	The City Council ratifies the eleventh revised version of the Aalborg Project
1983–84	Detailed planning and drafting of permanent solutions for individual subprojects
April 1984	The head of the project Executive Committee, the city engineer, retires
1984–85	Implementation of individual subprojects
January 1985	The acting city engineer proposes that the Aalborg Project be terminated
December 1985	The alderman for the Technical Department retires
1986	Project status unclear; the project lies dormant
July 1986	The project is revived by the new alderwoman for public transportation
1986–87	Project revisions

August 1987	The new alderman for the Technical Department declares that he does not share the Aalborg Project's objectives
December 1987	The chief of city planning retires; the head of the project Task Force resigns
1988	Minor construction work in connection with postponed parts of Stage One
1989	Introduction of fees and stricter short-term parking regulations in downtown Aalborg
1991–94	Elements of and lessons from the Aalborg Project are integrated into a new round of comprehensive planning for urban renewal, land use, traffic, and environment for downtown Aalborg
March 1995	The European Union in Brussels awards Aalborg the European Planning Prize for the city's new approach to planning

Appendix C

ELEMENTS IN THE ORIGINAL AALBORG PROJECT

The Aalborg Project seeks to address problems of urban renewal, land use, and traffic and environment. For each of these problem areas, specific plans and subprojects are produced, as described below.

A. URBAN RENEWAL

The original, official name for the Aalborg Project is "Urban Renewal of Downtown Aalborg." The intention is to structure the entire project, physically and organizationally, around issues of urban renewal. For reasons discussed in Chapter 5, however, urban renewal soon recedes into the background, to be replaced by other project activities. Urban renewal is reduced to a "Catalogue of Ideas" for specific isolated actions to be undertaken in the city center.

A.1 Catalogue of ideas for urban renewal. The objective is to help contribute to:

- A better linkage of the central shopping zones of downtown Aalborg.
- An improvement of the quality of the city center's public spaces, that is, streets, squares, and recreational areas.
- An improvement of the city center's residential areas.

A.2 To achieve the objectives of urban renewal, sixteen subprojects are proposed:

1. Establishment of improved pedestrian connection between the streets of Bispensgade and Reberbansgade (*gade* means "street").
2. Extension of the Bispensgade pedestrian mall to include part of Vesterå Street.
3. Establishment of street behind Bispensgade.
4. Establishment of pedestrian connection between the streets of Jomfru Ane Gade and Maren Turis Gade.
5. Establishment of a "green" pedestrian square in Maren Turis Gade.
6. Renovation and "greening" of C. W. Obels Square.
7. Integration of C. W. Obels Square into the Bispensgade pedestrian mall.
8. Integration of Aalborg Castle and its park into downtown Aalborg by means of a pedestrian connection through the park from Bispensgade to Slotsgade.
9. Construction of new buildings around Mølleplads and establishment of pedestrian zone on the square.
10. Establishment of pedestrian streets from Mølleplads to the Algade pedestrian mall and to Danmarksgade.
11. Establishment of green recreational area between Danmarksgade and Mølleplads.

12. Establishment of pedestrian connection through green areas between the Vor Frue and Mølleplads Squares.
13. Establishment of pedestrian malls on parts of the streets Niels Ebbesens Gade and Peder Barkes Gade.
14. Establishment of a recreational area around the Vor Frue church.
15. Establishment of recreational area and market place on Frederikstorv Square.
16. Integration of harbor areas in downtown Aalborg.

B. LAND USE

B.1 Land use plan with the following objectives:
- The total housing area in the city center should be maintained and improved.
- Urban renewal activities should be strengthened.
- The center's geographic limits should be maintained.
- Commercial, administrative, and regional functions should be located in secondary centers outside the city center.
- Extension of square footage for industry, workshops, and wholesale commerce should be avoided.
- Green areas are to be expanded and upgraded.
- Open spaces in residential zones are to be upgraded.

The land use plan indicates the existing and planned locations of various city center activities.

B.2 A report is announced that will develop and detail the land use plan. This report is never produced.

B.3 Plan for building use and preservation: the objective of the plan is to prevent banks, savings-and-loan associations, insurance companies, offices, and other nonretail businesses from occupying the street-level space in buildings in the most important shopping streets of the city center. The intent of the plan is to preserve these areas as genuine shopping streets.

C. TRAFFIC AND ENVIRONMENT

C.1 Plan for traffic and environment with the following objectives:
- To accord increased priority to the urban environment, the more vulnerable road users, that is, pedestrians and bicyclists, and public transportation.
- To downgrade automobile traffic—especially commuting motorists—where it causes conflict with other types of transport.

C.2 The plan is based on the following priorities for environment and transportation, listed in order of importance:
- Environment.
- Pedestrians.
- Bus passengers.
- Bicyclists.
- Handicapped drivers.
- Commercial traffic.

- Car-driving shoppers.
- Other car drivers.
- Residential parking.
- Home–workplace commuters using private cars.

C.3 Central to the plan for traffic and environment is a "traffic zone solution." Downtown Aalborg is to be divided into four zones having barriers which prevent their being traversed by cars. The objective is to make it more difficult to drive through the city center by car, thereby removing what are considered "unnecessary" cars from downtown streets, estimated at 35% of total vehicular traffic.

C.4 Forty-one subprojects to be implemented to achieve the objectives for traffic and environment. The subprojects eventually are divided into three stages:

Stage One:

1. Construction of a city bus terminal at Nytorv–Østeraagade.
2. Establishment of an integrated bus stop for city and regional buses at Vingaardsgade; in effect, a second bus terminal.
3. Restructuring the urban and regional bus network in the city center.
4. Provisional reduction of traffic and the introduction of bicycle paths on the main traffic artery of Vesterbro as part of north-south bicycle path through the city center.
5. An east-west bicycle path through the city center along the route Østerbro-Borgergade-Kastetvej.
6. Making Borgergade one-way between Vesteraa and Vesterbro in order to reduce traffic and create space for the construction of a bicycle path.
7. Reducing car traffic by creating a slowdown street (*stillegade*) on Danmarksgade-Løkkegade.
8. Zone boundary on Danmarksgade.
9. Pedestrian mall and bicycle path on the western section of Algade.
10. Zone boundary at the western part of Nytorv.
11. Closing of Østeraagade at Slotspladsen Square.
12. Opening of Ved Stranden to automobile traffic.
13. Shorter time limits and the introduction of fees for public parking places.
14. Closing of small parking lots and streets.

Stage Two:

15. Establishment of all four traffic zones.
16. Expansion of the bicycle path network.
17. Elimination of smaller parking areas.
18. Restructuring of the Railroad Station Square (John F. Kennedy Square).
19. Reduction and restructuring of traffic patterns in residential areas.
20. Conversion of Vesterbro to include a "buses-only" lane and bicycle paths.
21. Conversion of Boulevarden-Østeraagade to include bicycle paths.
22. Zone boundary at Østeraagade.
23. Closing of Ved Stranden to noncommercial auto traffic.
24. Possible elimination of traffic signals at the Østeraagade-Nytorv intersection.
25. Bicycle path on Algade (from Jernbanegade to Boulevarden).
26. Closing of Algade to cars east of Budolfi Plads.

27. Making the western part of Danmarksgade a one-way street.
28. Restructuring of the Danmarksgade-Prinsensgade intersection.
29. Making Vingaardsgade two-way east of Budolfi Plads.
30. Footpaths and bicycle paths through Kildeparken Park.
31. Tunnel for bicyclists and pedestrians under Prinsensgade between Kilde-
    parken and downtown Aalborg.
32. Bicycle paths along Jyllandsgade.
33. Bicycle paths along Kjellerupsgade.

Stage Three:

34. Footpaths and bicycle paths over the railroad zone between downtown Aal-
    borg and the Kærby residential area.
35. Footpaths and bicycle paths over the harbor areas.
36. Traffic lights for pedestrians and bicyclists at the intersection of Slotspladsen
    and Østeraagade.
37. Establishment of parking areas at Sauers Plads.
38. Establishment of parking areas at the western harbor area.
39. Establishment of parking areas at the freight railway yard.
40. Reserving of parking spaces in downtown residential streets for residents.
41. Continued traffic reductions on "slowdown" streets.

In addition to the plans, projects, and subprojects mentioned above, the Aalborg Project is closely linked with, and conditioned by, two other projects for the city center: a new civic center and a new "buses-only" street through the center (see Chap. 2). Implementation of these projects was already underway when the Aalborg Project began. For all practical purposes, the three projects are part of the same package.

Notes

PREFACE

1. The paper later developed into "Towards Phronetic Social and Political Sciences: An Aristotelian Approach to Integrating Context, the Particular, and Narrative in Social and Political Inquiry," forthcoming.

ONE

1. Friedrich Nietzsche, "On Truth and Lying in an Extra-Moral Sense," in Sander L. Gilman et al., eds., *Friedrich Nietzsche on Rhetoric and Language* (New York: Oxford University Press, 1989), p. 246.

2. By "modernity" is understood the tradition from the Reformation and the Enlightenment as manifested in efforts to strengthen the domains of cognitive rationality, moral autonomy, and social and political self-determination.

3. Niccolò Machiavelli, *The Prince* (Harmondsworth: Penguin, 1984), p. 91 (chap. 15).

4. For more background on the selection of the Aalborg case, see Bent Flyvbjerg, *The Aalborg Study: Case Selection and Data Collection,* research report (Aalborg: Aalborg University, Department of Development and Planning, 1997).

5. Friedrich Nietzsche, *Ecce Homo* (New York: Vintage Books, 1969), p. 256 (§10).

6. Michel Foucault, "Nietzsche, Genealogy, History," in Paul Rabinow, ed., *The Foucault Reader* (New York: Pantheon, 1984), p. 77.

7. Bernard Crick, "Introduction" to Niccolò Machiavelli, *The Discourses* (Harmondsworth: Penguin, 1983), p. 27.

8. Friedrich Nietzsche, *Twilight of the Idols* (Harmondsworth: Penguin, 1968), pp. 106-7 (§2).

9. Nietzsche's influence is obvious in Foucault's texts. E.g., in Book One of *The Gay Science* ([New York: Vintage Books, 1974], p. 81 [§7]) under the heading "Something for the Industrious" (Foucault said of himself, "I worked like a dog all my life" ["Michel Foucault," interview by Steven Riggins, *Ethos* 1, no. 2 (1983), p. 8]). Nietzsche here spells out some of the "histories" that need to be written in the study of moral matters, explicitly mentioning areas Foucault would later cover: "So far, all that has given color to existence still lacks a history. Where could you find a history of love, of avarice, of envy, of conscience, of pious respect for tradition, or of cruelty? Even a comparative history of law or at least of punishment is so far lacking completely." Similarly, Nietzsche's focus (in the second essay of *On the Genealogy of Morals* [New York: Vintage Books, 1969], p. 59 ff. [§2]) on the development of "calculable" individuals through "the labor performed by man upon himself" also would be central to Foucault's work. Part of the originality of Nietzsche lies in seeing that studies of such issues need to be carried out. The originality of Foucault lies in actually carrying out the studies. Even though Nietzsche's influence on Foucault is apparent, Foucault rarely

mentions Nietzsche in his writings. In an interview given a few weeks before his death, however, Foucault explained that Nietzsche was one of the philosophers he had read the most, describing himself as "simply Nietzschean" (Michel Foucault, "Final Interview," conducted by Gilles Barbadette and André Scala, *Raritan* 4, no. 1 [1985], p. 9).

10. A historical approach has been employed, however, to understand the genealogy and historical context of the case studied.

11. As regards substance, the focus of Nietzsche and Foucault is on biopower, i.e., the question of how power creates people ("calculable" individuals). My focus is on how power creates things, here man-made environments. While man-made environments have biopower effects, such effects are not the focus of my study.

12. Michel Foucault, "The Subject and Power," in Hubert Dreyfus and Paul Rabinow, *Michel Foucault: Beyond Structuralism and Hermeneutics* (Brighton: Harvester Press, 1982), p. 217.

13. Albert O. Hirschman, "Social Conflicts as Pillars of Democratic Market Society," *Political Theory* 22, no. 2 (May 1994).

14. For more on the methodology employed, see my *Science of the Concrete: Context, the Particular, and Narrative in Social and Political Inquiry,* forthcoming.

15. D. A. T. Gasking and A. C. Jackson, "Wittgenstein as a Teacher," in K. T. Fann, ed., *Ludwig Wittgenstein: The Man and His Philosophy* (Sussex: Harvester Press, 1967), p. 51.

16. Other attempts at summarizing and generalizing the case study could certainly be made, depending on from what perspective one would approach the study.

17. Friedrich Nietzsche, *The Wanderer and His Shadow* (§11), here quoted from Nietzsche, *The Antichrist* (Harmondsworth: Penguin, 1968), p. 191 (Appendix C).

TWO

1. The case study that follows is based on seven types of data sources: interviews, documents, informants, observations, participant-observation, media-coverage including TV and radio programs, and participants' feedback. The case study's interview data consists of thirty-five intensive, semi-structured, in-depth interviews with twenty-nine persons conducted during the period 1984–90, though with most interviews in the earlier period. Three persons were interviewed twice, one person five times, and one interview was carried out with two persons simultaneously. Two interviews were conducted by letter and one by telephone. Of the thirty-five interviews, thirty were recorded on tape, including the answers to one of the written interviews. The taped interviews varied in length from a single forty-five-minute session to five sessions totaling eight hours, with the typical interview lasting about two hours. Besides the formal interviews, numerous clarifying, informal interviews and discussions were conducted with both the interviewed persons and with others. I also have had continual access to several informants who helped clarify certain events and issues in the case. All the interviews and conversations were carried out by me personally. The recorded interviews have been transcribed in their full length, producing 1,500 pages of interview transcripts. These transcripts constitute the raw interview data for the case study. The documentary sources include publicly accessible and internal material on the Aalborg Project from the City Government's Technical Department, the Aalborg City Council, the Planning Office for Public Transportation, the Aalborg Chamber of Industry and Commerce, the Danish Cyclist Federation, the former Kayerød Neighborhood Association, the Aalborg office of the Social Democratic party, one of the local trade unions, the

North Jutland County administration, the Danish Environmental Protection Agency, the Danish Environmental Appeals Board, the National Agency for Physical Planning, various private consulting companies who have worked in Aalborg, and the Aalborg Archives for Local History. Several thousand documents, totaling tens of thousands of pages, have been analyzed. They include reports, correspondence, minutes of meetings, memoranda, and handwritten comments on letters and draft reports. The most important parts have been copied and organized in a fourteen-volume "case journal" for further analysis. Collection and analysis of the documents, like the interviews, took place between 1984 and 1990, but started prior to the interviews so that the initial interview questions could be better formulated. As with the interviews, the documentary investigation was conducted solely by myself, both in the field and at the desk. The Aalborg Project began in the autumn of 1977. My studies of the project first started in 1984. Observation and participant-observation therefore played a role as sources of data from this point. The settings included public meetings, electronic media, and my own participation as researcher in meetings, panel discussions, radio and television broadcasts about the Aalborg Project with politicians, professional staff, businessmen and community organizers in Aalborg. As other activities were inaccessible for observation and participant-observation, interviewing and written sources were also important in analyzing project activities in the period 1984–90. For more on data collection and case selection, see Bent Flyvbjerg, *The Aalborg Study: Case Selection and Data Collection,* Research Report (Aalborg: Aalborg University, Department of Development and Planning, 1997).

2. All quotes are from interviews by the author, unless otherwise stated.

3. Policies for improving transit are a general trend in Denmark at this time. Total person-kilometers traveled in bus and rail transport in the country as a whole increased by 32% during 1975–80. On the supply side, the seating capacity in bus transport (number of seats in buses operating) also increased 32% in the same period.

4. Implementation of these projects was already underway when the Aalborg Project began. For all practical purposes, the three projects were part of the same package. Considerations regarding timing of their implementation, however, distinguish them as separate projects.

5. The century-long history leading up to this situation is described and analyzed in Bent Flyvbjerg, *Da miljøet kom til byen* (Copenhagen: Danish Urban Planning Lab Press, 1991).

6. The municipality's total expenses for city buses increased from 23.5 million Danish *kroner* to 75.5 million kroner 1977–81 (U.S. $1.00 equated about 6 kroner). The municipality's subsidy for city buses increased from 2.9 to 30.2 million kroner during the same period. Aalborg Byråd, *Regnskabsoversigt* (Municipal accounts), Aalborg, 1977–81.

7. The Jens Bang Stone House is described in detail in Henry-Russell Hitchcock, *German Renaissance Architecture* (Princeton: Princeton University Press, 1981), p. 296.

8. *Notat vedrørende AOS' krav til busterminalen* (Memorandum concerning the Aalborg Bus Company's demands for the bus terminal), Aalborg Omnibus Selskab, May 11, 1978 (archives of the Office of the City Engineer, Aalborg).

9. Downtown Aalborg has an extensive network of pedestrian streets. When the first pedestrian streets were proposed in 1956, and established 1962–63, Aalborg was first among the major towns in Denmark, and among the first towns in the world, to have such streets.

10. As described in Appendix A, Aalborg city government consists of an elected City Council (*Byrådet*) and a Municipal Administration (*Magistraten*). The Municipal Adminis-

tration is subdivided into five "departments" (*afdelinger*), each having several "offices" (*kontorer*). The First Department carries out executive tasks and contains the Office of the Mayor, the tax and finance offices, and other administrative organs. At this point in time the Aalborg Bus Company is part of the First Department, headed by the mayor.

11. In Danish elections, voters have the option of voting for a specific individual or checking off a party, which then installs its candidates according to a ranked list.

12. The mayor was subsequently expelled from the Social Democratic party. See Chap. 13.

THREE

1. *Notat vedr. etablering af busterminal i Aalborg bykerne* (Memorandum concerning establishment of bus terminal in downtown Aalborg), Teknisk Forvaltning, Aalborg, July 26, 1978.

2. *Notat vedr. placeringsmuligheder af ny busterminal* (Memorandum concerning siting options for the new bus terminal), Teknisk Forvaltning, Aalborg, August 4, 1978.

3. Minutes of the thirteenth meeting of the Task Force, Technical Department, Aalborg, August 18, 1978.

4. Besides the seven placement possibilities named above, the consulting firm's evaluation included an eighth: the outskirts of Budolfi Square (*Budolfi Plads*). Inclusion of this latter option had no effect on the outcome of the evaluation.

5. *Bybusterminalens placering,* arbejdsnotat (Bus terminal's siting, memorandum), Teknisk Forvaltning, Aalborg, August 24, 1978.

6. Aalborg Kommune, *Aalborg bykerne, Forslag til busterminal* (Downtown Aalborg, proposals to bus terminal), (Aalborg: Teknisk Forvaltning, 1979).

7. Minutes of Executive Committee meeting, Technical Department, Aalborg, September 27, 1978.

8. Letter to the author.

9. In two written commentaries to the Aalborg Project from January 1979, the city engineer expresses skepticism of the evaluations. He comments on the consulting firm's work thusly: "It appears that the evaluation of the placement possibilities at Nytorv–Østeraagade is characterized too positively." Memorandum, January 15, 1979. And in a second memorandum (January 26, 1979), the city engineer presents the idea that the Nytorv half of the terminal could be built while no construction would take place at Østeraagade. This indicates that the city engineer, at least at this time, sees the evaluation work and the bus terminal as problematic.

10. Friedrich Nietzsche, *Beyond Good and Evil* (New York: Vintage, 1966), p. 9 (§1).

FOUR

1. *Betragtninger over busnettet* (Considerations concerning the bus network), Teknisk Forvaltning, Aalborg, December 12, 1978.

2. *Kommentar til notat* (Comment on memorandum), Aalborg Omnibus Selskab, December 20, 1978.

3. Ibid.

4. At the time of the interview, planning and operation of the city buses in Aalborg had been moved from the First Department (the mayor's office) to the Fifth Department (public utilities). The "alderman" referred to in the interview is the alderman responsible for the

Fifth Department. Responsibility for the city buses was placed under the mayor's office from 1976 to 1981, after the municipality acquired the city's bus company from a private firm in 1976. The motivation was to ensure a central political and administrative position during the expansion of public transportation. In 1982 the expansion had been completed, and public transportation was transferred to the same authority as the municipality's other public utilities. This change has severely weakened the position of public transportation and the Aalborg Bus Company within the municipal organization. We will return to this point below.

5. Friedrich Nietzsche, *The Birth of Tragedy* (New York: Vintage Books, 1967), p. 60 (§7).

6. Aalborg Kommune, *Aalborg bykerne: Forslag til busterminal* (Aalborg: Teknisk Forvaltning, 1979).

7. Alexander Nehamas, *Nietzsche: Life as Literature* (Cambridge, Mass.: Harvard University Press, 1985), pp. 32, 79, 123.

8. Friedrich Nietzsche, "On Truth and Lying in an Extra-Moral Sense," in Sander L. Gilman et al., *Friedrich Nietzsche on Rhetoric and Language* (New York: Oxford University Press, 1989), p. 246. In *Beyond Good and Evil* (New York: Vintage Books, 1966), p. 12 (§4), Nietzsche similarly talks about "untruth as a condition of life"; and in *The Will to Power* (New York: Vintage Books, 1968), p. 328 (§609), he says, "You need to grasp that without this kind of ignorance life itself would be impossible, that it is a condition under which alone the living thing can preserve itself and prosper."

9. Here quoted from Timothy Garton Ash, "Prague: Intellectuals and Politicians," *New York Review of Books* 42, no. 1 (1995), p. 39.

10. Niccolò Machiavelli, *The Prince* (Harmondsworth: Penguin, 1984), pp. 51–52 (chap. 6).

11. Friedrich Nietzsche, *Twilight of the Idols* (Harmondsworth: Penguin, 1968), p. 60 (§1).

12. Ibid., p. 76 (§14).

13. Ibid.

14. Nietzsche, *Beyond Good and Evil*, p. 35 (§24).

15. Friedrich Nietzsche, *The Antichrist*, in Walter Kaufmann, ed., *The Portable Nietzsche* (New York: Penguin, 1968), p. 582 (§15).

16. "[T]he rulers of our community: they can lie for the good of the community," from Plato, *Republic* (Oxford: Oxford University Press, 1993), p. 83 (bk. 3, sec. 389).

FIVE

1. Interview with the author.

2. Aalborg kommune, *Aalborg bykerne: forslag til målsætning og overordnet struktur, trafik og arealanvendelse*, report no. 3 (Aalborg: Teknisk Forvaltning, 1979), pp. 15–16.

3. The eight reports are all published by Aalborg municipality, the Technical Department, 1979. The titles of the reports are: *Registrering, arealanvendelse; Registrering, trafik; Forslag til målsætning og overordnet struktur: Trafik og arealanvendelse; Forslag til trafikplan; Idékatalog; Forslag til busterminal; Forslag til omprofilering af Vesterbro;* and *Centerstrukturanalyse.*

4. Aalborg kommune, *Forslag til målsætning og overordnet struktur*, pp. 13, 15.

5. Aalborg kommune, *Aalborg bykerne: forslag til trafikplan*, report no. 4 (Aalborg: Teknisk Forvaltning, 1979), p. 7. In Denmark, approximately 40% of all trips are made by pedestrians and bicyclists (20% each), 10% by public transportation, and 50% by car.

6. Ibid. The priority list is subsequently reduced to the following five items: (1) pedes-

trians, (2) passengers on public transportation, (3) bicyclists, (4) drivers of mopeds, (5) cars. Aalborg kommune, *Forslag til målsætning og overordnet struktur,* p. 16.

7. The expected consequences of the traffic plan are described in Aalborg kommune, *Forslag til trafikplan;* and in Flemming Larsen and Bent Johnsen, "Trafikplan for Aalborg bykerne," *Stads- og Havneingeniøren,* no. 8 (1979).

8. Aalborg kommune, *Aalborg bykerne: Idékatalog,* report no. 5 (Aalborg: Teknisk Forvaltning, 1979).

9. Ibid., p. 1.

10. The Gothenburg plan is well-documented in an OECD evaluation; see Bo Blide et al., *Traffic Zone System of Göteborg* (Paris: OECD Group of the Urban Environment, 1976). See also Municipality of Göteborg, *Göteborg: The Traffic Zone System and Its Extension* (Gothenburg: Town Building Office, 1988); and OECD, "Gothenburg," chap. 2, in *Cities and Transport* (Paris: OECD, 1988). In Aalborg, planners built on previous experiences from Gothenburg, both in the design of the traffic zone solutions and in the assessment of the traffic plan's expected consequences.

11. Minutes of the eighth meeting of the Aalborg Project's Executive Committee, Teknisk Forvaltning, Aalborg, August 31, 1978.

12. Memorandum from Aalborg's city engineer to the alderman heading the Technical Department and the Aalborg Project's Executive Committee, Teknisk Forvaltning, Aalborg, January 15, 1979.

13. The total costs of the Aalborg Project are later estimated at 60 million kroner (1982 level). *Notat vedrørende økonomisk overslag over forslaget fra den socialdemokratiske byrådsgruppe* (Memorandum concerning economic estimates of the proposal from the Social Democratic City Council group), Teknisk Forvaltning, Aalborg, September 9, 1982.

14. Aalborg kommune, *Forslag til trafikplan,* pp. 103 ff.

15. Introduction by the alderman for the Technical Department at the orientation meeting of the City Council, March 14, 1979, concerning Aalborg city center (Memorandum, Teknisk Forvalting).

16. Memorandum from Aalborg's city engineer to the alderman of the Technical Department and the project's Executive Committee, Teknisk Forvaltning, Aalborg, January 15, 1979.

17. Nordic Council of Ministers, *Trafik i nordisk tätort,* 3 vols. (Oslo: Nordisk Ministerraad, 1978); and Blide et al., *Traffic Zone System of Göteborg.*

18. In Gothenburg the effects achieved were those planned for Aalborg: a decline in automobile traffic, reduction of traffic accidents in the inner city and peripheral streets by 27% and 9%, respectively, and a reduction in noise levels of up to 8 dB(A). In addition, driving time for public transportation was reduced in downtown Gothenburg. The businesses in Gothenburg's center, after a period of adjustment, have indicated their satisfaction with the changes implemented. See OECD, *Cities and Transport,* pp. 35 ff.

19. Richard Rorty, "Unger, Castoriadis, and the Romance of a National Future," in *Philosophical Papers,* vol. 2 (Cambridge: Cambridge University Press, 1991), p. 189.

SIX

1. Minutes of the ninth meeting of the Aalborg Project's Task Force, Technical Department, May 26, 1978, p. 4.

2. Minutes of the twelfth meeting of the Aalborg Project's Task Force, Technical Department, July 24, 1978, item 9.

3. Minutes of the seventh meeting of the Aalborg Project's Executive Committee, Technical Department, August 2, 1978. The "publicity" prior to the local plan procedures refers to two local plans elaborated in connection with the Aalborg Project: the bus terminal at Nytorv, and a local plan for utilization of buildings along selected shopping streets in downtown Aalborg. The Danish Municipal Planning Law requires publicity for local plans, in the form of orientation of the concerned parties and public announcements in the mass media. The two local plans are discussed further in Chaps. 9 and 10.

4. Minutes of the ninth meeting of the Executive Committee, Technical Department, September 27, 1978, p. 3.

5. Law for Municipal Planning (*Kommuneplanloven*) of 1975, in effect from February 1, 1977.

6. *Aalborg Stiftstidende,* May 24, 1979.

7. Ibid., August 7, 1979.

8. This description is based on minutes of the meeting as recorded by the Aalborg Chamber of Industry and Commerce (*Aalborg Handelsstandsforening*) and the Technical Department (*Teknisk Forvaltning*), both dated August 7, 1979, and on my own interviews with key participants. The minutes and interviews have been cross-checked with each other and with a newspaper report of the meeting published in *Aalborg Stiftstidende* on August 8, 1979.

9. Minutes of the meeting at the White House Hotel, Aalborg Handelsstandsforening, August 7, 1979, p. 6.

10. Ibid.

11. Ibid., p. 4; also mentioned in *Aalborg Stiftstidende*'s report of August 8, 1979.

12. *Aalborg Stiftstidende,* August 8, 1979.

13. Editorial in ibid., August 9, 1979.

14. *Kommissorium for arbejdsgrupperne,* bykerneudvalget, Aalborg Handelsstandsforening, August 20, 1979.

15. *Vedrørende teknikerbistand til studiekredse oprettet under Aalborg Handelsstandsforening,* Teknisk Forvaltning, Aalborg August 23, 1979.

16. The names of participants in the working groups and Steering Committee are listed in Appendix 1 of the Chamber of Industry and Commerce's counterplan; see *Aalborg Handelsstandsforening, Aalborg bykerne—et alternativ* (Aalborg, 1979), p. 19.

17. *Kommissorium for arbejdsgrupperne,* bykerneudvalget, Aalborg Handelsstandsforening, August 20, 1979.

18. Minutes of the first meeting of the Steering Committee, Aalborg Chamber of Industry and Commerce, August 30, 1979, pp. 1–2.

19. *Aalborg Stiftstidende,* September 15, 1979.

20. The Aalborg Chamber of Industry and Commerce's five working groups are organized according to geographical zones of the city center corresponding to the four traffic zones and the area around Reberbansgade.

21. Conclusion and minutes concerning the Aalborg Project from the "North-East" working group under the Aalborg Chamber of Industry and Commerce, October 4, 1979. The North-East and South-East groups cover the geographic areas closest to the planned bus terminal. The groups' members have economic and other interests in the future of precisely this area, and they see the terminal as enhancing their future prospects.

22. Minutes of the South-East Working Group, Aalborg Chamber of Industry and Commerce, September 28, 1979.

23. Minutes of the second meeting of the Steering Committee under the City Center Committee, Aalborg Chamber of Industry and Commerce, September 6, 1979, p. 2. The

figure of 60% is an undocumented assertion which, as we shall see later, does not stand up to scrutiny.

24. *Spørgeskema: Kundernes indkøbsvaner* (Questionnaire: customers' shopping habits), with handwritten additions, Aalborg Handelsstandsforening, September 18, 1979.

25. Letter from Aalborg Chamber of Industry and Commerce to the "North-East" Working Group, Aalborg Handelsstandsforening, November 5, 1979.

26. Minutes of the first meeting of the City Center Committee, Aalborg Chamber of Industry and Commerce, August 20, 1979, p. 3.

27. *Vedrørende tidsfrist for aflevering af bemærkninger til forslaget til trafik- og arealanvendelses-plan for Aalborg bykerne*, Teknisk Forvaltning, Aalborg, August 20, 1979.

28. I was unable to determine the precise date when the Technical Department received the Chamber's report; the date is recorded neither in the Technical Department's records of incoming correspondence nor in the Aalborg Chamber of Industry and Commerce's list of outgoing correspondence. Articles in *Aalborg Stiftstidende* and *Midt-Vest Avisen* on November 15 and 21, respectively, however, indicate that the report was forwarded to the Technical Department around November 15.

29. Jürgen Habermas, *Moral Consciousness and Communicative Action* (Cambridge, Mass.: MIT Press, 1990), p. 198.

SEVEN

1. Letter from the Kayerød Neighborhood Association to the Technical Department, Aalborg, October 31, 1979 (Technical Department archives, Aalborg).

2. Letter from Danish Cyclist Federation to the Technical Department, Aalborg, October 31, 1979 (Technical Department archives, Aalborg).

3. Letter from Confederation of Semi-Skilled Workers in Denmark to the Technical Department, Aalborg, October 30, 1979 (Technical Department archives, Aalborg).

4. Aalborg Handelsstandsforening, *Aalborg bykerne—et alternativ* (Aalborg, 1979), p. 9.

5. The Technical Department's proposal for priorities are (1) pedestrians, (2) passengers on public transportation, (3) bicyclists, (4) moped drivers, (5) motorists. Aalborg kommune, *Aalborg bykerne: forslag til målsætning og overordnet struktur*, report no. 3 (Aalborg: Teknisk Forvaltning, 1979), p. 16.

6. Aalborg Handelsstandsforening: *Aalborg bykerne—et alternativ*, p. 14.

7. Minutes of meeting in the Retailer Committee, Aalborg Chamber of Industry and Commerce, September 18, 1979 (archives of the Aalborg Chamber of Industry and Commerce).

8. Aalborg Handelsstandsforening, *Aalborg bykerne—et alternativ*, p. 1; large type and italics in the original.

9. Letter from the chairman of the North-East working group to the board of Aalborg Chamber of Industry and Commerce, September 4, 1979 (archives of the Aalborg Chamber of Industry and Commerce).

10. Aalborg Handelsstandsforening, *Aalborg bykerne—et alternativ*, p. 15.

11. *Aalborg Stiftstidende,* August 30, 1979.

12. Letter from Ejerforeningen Budolfi Plads 9/Vingaardsgade 2-4 to the Technical Department, Aalborg, October 31, 1979 (Technical Department archives, Aalborg).

13. Aalborg Handelsstandsforening, *Aalborg bykerne—et alternativ*, pp. 17–18.

14. Ibid., p. 17.

15. Ibid., p. 15.

16. Ibid., p. 6.

17. Den socialdemokratiske byrådsgruppe i Aalborg, *Forslag til ændring i trafikplanlæg-ning m.m. for Aalborg bykerne* (Proposal for changing of traffic planning and other matters for downtown Aalborg), Aalborg, March 29, 1982, p. 1 (Technical Department archives, Aalborg).

18. Letter from the Danish Town Planning Association to the alderman for the Technical Department, December 3, 1979 (Technical Department archives, Aalborg). "Mayoral Baton" in Danish is also a name for a popular type of pastry. The recipient of the award receives a batch of the pastry.

19. *Aalborg Stiftstidende,* December 6, 1979.

20. Memorandum of "Monday Meeting," December 10, 1979; and minutes of the twentieth meeting of the Aalborg Project's Executive Committee, February 18, 1980 (Technical Department archives, Aalborg).

21. Minutes of meeting between the Technical Department and the Chamber of Industry and Commerce (Technical Department archives, Aalborg), January 30, 1980, p. 1. There exists two sets of minutes of the meeting, written separately by each of the two parties.

22. Technical Department's minutes of meeting, January 30, 1980, p. 4.

23. Minutes of meeting of the Aalborg Chamber of Industry and Commerce, January 30, 1980, pp. 1, 4 (archives of the Aalborg Chamber of Industry and Commerce).

24. Minutes of City Council orientation meeting, April 22, 1980 (Technical Department archives, Aalborg).

25. *Aalborg Stiftstidende,* editorial, April 22, 1980.

26. Voting protocol for Aalborg City Council, meeting of May 12, 1980 (City Council archives).

27. Ibid., meeting of June 9, 1980 (City Council archives).

EIGHT

1. Anthony Giddens, *The Constitution of Society* (Cambridge: Polity Press, 1984), p. 85.

2. Minutes of meeting between the Technical Department and the board of the Aalborg Chamber of Industry and Commerce, November 29, 1971 (archives of the Aalborg Chamber of Industry and Commerce).

3. Minutes of meeting between the Technical Department, the board of the Aalborg Chamber of Industry and Commerce, and representatives of business owners on Østeraagade and Nytorv, January 14, 1972, p. 3 (Technical Department archives, Aalborg).

4. Minutes of meeting in the City Center Group, Technical Department, November 1, 1974, p. 2 (Technical Department archives, Aalborg).

5. Aalborg's chief planner for public transportation believes that the Aalborg Police have had greater influence on the Aalborg Project than my analysis in this book would indicate: "Generally I think that you underplay the influence of the police. It may well be that they do not appear to do much in your data, but my memory is that the 'fear' of conflict with the police has played a great role, both in connection with the reductions in the extent of the project and later on, in connection with the follow up [on the project]" (personal correspondence, author's archives). The chief planner for public transportation does not, however, dispute my claim that the Chamber of Industry and Commerce has had more influence than the police on the Aalborg Project and on the Technical Department.

6. Aalborg Handelsstandsforening, *Beretning for året 1973* (Aalborg, 1974).

7. *Notat fra mødet med Teknisk Forvaltning* (Memorandum from meeting with the Technical Department), Aalborg Chamber of Industry and Commerce, February 7 , 1983, p. 3.

8. The quotes are from advertisements in *Aalborg Stiftstidende,* November 16 and 17, 1989.

9. Author's interview.

10. C. Klitgaard, *Aalborg Købmænd gennem 500 År* (Aalborg merchants over 500 years) (Aalborg: Adolph Holst, 1931), p. 4.

11. Ibid. See also Lars Tvede-Jensen and Gert Poulsen, *Aalborg under krise og højkonjunktur fra 1534 til 1680* (Aalborg during economic crisis and growth 1534–1680), in *Aalborgs Historie,* vol. 2 (Aalborg: Aalborg Kommune, 1988), pp. 108 ff.

12. Klitgaard, *Aalborg Købmænd gennem 500 År,* pp. 4–5.

13. Ibid., p. 5.

14. Ibid., p. 7.

15. In 1672, the population of Aalborg was counted at 4,181 inhabitants. This can be considered a minimum number. Only Copenhagen was larger in Denmark. See Tvede-Jensen and Poulsen, *Aalborg under krise og højkonjunktur,* pp. 222, 257.

16. See Chap. 13.

17. Gert Poulsen and Per Bo Christensen, *Aalborg fra politisk skandale mod økonomisk katastrofe fra 1680 til 1814* (Aalborg from political scandal toward economic catastrophe 1680–1814), in *Aalborgs Historie,* vol. 3 (Aalborg: Aalborg kommune, 1990), pp. 18–19.

18. Ibid., pp. 22 ff.

19. Michel Foucault, "What Is Enlightenment," in Paul Rabinow, ed., *The Foucault Reader* (New York: Pantheon, 1984), pp. 42, 46.

20. A study of civic traditions in Italy by Robert Putnam, Robert Leonardi, and Raffaella Y. Nanetti is one of the few other studies in the field that explores the effects of premodern social practices on modern democratic institutions. Putnam and his associates find that practices of communal life that go back a millennium have more influence on the possibilities to implement democratic reform today than do modern policies of institutional change. Putnam's conclusions thus correspond closely to the results of the Aalborg study on this point. See also Chap. 20, "Power Has a Rationality That Rationality Does Not Know," this vol. (Robert D. Putnam, with Robert Leonardi and Raffaella Y. Nanetti, *Making Democracy Work: Civic Traditions in Modern Italy* [Princeton: Princeton University Press, 1993]).

NINE

1. Voting records for Aalborg City Council, meeting of June 9, 1980, p. 4; minutes of "Monday Meeting," Technical Department, Aalborg, July 21, 1980 (Aalborg City Council archives and Technical Department archives, Aalborg).

2. Letter from Aalborg Municipality to the EPA regarding proposal to local plan no. 10-010 concerning a bus terminal at Nytorv, July 26, 1980 (Technical Department archives, Aalborg).

3. Statement from the EPA on local plan no. 10-010 for bus terminal at Nytorv, September 29, 1980, pp. 1–2.

4. Aalborg kommune, *Buscenter ved Nytorv-Østeraagade: miljøteknisk konsekvensbeskrivelse* (Aalborg: Teknisk Forvaltning, 1980), p. 21.

5. Vejstøjudvalget, *Vejstøj* (Road noise), Betænkning (White Paper) no. 844, Copenhagen, p. 118. *Vurdering of støjforhold ved etablering af busterminaler* (Evaluation of noise factors

in connection with construction of bus terminals), memorandum from EPA's noise office, December 11, 1980, pp. 1–2 (Technical Department archives, Aalborg).

6. *Vedr. buscenter på Nytorv/Østeraagade—miljøforhold,* Teknisk Forvaltning, Aalborg, October 23, 1980, p. 2. Later calculations show the nitrous oxide content to be $132 \mu g/m^3$ measured as yearly average. *Rettelser til Miljøteknisk beskrivelse,* Teknisk Forvaltning, Aalborg, January 14, 1981.

7. Minutes of meeting between EPA and Technical Department, Aalborg, October 23, 1980, p. 3 (Technical Department archives, Aalborg).

8. *Vedr. buscenter på Nytorv,* Teknisk Forvaltning, Aalborg, October 20, 1980, p. 1.

9. Minutes of meeting between EPA and the Technical Department, Aalborg, October 23, 1980, pp. 2, 4 (Technical Department archives, Aalborg).

10. *Forslag til lokalplan nr. 10-010, Buscenter m.m., Nytorv Aalborg,* memorandum from EPA to Technical Department, Aalborg, December 15, 1980; *Lokalplan nr. 10-010 for Aalborg kommune vedr. buscenter m.m. Nytorv Aalborg,* memorandum from National Planning Commission to Aalborg City Council, December 22, 1980 (Technical Department archives, Aalborg).

11. Statement from the EPA regarding local plan no. 10-010 for the bus terminal at Nytorv, September 29, 1980, p. 2 (Technical Department archives, Aalborg).

12. Letter from Technical Department to the city administration's First Department, Aalborg municipality, July 6, 1981 (Technical Department archives, Aalborg).

13. Invitation for meeting of the Aalborg Project Executive Committee plus others, Technical Department, Aalborg, April 6, 1981, p. 3 (Technical Department archives, Aalborg).

14. Danish towns and counties each have their respective politically elected mayors (*borgmester/amtsborgmester*); to avoid confusing the two posts, the county mayor will be referred to as "county supervisor."

15. County supervisor for North Jutland County, quoted in *Aalborg Stiftstidende,* March 18, 1981.

16. Ibid., March 21, 1981.

17. Ibid., March 23, 1981; and *Redegørelse vedrørende projekt nr. 2297 — ny busterminal — foranlediget af Fremskridtspartiets byrådsgruppes skrivelse af 1. april 1981* (Report regarding project 2297—a new bus terminal—in connection with the Progress party's city council group's letter of April 1, 1981) (Technical Department archives, Aalborg).

18. *Vejgaard Avis,* April 13, 1981. The newspaper either renders the figures incorrectly, or the chief of city planning has rendered them incorrectly to the newspaper. The latter is the most probable explanation, for the city planning chief mentions the same figures in a completely different context, in an interview with the author. It is not a matter of the number of passengers transferring from one line to another but of the total number of passengers getting on or off the buses. Hence, of the 25,000 daily passengers with errands in downtown Aalborg, about 12,500 get on or off at Nytorv and 1,600 at the railroad and bus stations (passenger counts, May 31, 1978, mentioned in memorandum of April 13, 1981 [Technical Department archives, Aalborg]). The error has no effect on the significance of the trend, however, in that the tendency is the same in both the incorrect and the actual figures.

19. The chief of city planning has seen my analysis of the decision-making process for the bus terminal's location at Nytorv, and he observes, "Would the author have written this if he had been a proponent of the bus terminal at Nytorv?" (personal communication). Hence, I find it appropriate to emphasize that I am neither a supporter nor an opponent of

the bus terminal's location. In this phase of the research process I am working as a disinterested archaeologist: the hermeneutic horizon of the case (its self-understanding) is maintained, and my task is to clarify the meaning of the various arguments within this horizon. Thereafter I try to point out that this meaning does not accord with those meanings within other horizons; e.g., the canonized understandings of "analytic rationality" or "democracy." It is this juxtaposition which the chief of city planning seems to be against. At the same time, he himself talks of a "weakness in the argumentation" regarding the placement of the bus terminal at Nytorv (quoted in the main text) which deals specifically with the juxtaposition of formal rationality and the actual rationalization used to argue for placing the terminal at Nytorv.

20. Harold Garfinkel, *Studies in Ethnomethodology* (Cambridge: Polity Press, 1984).

21. Erving Goffman, *Behavior in Public Places* (New York: Free Press, 1963).

22. See, e.g., the Danish Engineers Association, *Generelle regler for den ansatte ingeniør* (General rules for the employed engineer) (Copenhagen: Dansk Ingeniørforening, undated).

TEN

1. *Notat vedrørende bus-og rutebiltrafik i Vingaardsgade efter etablering af bus- og rutebilholdeplads* (Memorandum concerning bus and regional bus transport in Vingaardsgade following the establishment of a local and regional bus stop), Teknisk Forvaltning, Aalborg, March 11, 1981.

2. Aalborg kommune, *Trafikomlægning i Vingaardsgade: Miljøteknisk beskrivelse* (Aalborg: Teknisk Forvaltning, 1980).

3. Letter from the "Attorneys in Vingaardshus" to Aalborg City Council, August 1, 1981 (Technical Department archives, Aalborg).

4. Letter from North Jutland County to the Technical Department, Aalborg, March 24, 1981 (Technical Department archives, Aalborg).

5. Personal communication to author (author's archives).

6. Aalborg kommune, *Lokalplan 10-011: Etageanvendelse m.m.* (Aalborg: Teknisk Forvaltning, 1982); and Aalborg kommune, *Lokalplan 10-010: Buscenter m.m., Nytorv* (Aalborg: Teknisk Forvaltning, 1980).

7. A "Paragraph 17" Prohibition, according to the Municipal Planning Law, allows for restrictions in a local plan to take effect immediately, even as the plan is being drawn up and before its final approval.

8. Letter to Technical Committee, Aalborg City Council, September 15, 1978 (Technical Department archives, Aalborg).

9. Minutes of Aalborg Chamber of Industry and Commerce meeting on the Aalborg Project at Hotel Hvide Hus, August 7, 1979, p. 6 (archives of the Aalborg Chamber of Industry and Commerce).

10. *Aalborg Stiftstidende,* August 1, 1979.

11. Objection (*Indsigelse*) to local plan 10-011, February 9, 1981 (Technical Department archives, Aalborg).

12. Letter of objection (*Indsigelse*) from Aalborg Chamber of Industry and Commerce to local plan 10-011, February 13, 1981 (Technical Department archives, Aalborg).

13. Two different sets of minutes of negotiations between the Technical Department and the Aalborg Chamber of Industry and Commerce, January 30, 1980 (Technical Department archives, Aalborg; archives of the Aalborg Chamber of Industry and Commerce).

14. *Aalborg Stiftstidende,* April 22, 1980.

15. Ibid., editorial, August 9, 1979. See also Chaps. 6 and 7.

16. Michel Foucault, *The History of Sexuality,* vol. 1 (New York: Vintage Books, 1980), p. xxx.

17. Letter from the chief executive officer of *Aalborg Stiftstidende* to the board of the Aalborg Chamber of Industry and Commerce, September 4, 1979 (archives of the Aalborg Chamber of Industry and Commerce).

18. Minutes of board meeting of Aalborg Chamber of Industry and Commerce, September 23, 1980 (archives of the Aalborg Chamber of Industry and Commerce).

19. Minutes of meeting of the Municipal Planning Council (*Kommuneplanrådet*), Technical Department, Aalborg, October 6, 1980 (Technical Department archives, Aalborg).

20. Aalborg kommune, *Aalborg bykerne: Indkøb i bykernen* (Downtown Aalborg: shopping in the city center) (Aalborg: Teknisk Forvaltning, 1981). The survey is based on 2,242 representative interviews with consumers in Aalborg municipality. The total number of interviews attempted was 3,265, which corresponds to a 70% response rate.

21. *Aalborg Stiftstidende,* September 18, 1981.

22. Annual reports from Aalborg Chamber of Industry and Commerce (*Beretning og regnskab*), Aalborg, 1977–1985.

23. This expression stems from my colleague Jeppe Gustafsson. See also Jeffrey Pfeffer, *Power in Organizations* (Boston: Pitman, 1981).

24. *Aalborg Stiftstidende,* September 18, 1981.

25. Dansk Pressenævn, Regler for god presseskik, sec. A.6, undated.

26. Draft of commentary to be submitted to *Aalborg Stiftstidende,* written by Aalborg's chief of city planning, October 21, 1981 (Technical Department archives, Aalborg).

27. *Aalborg Stiftstidende,* December 16, 1981.

28. Friedrich Nietzsche, *The Will to Power* (New York: Vintage Books, 1968), p. 342 (§643); Friedrich Nietzsche, *On the Genealogy of Morals* (New York: Vintage Books, 1969), p. 77 (§2.12).

ELEVEN

1. Letter from the Aalborg City Association to alderman for the Technical Department, September 4, 1981 (Technical Department archives, Aalborg).

2. Letter from Ejerforeningen Jernbanegade 17/Sankelmarksgade 17 to the Technical Department, undated, received on October 14, 1981 (Technical Department archives, Aalborg).

3. Letter to *Aalborg Stiftstidende,* October 8, 1981.

4. Letter to the Technical Department, November 18, 1981 (Technical Department archives, Aalborg).

5. Letter to the alderman of the Technical Department, November 21, 1981 (Technical Department archives, Aalborg).

6. Letter to *Aalborg Stiftstidende,* November 22, 1981.

7. Letter to the alderman of the Technical Department, November 23, 1981 (Technical Department archives, Aalborg).

8. Ibid.

9. Statement from Falcks Redderklub to the Technical Department and to Aalborg City Council, November 25, 1981 (Technical Department archives, Aalborg).

10. The column *Byskriveren, Aalborg Stiftstidende,* November 30, 1981.

11. Interview with the author.

12. Stuart Meck, "From High-Minded Reformism to Hard-Boiled Pragmatism: American City Planning Faces the Next Century," *The Planner,* February 16, 1990, p. 12.

13. Niccolò Machiavelli, *The Prince* (Harmondsworth: Penguin, 1984), p. 91 (chap. 15).

14. Hans Magnus Enzensberger, "Gangarten: Ein Nachtrag zur Utopie," *Kursbuch,* Heft 100, *Die Welt von Morgen* (Berlin: Rotbuch Verlag, 1990), pp. 1–2, my translation.

15. Minutes of meeting in Technical Committee, November 26, 1981 (Technical Department archives, Aalborg).

16. Notes of conversation between the alderman for the Technical Department and Aalborg's city engineer, December 3, 1981 (Technical Department archives, Aalborg); minutes of board meeting of Aalborg Chamber of Industry and Commerce, December 7, 1981 (archives of the Aalborg Chamber of Industry and Commerce).

17. *Aalborg Stiftstidende,* December 10 and 11, 1981.

18. Open Letter from the Aalborg Chamber of Industry and Commerce to the alderman of the Technical Department, December 7, 1981 (archives of the Aalborg Chamber of Industry and Commerce).

19. Minutes of board meeting in Aalborg Chamber of Industry and Commerce, December 7, 1981.

20. Ibid.

21. Michel Foucault, "The Subject and Power," Afterword to Hubert L. Dreyfus and Paul Rabinow, *Michel Foucault: Beyond Structuralism and Hermeneutics* (Brighton: Harvester Press, 1982), p. 225.

22. Minutes of "Police Meeting," Technical Department, October 28, 1981 (Technical Department archives, Aalborg).

23. This and subsequent information on Dansk Supermarked is taken from Helge Andersen and Lennart Weber, *Magtens mange mænd* (The many men of power) (Copenhagen: Fremad, 1985), pp. 42, 58–63, 114.

24. *Aalborg Stiftstidende,* December 8, 1981.

25. Letter from chairman of Danish Cyclist Federation's Aalborg chapter to a member of the Aalborg City Council Technical Committee, December 9, 1981 (Danish Cyclist Federation archives, Aalborg).

26. The name "Deep Throat" is used in English, without translation, by the participants in the Aalborg Project. In view of the fact that both Washington and Aalborg each had their respective "Deep Throats," and in view of the fact that Richard Nixon was the only U.S. president to be forced to resign despite having been a landslide victor in the previous election, it might be pertinent to add that Aalborg's Mayor Marius Andersen, a major Social Democratic personality and top vote getter, is the only Danish mayor ever to go to prison for corruption. Like Nixon, Marius Andersen also was ultimately politically rehabilitated.

TWELVE

1. Letter from Danish Cyclist Federation to the alderman for the Technical Department, December 15, 1981 (Technical Department archives, Aalborg).

2. Niccolò Machiavelli, *The Prince* (Harmondsworth: Penguin, 1984), pp. 51–52 (chap. 6).

3. Letter of objection from the chief planner for public transportation to the Financial Office of Aalborg Municipality, December 14, 1981 (archives of the Planning Office for Public Transportation, Aalborg).

4. *Notat, Magistratens 5. afdeling* (Memorandum, Municipal Administration's Fifth Department), Aalborg municipality, December 14, 1981 (archives of the Planning Office for Public Transportation, Aalborg).

5. *Notat vedr. maksimal tidsforsinkelse i udvalgte kryds i Aalborg bykerne* (Memorandum concerning maximum time delay in selected intersections of downtown Aalborg), Teknisk Forvaltning, Aalborg, April 6, 1982.

6. *Aalborg Stiftstidende,* December 16, 1981.

7. Interview with the author.

8. Nytorv had been provisionally opened two days previously but is expected to be closed to car traffic again after the New Year.

9. *Aalborg Stiftstidende,* December 16, 1981.

10. Machiavelli, *The Prince,* p. 96 (chap. 17).

11. Letter from the president of Dansk Supermarked to Aalborg's city engineer, January 4, 1982. The letter, marked "personal," is written on Salling "Executive Office" letterhead (Technical Department archives, Aalborg).

12. *Aalborg Stiftstidende,* January 3, 1982.

13. Ibid.

14. Minutes of meeting between Salling, Føtex, and Aalborg's city engineer, January 25, 1982 (Technical Department archives, Aalborg).

15. Memo from the Technical Department alderman to Aalborg's city engineer, January 6, 1982 (Technical Department archives, Aalborg).

THIRTEEN

1. The press conference is held on April 7, 1982.

2. The Social Democratic City Council Group, *Forslag til ændring i trafikplanlægning m.v. for Aalborg bykerne* (Proposals for change of traffic planning, etc., for downtown Aalborg) (Aalborg, 1982), p. 1 (Technical Department archives, Aalborg).

3. Ibid.

4. The "Aalborg Scandal" began in February 1981 when a contractor who worked for Aalborg municipality was jailed for tax evasion. In August that same year, a former Social Democratic alderman for the Fifth Department, which administers public utilities, was convicted of having received a bribe from the imprisoned contractor and was himself sent to prison. In October, the police began to investigate Aalborg's Social Democratic mayor regarding the infamous "moss-green bathroom" and other gifts received from the convicted contractor. Aalborg's Social Democratic party then decided that the mayor would not be their leading candidate in the forthcoming City Council elections. The mayor reacted by creating his own candidate list, which in the November elections received 15,517 votes, of which 13,581 were given personally to the mayor. While this gave his list six out of the City Council's thirty-one seats, the mayor had to resign from his post, which he had held since the formation of Aalborg municipality in 1970. The Social Democrats lost six seats on the City Council and thereby the absolute majority they had held since 1925 (with the exception of wartime elections in 1943–46). In July and August 1982 the already imprisoned contractor, the former alderman for public utilities, and the ex-mayor were sentenced to prison. The former mayor decided not to appeal and started serving a six-month sentence right away. After four months he was released on parole. In 1985 he was reelected to the City Council on his own candidate list. In 1993 he voluntarily retired from the City Council.

5. *Aalborg Stiftstidende,* April 8, 1982.

6. Ibid., April 11, 1982.

7. Ibid.

8. Ibid., April 20, 1982.

9. Ibid., April 21, 1982.

10. Minutes of meeting of the Aalborg Chamber of Industry and Commerce Retail Committee, April 6, 1982 (archives of the Aalborg Chamber of Industry and Commerce).

11. Ibid.

12. Minutes of meeting between the Technical Department and the Aalborg Chamber of Industry and Commerce, April 13, 1982 (Technical Department archives, Aalborg).

13. *Aalborg Stiftstidende,* December 16, 1981.

14. Ibid., April 22, 1982.

15. Letter from the Danish Cyclist Federation to the alderman for the Technical Department, March 5, 1982 (Technical Department archives, Aalborg).

16. Letter from the alderman for the Technical Department to the Danish Cyclist Federation, April 5, 1982 (Technical Department archives, Aalborg).

17. Letter from the Danish Cyclist Federation to the Technical Department alderman, April 15, 1982 (Technical Department archives, Aalborg).

18. Letter from Kayerød Neighborhood Association to Aalborg's mayor, April 22, 1982 (Technical Department archives, Aalborg).

19. Here cited from the manuscript of the city engineer's speech. The quotation is cross-checked with interviews and with *Aalborg Stiftstidende*'s report of the City Council meeting published on April 29, 1982, in which the city engineer is quoted in the same words. The further quotation from the city engineer's speech comes solely from the manuscript, and it has not been possible to verify from other written sources whether the speech was in fact given as written in the manuscript. I view this as probable, however, as it appears that much work has been put into the manuscript to bring it into its final form so that it could be read to the City Council.

20. *Aalborg Stiftstidende,* April 29, 1982.

21. City engineer's manuscript prepared for speech at Aalborg City Council, April 28, 1982 (Technical Department archives, Aalborg).

22. First draft of city engineer's speech, April 28, 1982 (Technical Department archives, Aalborg).

23. Minutes of orientation meeting of the Aalborg City Council, April 28, 1982 (City Council archives, Aalborg).

FOURTEEN

1. Letter from the chairman of Aalborg Chamber of Industry and Commerce to Aalborg City Council members, June 10, 1982 (archives of the Aalborg Chamber of Industry and Commerce, Aalborg).

2. Ibid.

3. Personal interview with the author.

4. Ibid.

5. Minutes of municipal administration meeting (*magistratsmøde*), i.e., between the mayor and the four aldermen heading the muncipal departments, June 9, 1982, p. 4.

6. "*Borgerligt brud,*" literally "bourgeois break" or rupture; the Danish term *borgerlig,* like the German counterpart *bürgerlich,* may connote citizenship or class. The term, however, is

commonly used to refer to all political parties to the right of the Social Democrats. To vote "bourgeois" may mean voting for any one of several liberal, centrist, conservative, or populist parties: i.e., the Center-Democrats, Radical Liberals, Liberals, Conservatives, Christian People's party, or the populist Progress party. The confusion caused by translating Danish political parties into English is daunting: the Center-Democrats are conservative ex–Social Democrats, the Radical Liberals are not radical but a break-off centrist grouping from the Liberals (*Venstre*), who despite their name (*Venstre* meaning "left") are actually conservative. Finally, the Progress party is considered the most reactionary of Danish parliamentary parties. In contemporary Danish political terminology, Liberal has come to mean Conservative, Radical to mean Center, and Progress to mean Reaction.

7. A bicycle lane (*cykelstribe*) is simply marked out with a line of paint, whereas real bicycle paths (*cykelstier*) are raised asphalt paths with separate curbs over which cars cannot cross. Bicycle paths are thus a capital construction of a different order than bicycle lanes.

8. *Aalborg Stiftstidende,* editorial, June 17, 1982.

9. City Council member for the Socialist People's party (*Socialistisk Folkeparti*), in ibid., June 18, 1982.

10. Ibid., April 21, 1982. See also Chap. 13.

11. Ibid., June 15, 1982.

12. Letter from the Conservative alderman for the Technical Department to Aalborg's Social Democratic mayor, June 22, 1982 (Technical Department archives, Aalborg).

13. Ibid.

14. The Social Democrats' counterplan has been formulated with assistance from a private consulting firm in Aalborg. In Danish they are referred to as "teknikere" which would formally be glossed as "technician." Here we have called them professional planning consultants.

15. *Notat vedr det socialdemokratiske forslag til ny trafikplan for Aalborg bykerne* (Memorandum concerning the Social Democratic proposal for a new traffic plan for downtown Aalborg), Technical Department, Aalborg, July 12, 1982.

16. Ibid.

17. Minutes of meeting between representatives of the Social Democratic City Council Group and the Technical Department, Aalborg, August 17, 1982 (Technical Department archives, Aalborg).

18. *Forslag til hvilke dele af det socialdemokratiske forslag, der bør uddybes eller konkretiseres* (Proposals for what parts of the Social Democratic proposal should be expanded and made more concrete); and *Referat af møde mellem repræsentanter for den socialdemokratiske byrådsgruppe og Teknisk Forvaltning* (Minutes of meeting between representatives of the Social Democratic City Council Group and the Technical Department), August 17, 1982 (Technical Department archives, Aalborg).

19. *Notat vedrørende bemærkninger fra den socialdemokratiske byrådsgruppe til referatet af mødet den 17. august 1982* (Memorandum concerning remarks from the Social Democratic City Council Group to the minutes of the meeting on August 17, 1982), September 10, 1982 (Technical Department archives, Aalborg).

20. *Notat vedrørende økonomisk overslag over forslaget fra den socialdemokratiske byrådsgruppe* (Memorandum concerning economic estimates for the proposal from the Social Democratic City Council Group), September 9, 1982 (Technical Department archives, Aalborg).

21. Ibid.

22. Draft of sec. 2, "*Forslaget generelt*" in the planned report from the Technical Depart-

ment about the Social Democratic plan, undated and unpaginated, probably October 1982 (Technical Department archives, Aalborg).

23. Personal interview with the author.

24. The Social Democratic party has established working groups covering each of the five departments which make up Aalborg's municipal administration.

25. The Social Democratic Group chairperson, as mentioned earlier, refuses to see herself as the originator of the phrase "Dream Plan" to denote the Social Democratic counterproposal.

26. The actual amount was 100 million kroner according to the Social Democratic Group itself at the time of the publication of the plan (*Aalborg Stiftstidende,* April 8, 1982).

27. Written comments from a city official to my presentation of this point (author's archives).

28. Aalborg kommune, *Aalborg bykerne: Vurdering af ændringsforslaget fra den socialdemokratiske byrådsgruppe* (Downtown Aalborg: evaluation of proposal for change from the Social Democratic City Council Group) (Aalborg: Technical Department, 1982).

29. Minutes of meeting in the Aalborg Project's Executive Committee, Technical Department, Aalborg, October 27, 1982 (Technical Department archives, Aalborg).

30. Letter from Technical Department alderman to Aalborg's mayor, *Vedrørende den socialdemokratiske byrådsgruppes forslag til ændring i trafikplanen, m.v. for Aalborg bykerne* (Concerning the Social Democratic City Council Group's proposal for changes in the traffic plan, etc., for downtown Aalborg), November 10, 1982 (Technical Department archives, Aalborg).

31. *Aalborg Stiftstidende,* November 4, 1982.

FIFTEEN

1. Letter from the North Jutland Transit Authority to the Environmental Appeals Board, September 23, 1981 (Technical Department archives, Aalborg).

2. "Decision of the Environmental Appeals Board on the Environmental Certification of the Integrated Bus Stop on Vingaardsgade," Aalborg, November 10, 1981 (Technical Department archives, Aalborg). Translated from the Danish, the full text of the decision reads, "The letter of the Environmental Protection Agency on September 1, 1981 informing of the certification is sustained. In connection with the above-mentioned viewpoints, no special stipulations are set in attachment to the certification" (p. 12).

3. It lies outside the scope of this book to enter into a legal assessment of the Environmental Appeals Board's decision. See Ellen Margrethe Basse, *Miljøankenævnet: En analyse af nævnets organisation, arbejdsgrundlag og funktionsmåde ud fra retlige og andre samfundsvidenskabelige argumenter* (The Environmental Appeals Board: an analysis of the board's organization, work basis, and mode of operation based on legal and other social science arguments) (Copenhagen: Gads Forlag, 1987). Basse's study discusses the Environmental Appeals Board's decision concerning the integrated bus stop on Vingaardsgade along with similar decisions.

4. Aalborg kommune, *Trafikomlægning i Vingaardsgade: Miljøteknisk beskrivelse* (Traffic restructuring on Vingaardsgade: environmental and technical description) (Aalborg: Technical Department, 1980), p. 4.

5. *Notat om fællesstoppested i Vingaardsgade* (Aalborg: Technical Department, February 19, 1982).

6. Letter from the Fifth Department alderman (public utilities) to the Technical Department, March 31, 1982 (archives of the Planning Office for Public Transportation, Aalborg).

7. The decision to transfer public transportation to the Department for Public Utilities was made before the "Aalborg Scandal" and is not connected to it.

8. Letter from the Technical Department to the Fifth Department, May 4, 1982 (Technical Department archives, Aalborg).

9. Minutes of meeting concerning public transportation in downtown Aalborg between the North Jutland Transit Authority, the Office of the City Engineer, and the Aalborg Planning Office for Public Transportation, September 17, 1982 (archives of the Planning Office for Public Transportation, Aalborg).

10. Three different sources confirm this decision: the minutes of the meeting on public transportation in downtown Aalborg between the North Jutland Transportation Authority, the Office of the City Engineer, and the Aalborg Planning Office for Public Transportation, September 17, 1982 (archives of the Planning Office for Public Transportation, Aalborg); letter from the Fifth Department alderman to the Technical Department, September 24, 1982 (Technical Department archives, Aalborg); and letter from the North Jutland Transit Authority to the Technical Department, September 29, 1982 (Technical Department archives, Aalborg).

11. Friedrich Nietzsche, *Ecce Homo* (New York: Vintage Books, 1969), p. 256 (§10).

12. Letter sent from the North Jutland County Council's Committee for Technology and Environment (*Udvalget for teknik og miljø*), to the Technical Department, Aalborg municipality, to the Environmental Protection Agency, and to the National Planning Commission (*Planstyrelsen*), February 25, 1982 (Technical Department archives, Aalborg).

13. Friedrich Nietzsche, *The Birth of Tragedy* (New York: Vintage Books, 1967), p. 60 (§7).

SIXTEEN

1. Aalborg kommune, *Aalborg bykerne. Indkøb i bykernen* (Aalborg, 1981).

2. Aalborg kommune, *Detailhandelsundersøgelse i Aalborg bykerne* (Retail survey in downtown Aalborg), unpublished memorandum from the Technical Department, October 27, 1982 (Technical Department archives, Aalborg). The survey compares retail earnings in downtown Aalborg during the fourth quarters of 1981 and 1979. The data derive from a questionnaire survey of earnings in downtown shops and from the Danish National Statistical Agency, Danmarks Statistik. The survey covers about 85% of downtown shops, comprising 85% of its total sales as well.

3. Ibid., p. 2.

4. See, e.g., the open letter from the Chamber of Industry and Commerce to the alderman for the Technical Department, December 7, 1981 (archives of the Aalborg Chamber of Industry and Commerce).

5. The years 1980 and 1981 are the only years in the decade 1975–85 where personal consumption declined in Denmark: a fall of 3.8% in 1980 and 1.1% in 1981 (fixed prices). Gross investments declined by 13.8% in 1980 and 16.3% in 1981 (fixed prices). See Danmarks Statistik, *Statistisk tiårsoversigt 1982* (Copenhagen, 1982), p. 108; and Finansministeriet, *Finansredegørelse 86* (Copenhagen: Budgetdepartementet, 1985), pp. 189–93.

6. Letter from Aalborg Chamber of Industry and Commerce to the Technical Depart-

ment alderman, December 7, 1981 (Technical Department archives, Aalborg). The letter is discussed further in Chap. 11.

7. Carmen Hass-Klau, "Impact of Pedestrianization and Traffic Calming on Retailing: A Review of Evidence from Germany and the UK," *Transport Policy* 1, no. 1 (1993).

8. The "abyss" argument was widely used in the press by the director general of the National Bank of Denmark, Erik Hoffmeyer, during this period.

9. Aalborg Kommune, *Detailhandelsundersøgelse i Aalborg bykerne*, p. 6.

10. The memorandum was completed on October 27, 1982. The City Council approved the revised Aalborg Project on January 10, 1983. The memorandum is first mentioned in *Aalborg Stiftstidende* on January 16, 1983.

11. Aalborg Handelsstandsforening, *Beretning og regnskab 1982* (Annual report and financial situation, 1982) (Aalborg, 1983), p. 14.

12. Correspondence and conversations with the author (author's archives).

13. Decision protocol (*beslutningsprotokollen*) for Aalborg City Council, meeting of January 10, 1983.

14. Quoted in *Aalborg Stiftstidende*, January 11, 1983.

15. Ibid.

16. Jürgen Habermas, *Moral Consciousness and Communicative Action* (Cambridge, Mass.: MIT Press, 1990); Habermas, *Justification and Application: Remarks on Discourse Ethics* (Cambridge, Mass.: MIT Press, 1993).

SEVENTEEN

1. *Notat vedrørende de fremtidige trafikale forhold på Vesterbro mellem Hasserisgade og Limfjordsbroen* (Memorandum concerning future traffic conditions on Vesterbro between Hasserisgade and the Limfjord Bridge) (Aalborg: Technical Department, June 15, 1983). During the period 1977–82, 121 traffic accidents were recorded on Vesterbro, of which forty-eight involved personal injury. A total of 73% of the accidents producing personal injury involved pedestrians, bicyclists, and those on mopeds (*lette trafikanter*). See *Notat vedrørende trafikuheld på Vesterbro* (Memorandum concerning traffic accidents on Vesterbro), Technical Department, Aalborg, January 5, 1984.

2. Personal interview with the author.

3. Minutes of meeting on the rebuilding of Vesterbro attended by the Technical Department, Vesterbro Street Association, Aalborg Chamber of Industry and Commerce, and Aalborg Police Department, June 23, 1983 (Technical Department archives, Aalborg).

4. Decision protocol for Aalborg City Council, January 10, 1983, item 6 (Aalborg City Council archives).

5. Technical Department financial records, 1983 and 1984.

6. Ibid.

7. *Referat af borgermøde vedrørende etablering af stillevej i Danmarksgade* (Minutes of public meeting concerning establishment of slowdown street on Danmarksgade), Technical Department, November 22, 1984. *Stillevej i Danmarksgade* (Slowdown street on Danmarksgade), memorandum (*notat*), Technical Department, July 13, 1989 (Technical Department archives, Aalborg).

8. From Frederikstorv Square to Løkkegade, December 1988.

9. Minutes of meeting concerning the establishment of bicycle paths at Vesterbro between the Technical Department, Vesterbro Gadeforening, Aalborg Chamber of Industry

and Commerce, and Aalborg Police Department, June 23, 1983 (Technical Department archives, Aalborg).

10. Aalborg kommune, *Aalborg bykerne: Forslag til omprofilering af Vesterbro* (Aalborg: Technical Department, 1979).

11. From a Boulevard Street Association brochure, December 1984.

12. Minutes of meeting between Vesterbro Gadeforening and the Technical Department, October 24, 1984 (Technical Department archives, Aalborg).

13. Letter from shopkeepers on the western part of Algade to the Technical Department, November 14, 1984 (Technical Department archives, Aalborg).

14. Ibid.

15. Letter from alderman for the Technical Department to the business community on the western part of Algade, December 17, 1984 (Technical Department archives, Aalborg).

16. Some of those in the Technical Department even had to have the concept "second stage" explained to them when they were interviewed about the project.

17. Letter from Aalborg's retiring city engineer to the members of the Aalborg Project's Executive Committee, April 4, 1984 (Technical Department archives, Aalborg).

18. The Aalborg Project's core group consists of the alderman for the Technical Department, the city engineer, the chief of city planning, the chief of planning for public transportation, the head of the project's Task Force, and the Planning Office's staff member on the Task Force.

19. Minutes of the Aalborg Project's Executive Committee, January 9, 1985 (Technical Department archives, Aalborg).

20. Ibid., p. 5.

21. Ibid. The acting city engineer coauthored the minutes, but his is the only signature. This contrasts with seven years of practice, in which the head of the project's Task Force, who also functions as secretary for the Executive Committee, was responsible for the minutes of Executive Committee meetings.

22. Ibid., p. 6.

23. Ibid., p. 4.

24. Recommendation (*indstilling*) from Aalborg's acting city engineer to the alderman for the Technical Department, February 8, 1985 (Technical Department archives, Aalborg).

25. In March 1985, however, the Planning Office for Public Transportation makes an unsuccessful attempt to revive the issue of illegal auto traffic through the Nytorv bus terminal with the Technical Department and with the Aalborg Police Department. See the letter from the alderman for the Fifth Department to the Technical Department alderman, March 15, 1985 (Technical Department archives, Aalborg); minutes of meeting between the Technical Department and Aalborg Police Department, May 9, 1985 (Technical Department archives, Aalborg).

EIGHTEEN

1. The fact that the new leader of the Fifth Department is a woman does not stop people from continuing to refer to her as "alderman" (*rådmand*).

2. Letter from alderwoman for the Fifth Department to Technical Department alderman, Aalborg, July 28, 1986 (Technical Department archives, Aalborg).

3. Debate newspaper (*debatavis*) on public transportation in Aalborg municipality, published by the Fifth Department, Aalborg, September 1986, p. 7 (author's archives).

4. Ibid.

5. Ibid.

6. As mentioned previously, the reason that the groups were not formally dissolved is that the former alderman of the Technical Department never approved the acting city engineer's recommendation for their elimination. The groups therefore can meet again without the department formally having to restart the project.

7. Invitation issued by Aalborg's city engineer to the Aalborg Project's Executive Committee, October 1, 1986 (Technical Department archives, Aalborg).

8. Three main tasks are now defined as especially urgent in order of priority: (1) formulating prerequisites so as to elaborate a public transportation plan for Aalborg municipality; the Planning Office for Public Transportation is working on such a plan, and, with the hub-and-spoke structure of the public transportation network, it is seen as necessary that a comprehensive traffic plan be elaborated for the downtown area; (2) evaluation of proposals for several construction projects with "wide-ranging consequences for land use, parking, and traffic conditions in downtown Aalborg" (*Aalborg bykerne—det videre arbejde* [Downtown Aalborg: further work], memorandum, Office of the City Engineer, Technical Department, Aalborg, December 16, 1986, rev. January 5, 1987, p. 1); (3) general evaluation of the existing traffic and land use plan for downtown Aalborg with reference to a possible revision. As part of these tasks, attempts are made to resolve several well-known problems. These include: (1) reduction of automobile traffic on Nytorv/Østeraagade, (2) reduction of automobile traffic on Borgergade, (3) reduction of automobile traffic on Algade, (4) establishment of a bus stop for city and regional buses on Vingaardsgade, (5) reduction of traffic on Østeraagade by prohibiting through traffic on the street, (6) reduction of automobile traffic and of vehicle speed on Danmarksgade, (7) improvement of transfer possibilities between city and regional buses at the Aalborg Bus Depot (*Status for realisering af trafikplanen for Aalborg bykerne set i forhold til de politiske vedtagelser* [Status for realization of the traffic plan for downtown Aalborg seen in relation to political approvals], memorandum [*notat*], Office of the City Engineer, Technical Department, Aalborg, November 27, 1986, rev. December 16, 1986; *Yderligere foranstaltninger i Aalborg bykerne* [Further measures in downtown Aalborg], Office of the City Engineer, Technical Department, Aalborg, October 29, 1986, rev. December 16, 1986).

9. Hence, the Executive Committee again consists of Aalborg's city engineer as chairman and includes the chief of city planning, the chief planner for public transportation, the city architect, and the city landscape architect. The Task Force again consists of staff members from each of these administrators' respective offices.

10. *Status for realisering af trafikplanen for Aalborg bykerne set i forhold til de politiske vedtagelser*, p. 7.

11. *Aalborg Stiftstidende*, December 28, 1986.

12. Ibid.

13. *Status for realisering af trafikplanen for Aalborg bykerne set i forhold til de politiske vedtagelser*, p. 4.

14. *Aalborg Stiftstidende*, October 31, 1985.

15. Ibid., December 28, 1986.

16. Ibid., January 29, 1987.

17. Ibid.

18. Ibid., editorial, February 3, 1987.

19. Ibid.

20. Minutes of meeting between the Fifth Department alderwoman and the Technical Department alderman, January 9, 1987; minutes of Aalborg Project's Task Force meeting, January 16, 1987 (Technical Department archives, Aalborg).

21. *Aalborg bykerne: Opfølgning af trafikplanens 1. etape* (Downtown Aalborg: follow-up of the traffic plan's first stage), memorandum, Technical Department, January 27, 1987, rev. February 23, 1987, pp. 16 ff. To obtain better conditions for pedestrians in the Algade/Boulevard intersection and to reduce traffic in downtown Aalborg the planners propose that Algade be closed toward the west in this intersection. Only bus traffic and bicycles will be permitted to head west. For the present, it is decided for financial reasons to delay additional, more expensive plans to reconstruct Danmarksgade and rebuild John F. Kennedy Square (see also Chap. 17; and also p. 15 of *Aalborg bykerne*).

22. *Aalborg bykerne*, p. 18.

23. Ibid., pp. 6–7.

24. Minutes of Task Force meeting with Aalborg Chamber of Industry and Commerce, Technical Department, Aalborg, February 11, 1987 (Technical Department archives, Aalborg).

25. *Møde om forslag til ændring af de trafikale forhold i Aalbog bykerne* (Meeting regarding the proposal for change in the traffic conditions in downtown Aalborg), Technical Department, Aalborg, February 25, 1987 (Technical Department archives, Aalborg).

26. Minutes of meeting concerning traffic in downtown Aalborg, Fifth Department, November 20, 1986 (archives of the Planning Office for Public Transportation, Aalborg).

27. Minutes of Task Force meeting with Aalborg Chamber of Industry and Commerce and the Technical Department, Aalborg, February 11, 1987, p. 1 (Technical Department archives, Aalborg).

28. *Møde om forslag til ændring af de trafikale forhold i Aalborg bykerne*, Technical Department, February 25, 1987, p. 1 (Technical Department archives, Aalborg).

29. Ibid., pp. 5–6.

30. Ibid., p. 7. See also minutes of the meeting between the Aalborg Police Department and the Technical Department, *Vedr. eventuel ændring af de trafikale forhold på Nytorv*, Technical Department, Aalborg, April 22, 1987, p. 2 (Technical Department archives, Aalborg).

31. *Møde om forslag til ændring af de trafikale forhold i Aalborg bykerne*, Technical Department, February 25, 1987, p. 6.

32. Ibid., pp. 4, 7.

33. *Aalborg Stiftstidende*, February 26, 1987.

34. *Onsdagsmagasinet* (The Wednesday Show), TV-Aalborg, June 8, 1988.

35. Presentation by the Technical Department alderman at meeting of the Danish Town Planning Association, Local History Archives, Aalborg, August 13, 1987 (participant-observation by the author, verified with the alderman).

36. The "life or death meeting" is described in Chap. 6.

37. *Opfølgning af bykerneplanens 1. etape: Ensretning af Nytorv* (Follow-up of the city center plan's first stage: making Nytorv one-way), Technical Department, Aalborg, April 30, 1987, p. 5.

38. Decision protocol for Aalborg City Council, meeting of September 14, 1987, item 4.

39. The Danmarksgade subproject is described in more detail in Chap. 17.

40. Aalborg kommune, *Forslag til parkeringspolitik for Aalborg bykerne*, notat 76/2 (Proposal for parking policy for downtown Aalborg) (Aalborg: Stadsingeniørens Kontor, 1976).

41. *Parkeringsafgift* (Parking fee), Recommendation from Technical Department to Aalborg City Council, February 7, 1989 (Technical Department archives, Aalborg).

42. Decision protocol (*beslutningsprotokollen*) for Aalborg City Council, January 9, 1989, p. 19 (Aalborg City Council archives).

43. *Parkeringsafgift,* recommendation from Technical Department to Aalborg City Council, February 7, 1989, p. 2.

44. *Aalborg Stiftstidende,* August 31, 1988.

45. Ibid.

46. Ibid., December 4, 1988.

47. Ibid., January 7, 1989.

48. Ibid.

49. Following a controversy with the Socialist People's party over how to run the Fifth Department, the alderwoman left the party's City Council Group and became an independent.

50. Decision protocol for Aalborg City Council, January 9, 1989, p. 22 (City Council archives).

51. Editorial, *Aalborg Stiftstidende,* January 11, 1989.

52. Decision protocol for Aalborg City Council, February 27, 1989, p. 140 (Aalborg City Council archives).

53. For an analysis of the implementation status for the individual subprojects, see Chap. 19.

54. *Journalen,* Denmarks Radio, Program One, October 18, 1989 (author's archives).

55. Michel Foucault, "Nietzsche, Geneaology, History," in Paul Rabinow, ed., *The Foucault Reader* (New York: Pantheon, 1984), p. 85.

NINETEEN

1. The complete evaluation, with a substantially more detailed comparison of objectives and outcomes, can be found in Bent Flyvbjerg, *Rationalitet og Magt,* vol. 2, *Et case-baseret studie af planlægning, politik og modernitet* (Copenhagen: Akademisk Forlag, 1991), pp. 265–325.

2. Significant at 0.85 level of confidence.

3. Approaching significance at 0.85 level.

4. A nonsignificant increase of 6%.

5. *Aalborg Stiftstidende* has also had its own independent financial interests which conflicted with those of the project. See Chap. 10.

TWENTY

1. Svend Søholt, "Miljø, Trafik og Demokrati," *Byplan* 42, no. 2 (1990), p. 60.

2. Charles Taylor, "Interpretation and the Sciences of Man," in Paul Rabinow and William M. Sullivan, eds., *Interpretive Social Science: A Second Look* (Berkeley: University of California Press, 1987), p. 72.

3. Robert Dahl and most other students of power, be they pluralist, elitist, or Marxist in their orientation, begin their analyses by posing the Weberian question, "Who governs?" In this book, and in this final chapter, we ask, "What 'governmental rationalities' are at work when those who govern govern?" This does not mean that we evade the Weberian ques-

tion. As we have seen, the fate of the Aalborg Project was decided by a tiny elite of top-level politicians, high-ranking civil servants, and business community leaders. The study uncovered an informal, hidden business–government "council" in which decision about the Aalborg Project—and about other policies and plans of interest to the business community—were negotiated and enacted in corporative fashion before anyone else had a say over such decisions. Business interests also gained special weight in the Aalborg Project because of strong and coordinated support by the local press and the police. This is not to say that all decisions benefited the business community. Nevertheless, the trend in the overall pattern of decisions that comprise the Aalborg Project—from its genesis, through design and ratification, to implementation and operation—indicates a clear and irrefutable preference for business interests as a result of the initiatives by the business community. Democratically elected bodies of government such as the City Council, the magistrate, and political committees had very little influence. They merely rubber-stamped decisions already made elsewhere. Other community groups beside the business community lacked influence on outcomes, as did the general public. In sum, by democratic standards, and understood in terms of conventional power theory, decisions regarding the Aalborg Project were made by too few and the wrong parties. Read in this way, the Aalborg case can be seen as refuting pluralist power theories of the type propounded by Dahl and others and as corroborating theories of a more elitist and corporatist orientation such as those developed by C. Wright Mills, Floyd Hunter, and Nicolas Poulantzas (Robert A. Dahl, *Who Governs?: Democracy and Power in an American City* [New Haven: Yale University Press, 1961]. See also Dahl's updated reflections in "Rethinking *Who Governs?:* New Haven Revisited," in Robert Waste, ed., *Community Power: Directions for Future Research* [Beverly Hills: Sage, 1986]; C. Wright Mills, *The Power Elite* [Oxford: Oxford University Press, 1956]; Floyd Hunter, *Community Power Structure* [Chapel Hill: University of North Carolina Press, 1953], and Hunter, *Community Power Succession: Atlanta's Policy Makers Revisited* [Chapel Hill: University of North Carolina Press, 1980]. See also G. William Domhoff, *Who Really Rules? New Haven and Community Power Reexamined* [Santa Monica, Calif.: Goodyear Publishing Company, 1978]; Nicolas Poulantzas, *Political Power and Social Classes* [London: NLB, 1973]; Poulantzas, *State, Power, Socialism* [London: NLB, 1979]). The question of "Who governs?" has been addressed in numerous other studies, many of which have emerged with similar conclusions. This is one reason why in this book, instead of focusing mainly on the "who" and "where" of power, we have focused on the more dynamic question of "how" power is exercised and on the relationships between rationality and power. The latter questions have been studied and answered much less frequently than "Who governs?"

4. Friedrich Nietzsche, *The Will to Power* (New York: Vintage Books, 1968), p. 342 (§643); Friedrich Nietzsche, *On the Genealogy of Morals* (New York: Vintage Books, 1969), p. 77 (§2.12).

5. Jürgen Habermas, *The Philosophical Discourse of Modernity: Twelve Lectures* (Cambridge, Mass.: MIT Press, 1987), pp. 297–98. Habermas sees consensus seeking and freedom from domination as universally inherent as forces in human communication, and he emphasizes these particular aspects in his discourse ethics. Other important social thinkers have tended to emphasize the exact opposite. Machiavelli, e.g., whom students of politics do not hesitate to call a "most worthy humanist" and "distinctly modern," and whom, like Habermas, is concerned with "the business of good government," states: "One can make this generalization about men: they are ungrateful, fickle, liars, and deceivers" (Bernard Crick, "Preface" and "Introduction" to Niccolò Machiavelli, *The Discourses* [Harmondsworth: Penguin,

1983], pp. 12, 17; Machiavelli, *The Prince* [Harmondsworth: Penguin, 1984], p. 96 [chap. 17]). Less radically, but still in clear contrast to Habermas, are observations by Nietzsche, Foucault, Derrida, and others that communication is at all times already penetrated by power. Whether the communicative or rhetorical position is "correct" is not the most important starting point for understanding rationality and power, even though the Aalborg study clearly supports the latter. What is decisive, rather, is that a nonidealistic point of departure must take account of the fact that in actual communication both positions are possible, and even simultaneously possible. In an empirical-scientific context, the question of communicative rationality versus rhetoric must therefore remain open for test. To assume either position ex ante based on a Kirkegaardian "leap of faith," to universalize it, and build a theory upon it makes for speculative philosophy and social science. Without placing Habermas's discourse ethics in the same league as Marxism, it may be said that the problem with discourse ethics is similar to that of some forms of Marxism in the sense that when it comes to organizing a better society, both Marx and Habermas have no account of how to deal with human evil; both assume that the good in human beings will dominate. In effect, this assumption tends to turn both lines of thinking into dogma. It is also what makes them potentially dangerous. History teaches us that assuming the nonexistence of evil may instead give free reign to evil. Nietzsche acutely observes about "[t]his mode of thought" that it "advises taking the side of the good, it desires that the good should renounce and oppose the evil down to its ultimate roots—it therewith actually denies life, which has in all its instincts both Yes and No." "Perhaps," says Nietzsche, "there has never before been a more dangerous ideology—than this will to good" (*The Will to Power,* pp. 192–93 [§351]). The evidence of the Aalborg case is on the side of Foucault when, in a comment on Habermas, he observes that the problem is not one of trying to dissolve relations of power in the "utopia of a perfectly transparent communication" but to give the rules of law, the techniques of management, and also the ethics which would "allow these games of power to be played with a minimum of domination" (Michel Foucault, "The Ethic of Care for the Self as a Practice of Freedom," in James Bernauer and David Rasmussen, eds., *The Final Foucault* [Cambridge, Mass.: MIT Press, 1988], p. 18). For more on the issues covered in this note, see my paper, "Empowering Civil Society: Habermas, Foucault, and the Question of Conflict," paper for symposium in Celebration of John Friedmann, School of Public Policy and Social Research, University of California, Los Angeles, April 11–13, 1996.

6. Here quoted from Timothy Garton Ash, "Prague: Intellectuals and Politicians," *New York Review of Books* 42, no. 1 (1995), p. 39.

7. Friedrich Nietzsche, *The Birth of Tragedy* (New York: Vintage Books, 1967), p. 60 (§7).

8. Machiavelli, *The Prince,* pp. 51–52 (chap. 6).

9. Friedrich Nietzsche, *Twilight of the Idols* (Harmondsworth: Penguin, 1968), p. 60 (§1).

10. Ibid., p. 76 (§14).

11. Ibid.

12. Friedrich Nietzsche, *Beyond Good and Evil* (New York: Vintage Books, 1966), p. 35 (§24).

13. Friedrich Nietzsche, *The Antichrist,* in Walter Kaufmann, ed., *The Portable Nietzsche* (New York: Penguin, 1968), p. 582 (§15).

14. "[T]he rulers of our community: they can lie for the good of the community," from Plato, *Republic* (Oxford: Oxford University Press, 1993), p. 83 (bk. 3, sec. 389).

15. Bernard Crick, "Introduction" to Machiavelli, *The Discourses,* p. 27.

16. Michel Foucault, "What Is Enlightenment," in Paul Rabinow, ed., *The Foucault Reader* (New York: Pantheon, 1984), pp. 42, 46.

17 Michel Foucault, "Questions of Method: An Interview," *I&C*, no. 8 (Spring 1981), p. 11.

18. Michel Foucault, "The Regard for Truth," *Art and Text,* no. 16 (1984), p. 31.

19. A prominent current example of the reliance on constitution writing and institutional reform for democratic progress is Habermas's trust in *Verfassungspatriotismus* (constitutional patriotism) as a main means to have the democratic principles of his discourse ethics take root in society. See Habermas, *Justification and Application: Remarks on Discourse Ethics* (Cambridge, Mass.: MIT Press, 1993); "Burdens of the Double Past," *Dissent* 41, no. 4; and Habermas, *Between Facts and Norms: Contributions to a Discourse Theory of Law and Democracy* (Cambridge: Polity Press, 1996). For an analysis of Habermas's *Verfassungspatriotismus,* see my "Empowering Civil Society."

20. Robert D. Putnam with Robert Leonardi and Raffaella Y. Nanetti, *Making Democracy Work: Civic Traditions in Modern Italy* (Princeton: Princeton University Press, 1993), p. 17.

21. Ibid., p. 183.

22. For more on this point, see my "Empowering Civil Society." See also Charles Spinosa, Fernando Flores, and Hubert Dreyfus, "Disclosing New Worlds: Entrepreneurship, Democratic Action, and the Cultivation of Solidarity," *Inquiry* 38, nos. 1–2 (June 1995).

23. Machiavelli, *The Prince,* p. 91 (chap. 15).

POSTSCRIPT

1. Bent Flyvbjerg, *Rationalitet og magt,* vol. 2, *Et case-baseret studie af planlægning, politik og modernitet* (Rationality and power, vol. 2, a case-based study of planning, politics, and modernity) (Copenhagen: Akademisk Forlag, 1991).

2. Written comments to the author (author's archives).

3. Michel Foucault, "What Is Enlightenment," in Paul Rabinow, ed., *The Foucault Reader* (New York: Pantheon, 1984), p. 47.

Index

alliances are important. 152
stable power relations 141
power is restored↗ 149
Danish Cycling Federation
Businesses doing well from bus & bike traffic
The Dream Plan
  Newspaper & chamber
  retail sales 184
  over intrepet 190
        ^193
      209